PELICAN BOOKS

A259

THE HITTITES

O. R. GURNEY

O. R. Gurney was born in London in 1911, and was educated at Eton College and New College, Oxford, where he was an Exhibitioner. He took up Assyriology in 1934 and has been Shillito Reader in Assyriology at Oxford University since 1945. He has made a special study of the Hittites, and spent a term at Berlin University (1935–6) as a pupil of the late Professor H. Ehelolf in order to learn their language. In 1939 he gained the degree of Doctor of Philosophy for a critical edition of the Hittite Prayers of Mursilis II, since published in the Annals of Archaeology and Anthropology, Liverpool 1940. During the war he served in the Royal Artillery and was attached for four years to the Sudan Defence Force, taking part in the campaigns in Eritrea and Abyssinia. He has taken part in excavations with Professor J. Garstang and Mr Seton Lloyd at sites in Southern Turkey. He was elected a Fellow of the British Academy in 1959 and a Fellow of Magdalen College, Oxford, in 1963.

THE HITTITES

O. R. GURNEY

PENGUIN BOOKS
BALTIMORE · MARYLAND

Penguin Books Ltd, Harmondsworth, Middlesex, England
Penguin Books Inc., 3300 Clipper Mill Road, Baltimore 11, Md, U.S.A.
Penguin Books Pty Ltd, Ringwood, Victoria, Australia

—

First published 1952
Second Edition 1954
Revised 1961 1962, 1964

—

—

Made and printed in Great Britain
by Richard Clay & Company, Ltd, Bungay, Suffolk
Collogravure plates by Harrison & Sons Ltd
Set in Monotype Bembo

Editorial Foreword

BY M. E. L. MALLOWAN

Professor of Western Asiatic Archaeology,
University of London

Dr O. R. Gurney's book on the Hittites describes what is known about this remarkable people, mostly from the evidence obtained on sites where they once lived. It seems that the Hittites had notions about civilization and the right way of life based on a standard of conduct which might with advantage be emulated to-day. Here we may read how they lived, what they thought and what they made. A splendid series of stone monuments and of architectural remains survives to give a strong impression of their character.

It is hoped that later on another book in this series will be written to illustrate the archaeological evidence and the achievements of the many other peoples who lived in the sub-continent of Asia Minor in addition to the Hittites. Meanwhile the reader may be interested to turn to previous Pelicans in order to compare Hittite accomplishments with those of other great civilizations in the Ancient Near East. Volumes by Prof. W. F. Albright on Palestine; by Prof. Stuart Piggott on Prehistoric India; by Dr I. E. S. Edwards on the Pyramids; and by Sir Leonard Woolley on a Forgotten Kingdom in ancient Syria which has a close bearing on Hittite civilization have already appeared.

Professor Mallowan is the general editor of the
Pelican series of Near Eastern and
Western Asiatic archaeologies

TO MY UNCLE, JOHN GARSTANG

Contents

CONTENTS

List of Plates

(between pages 128 and 129)

List of Text Figures

Foreword

THIS small work was undertaken at the invitation of Professor M. E. L. Mallowan, and is an attempt to present for English readers a concise account of Hittite history and civilization within the limits of our present knowledge. I do not claim that the work contains much that is original. Nearly all the conclusions presented here may be found in the writings of German or French scholars over the last twenty-five years. However, no synthesis of these results has yet been published in the English language, and it may therefore be hoped that this book may go some way to meet a real need.

It is my pleasant duty to acknowledge the kindness of all those who have assisted me in the production of the book. The following have provided photographs, from which the plates have been made: Dr H. Otten, on behalf of the Berlin State Museum (Plates 1a, 4, 5a, 10, 15b, 17, 25 and 28); Dr Hamit Z. Koşay (Plates 9, 20a, and 27), Mme Nimet Özgüç (Plates 5c and 24), Professor H. T. Bossert (Plate 29), Professor J. Garstang (Plates 6, 13b, 16, 19 and 32), the Director of the National Museum of Antiquities at Leiden (Plate 2b), the Keeper of the Ashmolean Museum (Plates 20b, 21, 22b and 23), and Mr R. A. Crossland (Plates 8, 13a, 15a and 30). Professor Garstang has also generously placed at my disposal a number of drawings originally made for his book *The Hittite Empire*. I am particularly indebted to Professor A. Goetze for allowing me to read the typescript of his forthcoming paper on the predecessors of Suppiluliumas. The chapter on Law and Institutions owes much to the guidance and advice of Sir John Miles. Professor Garstang again has contributed many valuable suggestions at all stages, but especially in reading the proofs. To all these friends and colleagues I offer my most sincere thanks for their assistance. A special word of thanks is due to my mother, Mrs S. G. Gurney, for her preparation of the index.

O. R. GURNEY

Boars Hill, Oxford

Note on Spelling of Proper Names

1. *Hittite Names*

In principle, the spelling is intended to render the Hittite pronunciation as closely as possible in terms of English letters; the vowels should be pronounced as purely as possible (as in German), the consonants as in English. The Hittite pronunciation itself is, of course, only approximately known, but the possible degree of error is not very large. Valuable clues have been obtained from contemporary transliterations into other scripts, such as Egyptian and Ugaritic. With regard to the case-endings which the Hittites attached freely to all names, whatever their origin, an artificial distinction has been made; the nominative case-ending -s has been kept for all personal names, mainly in order to give some idea of the Indo-European appearance of these names in Hittite, but it has been omitted from geographical and divine names, except where the latter are obviously of Hittite and not Hattian origin. An exception has also been made in the case of the city-name Hattusas, which has become widely known in this form; it would have been more consistent to give the Hattian form Hattus.

2. *Turkish Place Names*

The official Turkish spelling has been taken as a basis, but as certain letters in the Turkish alphabet are misleading for English readers and those with diacritical accents are difficult to print, the following substitutions have been made:

j for Turkish c		gh for Turkish ğ	
ch	„ ç	sh	„ ş

Notes to Revised Edition

P. 26. There is some reason to suppose that the dynasty founded by Tudhaliyas II was of Hurrian origin. For the Hittite names borne by these kings appear to have been in fact throne-names; their personal names, in so far as they are known, were, like those of their queens and brothers, Hurrian. Two such Hurrian names are Urhi-Teshub and Shar-Kushukh; Urhi-Teshub took the throne-name Mursilis III on ascending the throne of Hatti (p. 35), and Shar-Kushukh, the brother of Mursilis II (p. 33) is unquestionably the same person as the son of Suppiluliumas who took the Hittite name Piyassilis on his appointment as King of Carchemish (p. 30). This would explain the strong Hurrian influence on Hittite civilization during the period of the Empire (pp. 27, 123, 129, 190), and above all the introduction of the Hurrian pantheon (pp. 134, 140), which can be traced long before the time of Queen Puduhepa.

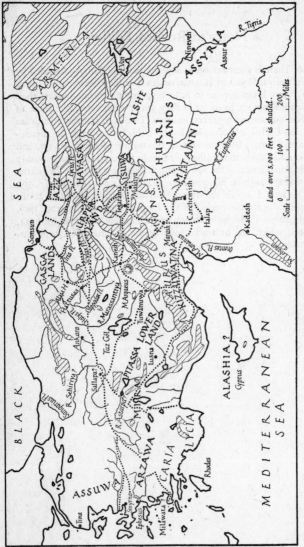

Fig. 1 – Map of Asia Minor

The Discovery of the Hittites

THE Hittites figure in the Old Testament mainly as one of several tribes which the Israelites found inhabiting Palestine when they entered the Promised Land. Most familiar are the lists of tribes such as Genesis xv. 19–21 (Kenites, Kenizzites, Kadmonites, Hittites, Perizzites, Rephaims, Amorites, Canaanites, Girgashites, Jebusites), or more briefly Joshua iii. 10 (Canaanites, Hittites, Hivites, Perizzites, Girgashites, Amorites, Jebusites). It is part of the same conception of the Hittites as one of the aboriginal tribes of Palestine when Abraham is described as buying the cave of Machpelah near Hebron from the Sons of Heth (Gen. xxiii.), Esau as marrying Hittite wives (Gen. xxvi. 34; xxxvi. 1–3), Heth as one of the sons of Canaan (Gen. x. 15), or Jerusalem as the bastard offspring of an Amorite and a Hittite (Ezek. xvi. 3). One passage, Numbers xiii. 29, specifies the particular area of Palestine inhabited by the Hittites: 'Amalek dwelleth in the land of the South: and the Hittite, and the Jebusite, and the Amorite, dwell in the mountains: and the Canaanite dwelleth by the sea, and along by the side of Jordan.' In Joshua i. 2–4 it seems to be implied that they occupied all the land between the Lebanon and the Euphrates, but the meaning is not very clear.

There is nothing in all this to suggest that the Hittites were of more importance than the Jebusites or the Girgashites. But when we come to the time of the monarchy the picture is rather different. Solomon's Hittite wives (1 Kings xi. 1) are foreigners, grouped with Moabites, Ammonites, Edomites, and Sidonians. Above all, there are two passages referring to the 'Kings of the Hittites'. In 2 Chronicles i. 17

it is described how Solomon imported horses from Egypt and sold them to the 'Kings of the Hittites and the Kings of the Arameans'; and in 2 Kings vii. 6–7 we read that a Syrian army, hearing a noise of horses and chariots, said one to another: 'Lo, the king of Israel hath hired against us the kings of the Hittites and the kings of the Egyptians, ... wherefore they arose and fled in the twilight.' Kings whose reputation inspired such terror must have been of more than local importance.

When the historical records of the Egyptians were deciphered it was revealed that the kings of the Eighteenth Dynasty had been in contact with a country called Kheta from the time when Tuthmosis III penetrated to the north of Syria and crossed the Euphrates in the fifteenth century B.C. The people of Kheta with their numerous allies had fought against Ramesses II at the battle of Kadesh on the River Orontes, a battle which was described in great detail by the Egyptian poet Pentaur, and the same king had made a treaty with them later in his reign, the text of which was carved on the wall of the great temple at Karnak. Who could doubt that the Kheta-folk of the Egyptian texts and the Hittites of the Old Testament were one and the same? The fact seemed to be confirmed when the cuneiform inscriptions of Assyria began to be deciphered and it was found that from the time of Tiglath-pileser I (*c.* 1100 B.C.) Syria was known to the Assyrians as the 'Land of Hatti' with its capital at Carchemish. No difficulty was then felt in the presence of Hittite settlements in Palestine at the time of the Israelite occupation or even in the time of Abraham.

Such was the position in 1876, when A. H. Sayce, in a paper read to the Society of Biblical Archaeology, proposed to ascribe to the Hittites the basalt blocks inscribed with a peculiar form of writing which had been found at Hama (bibl. Hamath) and at Aleppo. One of the Hamath stones had been noticed as early as 1812 by the traveller Burckhardt, who in his book *Travels in Syria* reported that in the corner of a house in the Bazaar there was 'a stone with a number of small figures and signs which appears to be a kind of hieroglyphic writing, though it does not resemble that of Egypt'. Yet this report attracted little attention until 1870, when two American travellers, Johnson and Jessup, succeeded in locating five such stones in the houses of Hamath. The hostility of the natives, however, prevented them from obtaining reliable copies of the inscriptions, and it was only in 1872, when William Wright, a missionary in Damascus, visited Hamath in the company of the Turkish governor of Syria, that the inscriptions were finally made available to science. The Pasha actually had the five stones removed from the houses into which they were built and sent to the Museum at Constantinople, but not before Wright had obtained casts of them, one set of which was sent to the British Museum and the other to the Palestine Exploration Fund.

The Aleppo stone was first seen in 1871 built into the wall of a mosque; it was believed by the natives to possess the power to cure ophthalmia, and generations of sufferers from this disease had worn the surface smooth by rubbing their eyes upon it. It was afterwards reported lost for a number of years, but it had in fact been removed by the local inhabitants and was later replaced.

Now the same script had been noticed by E. J. Davis on the great rock-carving over a stream at Ivriz in the Taurus Mountains. Davis had then called the script 'Hamathite'. This combination of script and relief at Ivriz enabled Sayce to bring into the same category a number of similar monuments which had been reported from distant parts of Asia Minor over a period of many years. Foremost among these were the remains of buildings and rock-carvings near Boghazköy (Boghazkeui) and at Alaja Hüyük (Euyuk) within the bend of the Halys River (now Kizil Irmak), which had been described by Charles Texier in 1839 and by William Hamilton in 1842. On the scarp of the hill-side above Boghazköy were to be seen the massive walls and ramparts of what had clearly been an important fortified city, and two miles away was the outcrop of rock known as Yazilikaya ('Inscribed Rock') with its natural recess, the walls of which had been used to depict in high relief a double procession of figures meeting in the centre of the back wall. In the middle of the city-area at Boghazköy stood a much-weathered stone (Nishan Tash) bearing an inscription in Hittite 'hieroglyphs', and the figures at Yazilikaya also had 'hieroglyphic' symbols by their sides. At Alaja Hüyük was a gateway flanked by huge sphinxes leading to a mound of debris which clearly covered an ancient city or large building. Farther to the west were the rock-reliefs at Gavur (Giaour) Kalesi ('Unbeliever's Fortress'), and in the hills above Smyrna were other rock-sculptures known since the time of Herodotus, who had described them as representations of the nymph Niobe and of the Egyptian king Sesostris. Sayce himself visited the 'Niobe' and 'Sesostris' figures in 1879, and in 1880 he read another paper to the Society for Biblical Archaeology in which he declared confidently that these and the other Anatolian sculptures were all monuments of the Hittites and that all the mountainous country to the north of Mesopotamia and including the whole of Asia Minor must have been inhabited in ancient times by Hittite tribes.

Widespread interest was now aroused, and during the next twenty years archaeologists visited Turkey in increasing numbers and were rewarded by the discovery of many more similar sculptures, particularly in the region of the Taurus and Anti-Taurus Mountains. The outstanding journeys were those of Humann and Puchstein (1882-3), Ramsay and Hogarth (1890), Chantre (1893), Hogarth and Headlam (1894), Anderson and Crowfoot (1900). The excavations at Carchemish (Kargamish) undertaken on behalf of the British Museum in 1879 had produced a number of inscriptions in the hieroglyphic script, as well as other monuments. A similarly inscribed stela was found during excavations at Babylon in 1899, and many monuments in a similar style were excavated by a German expedition at Zinjirli (Sinjerli) in North Syria between 1888 and 1892. Thus when in 1900 L. Messerschmidt undertook the publication of a Corpus of Hittite inscriptions the work contained some ninety-six major inscribed monuments, in addition to numerous seals and seal-impressions (cf. p. 203).

Meanwhile the history of the Hittites had been greatly illuminated by the discovery in 1887 of the Tell El Amarna letters – clay tablets, inscribed in cuneiform characters and for the most part in the Akkadian language, which had formed the diplomatic and administrative correspondence of King Akhenaten and (for the last few years of his reign) of his father Amenophis III, thus covering roughly the period 1370–1348 B.C. Not only did the letters from Palestinian and Syrian vassals contain frequent references to the King of Hatti and the movements of his armies, but among the letters was one from Suppiluliumas himself, the King of Hatti, congratulating Akhenaten on his accession. There were also two letters in an unknown language, one of which was addressed to the king of a country called Arzawa; these were studied in 1902 by the Norwegian scholar J. A. Knudtzon, who pointed out that the language had an apparent affinity with the Indo-European family of languages, but this view was treated at the time with great scepticism. A few fragments of texts in this same language were also acquired by E. Chantre near Boghazköy in 1893.

Many scholars now realized that the excavation of Boghazköy would be likely to yield rich rewards. The concession was eventually secured by Dr Hugo Winckler on behalf of the German Orient Society, and excavations under his direction began in 1906. The results justified and exceeded all expectations. About 10,000 cuneiform tablets came to light, and it was at once evident that the excavators had found a royal archive. The majority of these tablets were seen to be inscribed in the language of the two 'Arzawa' letters and could not be understood, but some were in the well-known Akkadian language of Babylonia, and a preliminary study of these revealed that this was indeed the capital of the 'Land of Hatti'. The 'Arzawan' language was evidently the official language of this kingdom of Hatti, and just as previously the name 'Hittite' had become attached to the hieroglyphic writing of Hamath, so this name now replaced 'Arzawan' to denote the language of the cuneiform texts. For what was 'Hittite' but the English rendering of the original Hatti? As to the date of the tablets, a most fortunate chance brought to light during that first season a document which proved to be the Hittite version of the treaty already mentioned between Ramesses II and the King of Hatti, the Egyptian version of which was dated in the twenty-first year of the Pharaoh.[1] Here then, not in Syria, was the capital of that 'Great Kheta' which had paid tribute to Tuthmosis III and fought and made peace with Ramesses II. Winckler's preliminary report on the tablets, published in 1907, gave a list of the kings of Hatti from Suppiluliumas in the first half of the fourteenth century to Arnuwandas at the end of the thirteenth, after which the records came to an abrupt end. It was inferred that for these 200 years the Cappadocian Hittite kingdom had dominated the other states of a great Hittite confederacy such as Carchemish, Milid, and Hamath, which were mentioned in the Assyrian records, that it had been overrun about 1200 B.C. by the invading Mushki, whom the Assyrians found in

1. Actually the 'Egyptian' version represents a translation of the text drawn up by the Hittites and sent to Egypt, whereas the 'Hittite' version is a copy of the Akkadian text drawn up by the Egyptians.

6

occupation of that part of the country in the eighth century, and that the other Hittite states then simply resumed their independence under the hegemony of Carchemish. We shall see, however, that the Syrian Hittite kingdoms of the first millennium B.C. were, with the exception of Carchemish itself, new states, which had come into existence after the Cappadocian kingdom fell; but continuity in the use of the hieroglyphic script was established not only by the fact of the inscribed stone Nishan Tash standing in the middle of the enceinte of Boghazköy, but also by the presence of hieroglyphic signs on a seal impression on one of the cuneiform tablets.

A most valuable summary of the progress made up to that time in the re-discovery of the Hittites and their monuments was published in 1910 by John Garstang, who had himself travelled widely in Asia Minor in the spring of 1907 and visited Dr Winckler at Boghazköy. His book, *The Land of the Hittites*, combined a corpus of Hittite monuments with an attractive description of the countryside which forms their setting and a *résumé* of Hittite history as revealed by Winckler's report. It remained for many years the standard work on the subject. Garstang's excavations at Sakje-gözü (Sakje-geuzi) in North Syria brought to light the remains of a palace of the latest Hittite period adorned with bas-reliefs, but failed to add to our knowledge of Hittite history; indeed, the ancient name of the place is still unknown.

The outbreak of war in 1914 prevented further exploration and also cut off English scholars from their German colleagues, who were now engaged in studying the great mass of source-material contained in the Boghazköy archives. The pioneer work on the grammar of 'cuneiform Hittite' and the first publication of Hittite texts in facsimile took place in Germany during the war years, and when contact was resumed after the war there already existed a considerable literature on the subject in which English scholarship had no part. The British Museum, however, had in the years 1911–14 been enriched by the accession of many stone monuments and hieroglyphic inscriptions excavated by a second expedition to Carchemish under the direction of D. G. Hogarth, C. L. (now Sir Leonard) Woolley, and T. E. Lawrence. Thus it came about that while there developed an entirely German science of Hittitology devoted to the study of the cuneiform tablets, the small band of British enthusiasts tended to concentrate on the decipherment of the hieroglyphic script and the study of Hittite art. Attempts at decipherment were published by Sayce, Cowley, and Campbell Thompson. But in fact this was a very difficult task, and their labour was largely in vain. For the only bilingual text of any importance was the silver 'Boss of Tarkondemos' (see Plate 20b), in reality the plating of a hemispherical seal, on which Sayce had written a paper in 1880, but this contained only ten cuneiform and six hieroglyphic signs, the cuneiform legend itself being open to more than one interpretation. More useful for the purpose of decipherment was the identification of a number of place-names and some personal names known from contemporary Assyrian inscriptions. Starting from these, five scholars – Bossert (German), Forrer (Swiss), Gelb (American), Hrozný (Czech), and Meriggi (Italian) – working independently, reached a considerable measure of agreement on the values of most of the signs in so far as they are used phonetically and determined the general structure of the language. But it was only the discovery of a long bilingual inscription at Karatepe in 1947, described below, that provided the clue to the meaning of the numerous ideograms and has enabled decipherment to reach its present stage, in which all but the most archaic inscriptions are more or less intelligible.

In Berlin the study of the cuneiform tablets from Boghaz-

köy was entrusted by the German Orient Society to a group
of Assyriologists, and the publication of the cuneiform texts
in facsimile was begun. In the linguistic field it was not long
before sensational results were achieved. In 1915 B. Hrozný
published his first sketch of the grammar of the Hittite language and showed that its structure was undoubtedly Indo-
European, as had been claimed by Knudtzon in 1902. A
more elaborate study of the language by the same author
appeared shortly afterwards under the title *Die Sprache der
Hethiter*. Unfortunately Hrozný, who was not an Indo-
European philologist, extended his thesis to the vocabulary
of the language and freely assigned meanings to Hittite
words merely by reason of their similarity to words in the
other Indo-European languages. As a result, many philologists rejected his thesis in its entirety, though much of it
was in fact sound.

The necessary corrective was introduced in 1920 by F.
Sommer, a distinguished philologist who had acquired
enough of the technique of Assyriology to read the published texts. Sommer insisted that progress could be made
only by the exercise of a strict discipline; meanings should
be assigned to words only on the basis of a comparison of
all the contexts where they were known to occur and not
by means of deceptive etymologies. This process would
hardly have been possible were it not for the extensive use
of 'allography' in the Hittite texts, whereby the scribes
often replaced common Hittite words by the corresponding Sumerian or Babylonian word by way of abbreviation
(see below, p. 121). Since this occurs irregularly, duplicate
texts often provide at once the Akkadian or Sumerian equivalent of a Hittite word; and even where there are no duplicates, many sentences are so full of these Akkadian or
Sumerian words that the meaning of the intervening Hittite
words is quite evident. A certain amount of help was obtained from the fragments of vocabularies giving Sumerian,

Akkadian, and Hittite words in parallel columns; but on the whole these vocabularies were a disappointment, partly on account of their mutilated condition and partly because they dealt with words which rarely occurred in the texts themselves. When once a number of Hittite words had been determined by the above method, it was possible to extend it to sentences which appeared in their natural Hittite guise, and so Sommer and his colleagues J. Friedrich, H. Ehelolf, and A. Götze, by constantly proceeding from the known to the unknown, have gradually brought our knowledge of Hittite to a point where historical texts can generally be translated throughout with almost complete certainty, though many religious and other texts contain passages which still baffle interpretation. In fact, most of the better-preserved historical texts had been edited and translated into German by 1933.

Meanwhile E. Forrer had applied himself with enthusiasm mainly to the reconstruction of Hittite history. Working independently of Hrozný, he also produced a sketch of Hittite grammar, but he cannot claim the credit of being the first in this field. He succeeded in collecting together and publishing in a single volume almost all the historical texts belonging to the period of the Old Kingdom (see below) and in reconstructing a complete table of kings of Hatti from the beginning to the end. This work was of lasting importance. His *résumé* of the linguistic character of the Hittite archive as a whole, with its eight languages, became well known. But his most sensational paper was that published in 1924 in which he announced that he had discovered references to the Homeric Greeks, or Achaeans, and even to particular personalities such as Andreus and Eteocles of Orchomenos and Atreus of Mycenae. His statements were based on unpublished sources, but many scholars, including Sayce, accepted them in the same spirit of enthusiasm in which they had been made. They were, however, sharply criticized by Friedrich in a paper published in 1927, and then, as in the case of Hrozný's Indo-European theory, many scholars began to treat the matter with extreme scepticism. Here again it was F. Sommer who undertook the scientific scrutiny of all the relevant material, and the results of his work were published in a monumental volume, *Die Ahhijava-Urkunden*, in 1932. The present state of the question consequent upon this and other more recent publications is discussed below, pp. 46-58.

The article on the Hittites contributed by Hrozný in 1929 to the fourteenth edition of the *Encyclopaedia Britannica* was the first attempt to synthesize the knowledge of Hittite life and culture that had been gained from the texts. But it was Götze who in his volume on Asia Minor, contributed to Müller's *Handbuch der Altertumswissenschaft* in 1933, produced the first fully documented and systematic description of Hittite civilization. So sure was his touch and so clear his presentation of the subject that, although some gaps have since been filled, the edifice which he built still remains unshaken. His work inevitably forms the basis of the present volume, as it has of others before it.

The first notable undertaking in the field of Hittite studies outside Germany was the *Éléments de la Grammaire Hittite*, by L. Delaporte, published in 1929. In 1930, at the instigation of L. Delaporte, E. Cavaignac, and A. Juret, there was founded in Paris the *Société des Études Hittites et Asianiques*, which publishes a Journal, *Revue Hittite et Asianique*, devoted to the study of Hittite and Anatolian problems. In America E. H. Sturtevant, the leader of a group of Indo-European philologists who had interested themselves in the Hittite language from the comparative point of view, published in 1933 *A Comparative Grammar of the Hittite Language*, a work which was severely criticized for its premature speculations in comparative etymology, but which as a descriptive grammar, summarizing the work of German scholars, supplied a real need and superseded all previous attempts of the kind, included that of Delaporte.

Sturtevant's Grammar held the field for seven years. It was only in 1940 that there appeared a definitive descriptive grammar of the Hittite language from the pen of one of the pioneers of Hittitology. This was the *Hethitisches Elementarbuch*, by J. Friedrich, which will probably remain the standard work of its kind for a long time to come. The same author's *Hethitisches Wörterbuch* (1952) has now provided scholars with a similar standard work in the field of lexicography, superseding Sturtevant's *Hittite Glossary* (1935).

In the Hittite lands themselves exploration was resumed in the late twenties, encouraged by conditions which differed markedly from those which obtained under the pre-war Turkish régime. H. H. Von der Osten and I. J. Gelb travelled widely in Asia Minor for the University of Chicago and discovered a number of new monuments. Von der Osten also undertook the excavation of the Hittite site of Alishar, which established the pottery sequence of the Bronze Age in Anatolia. Delaporte began excavations at Malatya in 1932. At Boghazköy itself excavations were resumed in 1931 under the direction of K. Bittel and continued year by year until the outbreak of the Second World War. In Syria excavations were conducted at Hama (Hamath) by a Danish expedition under Harald Ingholt, at Tell Tainat by an expedition from Chicago, and finally by Sir Leonard Woolley at Tell Atchana. A most significant fact has been the increasing part taken by the Turks themselves in all branches of Hittite studies under the guidance of H. G. Güterbock, Professor of Hittitology at Ankara University from 1935 to 1948,[1] and H. T. Bossert, Director of the Department of Near Eastern Studies at the University of Istanbul. To the latter and his Turkish assistants is due the dis-

[1]. Professor Güterbock has been worthily succeeded by the Turkish Hittitologist Dr Sedat Alp, who received his training in Germany.

covery of one of the most important of all the Hittite hieroglyphic monuments – the bilingual inscription of Karatepe.
At the summit of this mound, which is situated far up in the
foot-hills of Taurus beside the River Jeyhan (the classical
Pyramus), is a late Hittite fortress which first attracted the
attention of Professor Bossert in 1946. Excavations were
begun in autumn 1947, and it was found that the fortress
had two entrance buildings, to the north and to the south,
each approached by a corridor flanked by inscribed slabs. In
each case the inscription on the left is in old Phoenician,
while that on the right is in Hittite hieroglyphs, and it appears that the content of the inscriptions is everywhere the
same, that in fact we have here twice repeated a single bilingual text in Phoenician and hieroglyphic Hittite. A
further copy of the Phoenician text is inscribed on a statue
which was found lying on the surface. It is indeed a strange
chance that a monument of this size and importance should
have eluded explorers for so many years. The Hittite and
Phoenician texts are not identical, but the correspondence
between them is very close. Consequently, though many
problems remain unsolved, this discovery has brought about
a great advance in our understanding of the hieroglyphic
inscriptions.

The tale of excavations in Hittite lands would not be
complete without reference to the American expedition
under Professor Hetty Goldman which worked at Tarsus in
Cilicia from 1935 to 1949, the Neilson expedition under Professor John Garstang which excavated part of a Hittite fortress and some earlier Hittite material at Yümük Tepe near
Mersin, and the Turkish excavations at Alaja Hüyük under
Dr Hamit Koşay, at Kültepe, Fraktin, Karahüyük (Elbistan)
and Horoztepe under Professor Tahsin Özgüç, and at Karahüyük (Konya) under Professor Sedat Alp. At Tarsus and at
Alaja Hüyük one Hittite tablet was found, while Karahüyük
(Konya) has yielded many Hittite seals and seal-impressions.

It will be seen from this narrative that, largely through extraneous circumstances, the several branches of Hittite studies tended for a while to become separated. The British public has come to associate the Hittites with the hieroglyphic writing and the stone monuments rather than with the clay tablets and cuneiform texts from Boghazköy, of which comparatively few have ever reached this country. On the other hand, the Anatolian Hittite kingdom was treated culturally, as well as historically and linguistically, in isolation, a tendency which was accentuated by the fact that Götze's epoch-making book was devoted exclusively to Asia Minor as such. Götze indeed took up the extreme position that only the Anatolian kingdom was entitled to the name of Hittite and that the so-called Hittite monuments represented the art not of the Hittites but of the Hurrians. But of recent years, since it was established that 'hieroglyphic Hittite' is closely related to, though not identical with, 'cuneiform Hittite', there has been a new tendency towards synthesis and renewed recognition that the Anatolian and Syrian kingdoms must after all be treated as parts of a single whole. None the less, owing to the fact that the hieroglyphic inscriptions in so far as they have been read, are for the most part rather formal dedications, we still know little about the Syrian Hittites except the characteristics of their art and the bare outline of their external political history. It is at present the tablets of Boghazköy and they alone that enable us to appreciate something of the life and thought of this ancient people, and it is for this reason that in the present survey the Anatolian kingdom occupies a space which is out of proportion to its duration in time as compared with the Syrian states. It is hoped that the intrinsic interest of the cuneiform texts will be thought to provide sufficient excuse for this treatment.

CHAPTER I

Outline of History

I. THE EARLIEST PERIOD

WE have seen how the quest for the Hittites led up from Palestine through Syria, until in 1907 the capital of the 'Land of Hatti' was discovered at Boghazköy in the north of Asia Minor. The last step is significant because of the fundamental contrast between the plains of Syria and the essentially highland country which formed the homeland of the Hittites. Asia Minor (Anatolia) is a high table-land which rises in general from the Aegean coast in the west to the great ranges of Eastern Turkey: structurally it is part of the mountain system which extends eastward, and then southward, to the borders of India. Seen from the Syrian plains, these northern mountains form a mighty wall known to the Romans as Taurus, which seemed to the ancient geographers to divide the whole world east of the Mediterranean into 'inner' and 'outer' (i.e., northern and southern) halves. From the Anatolian plateau, however, it is only the western extension of the Taurus range that bounds the view to the south. To the east other mountains dominate the landscape, foremost among them the great cone of the extinct volcano Erjiyes Dagh, the ancient Argaeus, rising to a height of over 12,000 feet, and behind it the chain of Anti-Taurus running obliquely northeastwards from Taurus to merge in the great massif of the eastern highlands. This range of Anti-Taurus is the watershed which divides the rivers of the plateau from those of Mesopotamia to the east and of Cilicia to the south. The centre of the plateau is occupied by a shallow basin, from which the waters can find no outlet to the sea and drain into a salt lake (Turkish Tuz Göl). North of this the land rises again to a series of transverse ridges running out from the eastern massif, before it sinks ultimately down to the Black Sea coast. This region has always been rendered difficult of access by the thick forests nourished by the waters drawn up from the Black Sea and precipitated on the hill-sides.

The river Kizil Irmak, familiar to classical scholars as the Halys and probably known to the Hittites as Marassantiya, after emerging from the eastern mountains and flowing for a considerable distance in a south-westerly direction, is turned aside by a secondary ridge as it approaches the salt lake, and so bends round in a great loop, until its course is completely reversed and it cuts through the northern hills in a north-easterly direction to enter the Black Sea. The Hittite area with which we shall be chiefly concerned comprises the bend described by the Halys in its middle course and the plain to the south of the lake; it is bounded on all sides by the highlands, on the east by the Anti-Taurus and the mountains beyond, on the south by Taurus, and on the west and north by more broken ranges. The coastal areas to the north and south were excluded from it, and the western half of the peninsula seems to have been dominated for long periods by the rival kingdom of Arzawa.

Hattusas, the Hittite capital, lay on the northern slope of one of the ridges where the plateau begins to break down towards the Black Sea. Two torrents flowing northward from this range in steep rocky beds unite at the foot of the slope near the modern village of Boghazköy, leaving between them a spur on which the oldest settlement at Hattusas has been found. The site commands a fine view of the valley to the north bounded only by the next range of Pontic hills some fifteen miles away, and is a natural stronghold. It also lies near the junction of the two most ancient trade-routes, the one leading from the Aegean coast across the lower Halys to Sivas and the East, the other southwards from the Black Sea port of Amisus (Samsun) to the Cilician gates. It was only necessary to link the city with these routes in order to make it the centre of a radiating web of strategic roads.

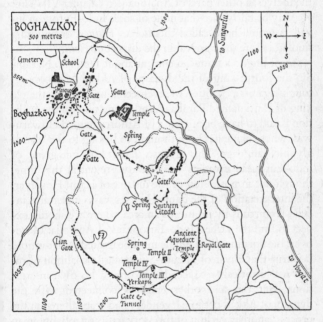

Fig. 2 – Plan of Boghazköy (Hattusas)

The historical 'Land of Hatti', as we know it in the second millennium B.C., was a state, later an empire, created by kings ruling from this mountain fastness. This kingdom and its official language have become known as 'Hittite', and the name must now be accepted. But the 'Hittite' language was not indigenous in Asia Minor, and the name of Hatti was given to the country by the earlier people of the land, whom we call Hattians. The Indo-European Hittite language was superimposed on the non-Indo-European Hattian by an invading people, and it was presumably at the same time that other Indo-European dialects (Luwian, Palaic, Lycian, and 'Hieroglyphic Hittite') established themselves in other parts of Anatolia (see Chapter VI). Thus we may be fairly sure that none of these Indo-European invaders would have called themselves *Hittites*, or anything similar, before their arrival in the district of *Hatti*.

According to a tradition current about 1400 B.C. Naram-Sin the fourth king of the dynasty of Akkad (*c.* 2200 B.C.) fought against a coalition of seventeen kings, among them a king of Hatti named Pamba. Another member of the coalition is said to have been a king of Amurru named Huwaruwas, whose name has been thought to belong to the 'hieroglyphic' language. This suggests that at least one group of Indo-European invaders was already present at that time, though not in possession of the district of Hatti. However, the interpretation of the name Huwaruwas is uncertain; indeed Amurru is by no means an area where we should expect to find the earliest Indo-Europeans of Anatolia. Moreover, the document as a whole must be treated with caution. It is true that a war of Naram-Sin against a coalition of rebels is a historical fact recorded in one of his own inscriptions. But this and other episodes connected with the dynasty of Akkad became legendary and were altered in the process; another version of this story exists on a Babylonian tablet of *c.* 1700 B.C., and the names on the two versions do not correspond. It is therefore unsafe to use this text or others like it as a historical document.

True history begins in Anatolia with the arrival on the plateau of Assyrian traders about 1900 B.C. At this time the people of Assur were already familiar with the cuneiform script of Babylonia, and the clay tablets on which these Assyrian merchants inscribed their day-to-day business correspondence with their capital city have been found in large numbers at several sites, but chiefly at Kültepe, the ancient Kanesh, near Kayseri. Among the many non-Assyrian names to be found in these documents there are a few which can be interpreted as Hittite, and, scanty though this material is, it is enough to establish a probability that Hittites were already settled in the country.

Little enough is learnt from these tablets of the indigenous population and their history. But we hear of local princes and their palaces, and it is evident that the country was broken up into at least ten small principalities, among which the city of Burushkhatum (the Hittite Puruskhanda) seems at first to have held a dominant position, since its ruler is distinguished from the rest as a 'Great Prince'. Very few of the local princes are known to us by name. But we have been fortunate in recovering three tablets bearing the names of a certain Pitkhana and his son Anitta, for these two are known to us from a remarkable Hittite text, which in its present form at least dates from about 1300 B.C. In it Anittas (for this is the Hittite form of his name) son of Pitkhanas, King of Kussara, records – ostensibly in his own words – the story of his and his father's struggle for power against the rival cities of Nesa, Zalpuwa, Puruskhanda, Salatiwara, and Hatti (or Hattusas). These cities were successfully subdued, the last named (otherwise well known as the capital of the Hittite kingdom) being utterly destroyed and declared accursed. Having overcome all opposition, King Anittas transferred his residence to Nesa, possibly to be identified with Kanesh (Kültepe), where a dagger inscribed with his name has been found. It would seem, then, that by the end of his reign this king must have controlled the greater part of the Cappadocian plateau.

The natural assumption that the inscription of Anittas is simply a late copy of one composed by the king himself leads to serious difficulties. For the style of cuneiform used by the Hittites is totally unlike that employed by the Assyrian merchants, and we must infer that the Hittites adopted their script from a source as yet unknown at a time when the Assyrians were no longer living in their midst. Therefore, Anittas, who was contemporary with the Assyrians, could hardly have written in 'cuneiform Hittite' if the script was not introduced into the country until after his time. In what language then did he write? Such elaborate inscriptions as this are not produced out of a literary vacuum. Yet not a single example of an Anatolian royal inscription of this period has yet come to light. It has been suggested that a whole literature inscribed on some perishable material, such as wood, possibly in Hittite hieroglyphs, has been lost to us; but in view of the very brief and formal nature of the earliest extant hieroglyphic inscriptions, it does not seem very likely that such a literature can have existed in these early times, even though 'scribes of wood' are frequently mentioned in the later Hittite texts. Perhaps further excavation will produce evidence that these native princes composed inscriptions in Akkadian; we might then believe that our inscription of Anittas is a translation from that language. At present we seem driven to conclude that the deeds of Anittas became legendary, and were later worked into the form of an apocryphal 'royal inscription'. The statement that Anittas received among the tribute from Puruskhanda such large iron objects as a sceptre and a throne certainly looks like an anachronism.

It was probably during the reign of Anittas that the commercial activity of the Assyrians in Cappadocia, having flourished for more than a century, came to a sudden end. Whether this was the result of the conquests of Anittas, or of some disaster which befell the city of Assur at this time, is unknown. There is nothing to suggest that the attitude of the indigenous rulers to the Assyrians was anything but friendly. Indeed, we may well suppose that the foreign merchants were welcome to the native princes, to whom they brought the benefits of the higher civilization of the Mesopotamian valley.

What is the relation of Anittas to the kingdom of Hatti? On the one hand, Kussara, his city, was evidently a royal residence in early Hittite times, if not the actual administrative capital, and this has suggested to many scholars that the Hittite royal line was really descended from Anittas. But no Hittite king ever claimed Anittas as his forebear, and it has been argued that the episode of the destruction of Hattusas and the peculiar animosity shown by Anittas against that city proves him to belong to a tradition foreign to the kings who later made Hattusas their capital. His story would then have been preserved only as a saga with which the Hittites claimed a spiritual connexion. There is much force in this argument, but it does not amount to proof, and the question must at present remain open.

2. THE OLD KINGDOM

The later Hittite kings liked to trace their descent back to the ancient King Labarnas, and with him therefore Hittite history may be said to begin, although he does not appear to have been the first of his line. No authentic inscription of this monarch has survived, but his deeds are narrated by one of his successors, and there is no reason to doubt the record.

Formerly Labarnas was king; and then his sons, his brothers, his connexions by marriage and his blood-relations were united. And the land was small; but wherever he marched to battle, he subdued the lands of his enemies with might. He destroyed the lands and made them powerless, and he made the seas his frontiers. And when he returned from battle, his sons went each to every part of the land, to Hupisna, to Tuwanuwa, to Nenassa, to Lānda,

to Zallara, to Parsuhanda and to Lusna, and governed the land,
and the great cities of the land were assigned to them.

This inscription was written to point a moral, namely
that the strength of the kingdom lay in the existence of har-
monious relations between the members of the royal family.
We have a glimpse of a strong and united clan pushing forward ambitiously in all directions. Of the seven cities mentioned, Tuwanuwa is certainly the classical Tyana, and Hupisna is generally equated with Kybistra; Lusna may be the
classical Lystra, well known from the mission of Saint Paul.
Zallara and Nenassa have not been identified with any certainty, but Parsuhanda must have been in the same general
area, since it is said elsewhere to have been in the province
called the Lower Land, which is the plain to the south-east
of the salt lake within the curve of the Taurus. With the
exception of Lānda, which was probably in the north,
the cities thus form a compact group separated by a considerable distance from Hattusas, and it is therefore not surprising to find that the capital of the kingdom at this time
was most probably not Hattusas but the ancient city of Kussara, which has not indeed been located, but may well have
been south of the Halys.

The statement in the inscription that Labarnas made the
seas his frontiers is confirmed by another, much later, document, according to which he subdued the kingdom of Arzawa, a country certainly situated in the western half of
Asia Minor, though its exact location is disputed. It seems
therefore that already in the reign of its first king the Hittite
kingdom dominated a territory which, in the south and
west at least, represented the farthest limit of expansion attained by the most powerful monarchs of the later empire.

The successor of Labarnas, Hattusilis I, was remembered
in later times as King of Kussara, and it was at this city that
he delivered the speech which is our main source of infor-

mation for political conditions in the early kingdom (see below, pp. 67–9 and 171). However, the same document shows clearly that the administrative capital at the end of his reign was Hattusas; it also indicates that his original name was not Hattusilis but Labarnas, like his father. Hence we may conclude that this king during the course of his reign transferred his capital from Kussara to Hattusas and adopted in consequence the name of Hattusilis. His choice of this northern stronghold as his capital was doubtless guided by strategical considerations.

During this and the following reign the Hittite kingdom began to expand southward and eastward. This meant the emergence of the Hittite armies from behind their mountain barrier and the crossing of the formidable range of Taurus, through which only a few passes lead. Perhaps it was the wealth of the southern plains and their ancient civilization that tempted them to this difficult operation. Hattusilis appears to have come into collision first with the prosperous kingdom of Yamhad, with its capital at Aleppo (Hittite Halap), which at that time controlled northern Syria. There can be little doubt that Yamhad was defeated at this time and Aleppo reduced to vassalage, but it must have revolted again, for the next king, Mursilis I, is said to have destroyed it. The siege of Urshu, a literary description of which has survived (see below, Chapter VIII), must have occurred during one of these campaigns.

Mursilis, not content with his conquest of North Syria, pressed on down the Euphrates and fell upon the great Amorite kingdom of Babylon, which collapsed before him. The Babylonian Chronicle records this event – the end of the First Dynasty of Babylon, of which Hammurabi is the most notable figure – as follows: 'In the time of Samsuditana the men of Hatti marched against the land of Akkad.' This epoch-making victory links Hittite chronology firmly with that of Babylonia. Unfortunately the latter is itself still a matter of controversy. A very plausible view places the Hittite capture of Babylon shortly after 1600 B.C., though some would either raise or lower this date by about sixty years.

However, the internal organization of the Hittite kingdom had not yet reached a stage which would enable it to stand the strain of such a formidable adventure. Signs of this instability had already become manifest during the reign of Hattusilis. The princes of the royal house, led by the son whom Hattusilis had himself proclaimed as his successor, had started an insurrection, but the king was strong enough to stamp out the rebellion. The heir to the throne was disowned and banished from Hattusas, and Mursilis, then a minor, was adopted in his place. But the prolonged absence of this young king on his foreign campaigns was an invitation to conspiracy, and on his return from Babylon Mursilis was assassinated by one Hantilis, who had married the king's own sister. A sorry period of palace murders and intrigues was thus inaugurated which lasted for several generations and reduced the kingdom to a condition little short of anarchy.

The reign of Hantilis was marked by external disasters. The Hurrians, a people whose home was in the mountains around Lake Van, and who had been the victims of an attack by Mursilis, invaded the eastern part of the Hittite realm. A short distance east of the capital Nerik and Tiliura were destroyed by invaders, and the king found it necessary to strengthen the fortifications of Hattusas itself. In the south Hantilis and his successors seem to have lost most of the territory conquered by Labarnas, Hattusilis, and Mursilis.

The position was to some extent restored when about 1525 B.C. Telipinus, the husband of a royal princess, seized the throne, and succeeded in securing his position by disposing of all rival claimants. The chaotic conditions of the previous fifty years had demonstrated only too clearly the need for a law of succession and for a consolidation of the Hittite state from within, and this seems to have been the main task which Telipinus set himself to accomplish. He composed an elaborate edict, in which a brief survey of Hittite history (the beginning of which is quoted above), illustrating the dangers of discord and disunity in high quarters, led up to the proclamation of a precise law of succession and of a number of other rules for the conduct of the king and the nobles. The laws thus promulgated seem to have been observed down to the last days of the Hittite Empire.

In external policy Telipinus was content to establish a safe and defensible frontier. To the north and east of the capital the barbarian invaders were pushed back to a safe distance, and a certain amount of territory seems to have been reconquered. But to the west and south the loss of Arzawa and the countries beyond the Taurus, including the whole of Syria, was accepted. It is perhaps typical of this king that he is the first of whom it is stated that he made a treaty with a foreign power. The treaty was with Kizzuwatna (the Cataonia of Roman times), which at this date probably comprised the eastern part of the Cilician plain with an extension up the valley of the river Pyramus. The treaty itself has not survived, and we do not know its terms. But as the ruler of Kizzuwatna apparently claimed the title of 'Great King', and as Kizzuwatna is known as a powerful state in the following century, we may suppose that Telipinus recognized its king on terms of approximate parity.

Telipinus is usually regarded as the last king of the Old Kingdom. From the middle of his reign the historical sources fail, and the names of his immediate successors cannot be stated with certainty. This rather obscure period fills the interval between Telipinus and Tudhaliyas II, the founder of a new dynasty and the first king of the Empire. During this interval of about half a century the archaeological evidence proves that there was no serious break in continuity, and indeed the period is not entirely devoid of written evidence. The law code, one of the most important of all the texts found at Boghazköy (see Chapter IV), was compiled by one of Telipinus' successors, who thus continued the process of consolidation begun by his predecessor; and it is probably a sign of the same tendency that a particular kind of land-deed or charter, bearing an impression of the royal seal, belongs exclusively to this period.

3. THE EMPIRE

Tudhaliyas II, the founder of the dynasty which later created the Hittite Empire, is himself a shadowy figure. The only fact recorded of him is that he attacked and destroyed Aleppo, but this is enough to show that the Hittite kingdom had recovered its inner stability and was again able to impose its will upon rebellious vassals.

The date and circumstances of this attack on Aleppo are uncertain, and the event has to be fitted into the known history of Syria during the fifteenth century B.C. During the long period of Hittite weakness following the murder of Mursilis I North Syria seems to have fallen under the domination of Hanigalbat, one of the political units into which the Hurrian people became organized about 1500 B.C. The powerlessness of Hatti is shown by the fact that a Syrian vassal of the Hurrian kingdom was able to make border raids into Hittite territory with impunity. In 1457 B.C. the Hurrian domination was brought to an end by the victories of Tuthmosis III in his eighth campaign, and for some thirty years the Egyptians were supreme in Syria. But the Egyptian hold on northern Syria did not long survive the death of the energetic Tuthmosis, and shortly after the accession of Amenophis II the Egyptians were forced to retire in their turn before another Hurrian power, Mitanni. This kingdom of Mitanni, under the leadership of an Aryan dynasty, became indeed for a time the dominant power in western Asia. The inner history of this movement is unknown to us, for the records of the kings of Mitanni have yet to be found. But in the following century, when the strength of Mitanni was broken, and records again become plentiful, the Hurrian language and the influence of Hurrian culture is very marked in all the lands from Hittite Anatolia to Canaanite Palestine.

The Hittite attack on Aleppo is said to have been in punishment for the defection of that city to Hanigalbat. It can therefore hardly be later than the defeat of Hanigalbat by Tuthmosis III in 1457 B.C. In fact, it is not unlikely that the Hittites carried out this attack in conjunction with the Egyptian campaign, as allies of the Egyptian king, for we know that Tuthmosis received gifts from 'Great Kheta' at this time. This would explain the omission of any reference to the capture of Aleppo in the accounts of the Egyptian campaign.

The rise of Mitanni brought renewed crisis to the Hittite kingdom. A number of principalities which had formerly come within the Hittite orbit either went over to the rival power or asserted their independence, and under Hattusilis II and Tudhaliyas III the kingdom was brought to the verge of catastrophe. The following description of the crisis by a later king seems to refer to this period:

In earlier days the Hatti-lands were sacked from beyond their borders(?). The enemy from Kaska came and sacked the Hatti-lands and made Nenassa his frontier. From beyond the Lower Land came the enemy from Arzawa, and he too sacked the Hatti-lands and made Tuwanuwa and Uda his frontier.

From beyond, the enemy from Araunna came and sacked the whole of the land of Gassiya.

From beyond again, the enemy from Azzi came and sacked all the Upper Lands and made Samuha his frontier. And the enemy from Isuwa came and sacked the land of Tegarama.

From beyond too the enemy from Armatana came, and he too sacked the Hatti-lands and made the city Kizzuwatna his frontier. And Hattusas, the city, was burned down and ... but the mausoleum of ... escaped.

It seems scarcely credible that all these attacks could have occurred simultaneously, for the kingdom would have been reduced to a barren patch of territory south of the Halys river. But the account fits in with the known facts of the situation at about this time in so far as the attacks of Hatti's eastern neighbours can be ascribed to the backing of Mitanni, while the independence and expansion of Arzawa are confirmed by the presence of letters to its king from the Pharaoh among the archives of Tell El Amarna.

The end of this period of impotence and the beginning of a new era are marked by the rise to power of King Suppiluliumas. The circumstances of his accession about 1380 B.C. seem to have been irregular, though he was a son of Tudhaliyas III and had accompanied his father on certain campaigns.

Of the struggle for consolidation in the home-lands of Hatti which must have occupied the first few years of this king's reign we know little. It was probably he who laid out the line of the great protective wall on the south side of the city of Hattusas and the other fortifications of the capital which are described below (pp. 110–13). He was then able to devote himself to the main task of his reign, the settling of accounts with Mitanni, the enemy who had been responsible for the distressful condition of his kingdom in the previous generation.

A first raid through the Taurus passes into Syria was repulsed with heavy losses; Tushratta, King of Mitanni, was able to forward a portion of the booty to his ally the King of Egypt. The next attack was therefore more carefully prepared. Perhaps it had been found that the main defences of Mitanni were in northern Syria. At any rate the new plan was to cross the Euphrates at Malatya and take the Mitannian kingdom itself in the rear. The route was dangerous on account of the wild tribes who inhabited the northern mountains, and a preliminary campaign was necessary to reduce them to submission; a treaty was concluded with a somewhat nebulous kingdom called alternatively Azzi and Hayasa, and was cemented by the marriage of the king's sister to the chieftain. Thus was the left flank secured. Crossing the Euphrates, Suppiluliumas recovered without difficulty the lost province of Isuwa and descended suddenly upon the Mitannian capital, Wassukkanni, which he entered and sacked. The Mitannian king apparently offered no resistance and avoided battle. Suppiluliumas then re-crossed the Euphrates into Syria, where the local princelings, deprived of Mitannian support, hastened to offer submission. It was no part of his plan to provoke hostility with Egypt, and he would probably have been content to make the Orontes River his frontier; but the King of Kadesh (an outpost of Egyptian influence) came out to battle and was overwhelmed by the Hittite chariotry. The Hittite army penetrated southwards as far as Abina (the Hobah of Genesis xiv. 15) near Damascus, and Suppiluliumas claims that he made the Lebanon his frontier. Fortunately for him, the Egyptian kings at this time had ceased to concern themselves with their imperial defences and were preoccupied with an internal religious reform.

As a result of this brilliant expedition, which is to be dated about 1370 B.C., Halap (Aleppo) and Alalakh (Atchana) became Hittite. The extant treaties with the kings of Nuhassi (central Syria) and Amurru, which included the Lebanon region and much of the coastal strip, were perhaps concluded at this time. However, Carchemish, which controlled the main Euphrates crossing, and the district known to the Hittites as Astata, which extended down the Euphrates from Carchemish to the mouth of the Habur, remained hostile and could still expect support from the undefeated, though discredited, forces of Tushratta.

At this point Suppiluliumas was recalled to his capital by pressing affairs at home. The task of holding Syria, which he left to his son Telipinus, 'the priest', can have seemed no easy one. The Syrian principalities were split into pro-Hittite and pro-Mitannian factions, each watching eagerly for the outcome of the struggle of the great powers. But fortunately for the Hittites Mitanni was itself torn by faction. King Tushratta and his predecessors had allied themselves with the kings of Egypt, and the two dynasties were closely linked by diplomatic marriages. But now Egypt had proved itself a broken reed, and a rival branch of the Mitannian royal family saw in Tushratta's embarrassment its own chance of power. This party looked for aid and support to Assur-uballit, the ambitious King of Assyria, whose forebears had done homage to the Mitannian kings. So it came about that Tushratta was assassinated and the new King Artatama, followed by his son Shutarna, acknowledged the independence of Assyria and rewarded its king with sumptuous gifts from the palace.

Whatever dangers this sudden rise of a vigorous new state on the Tigris held for the future, the collapse of Mitanni undoubtedly facilitated the Hittite conquest of Syria. When Suppiluliumas returned there about 1340 B.C. to complete his task, it needed only an eight-days' siege to reduce the great fortress of Carchemish, and Syria from the Euphrates to the sea became a Hittite dependency. Telipinus was installed as King of Aleppo and another of the king's sons, Piyassilis, as King of Carchemish. Finally, the kingdom of Kizzuwatna, now isolated, made peace, and was recognized as a friendly power almost on a basis of equality (see below, p. 74).

The fame which Suppiluliumas had achieved may be judged from an incident which occurred while he was encamped before Carchemish. There arrived a messenger from Egypt bearing a letter from his queen in the following words: 'My husband has died and I have no son, but of you it is said that you have many sons. If you would send me one of your sons, he could become my husband. I will on no account take one of my subjects and make him my husband. I am very much afraid.' So astonished was Suppiluliumas at this request that he sent his own envoy to the Egyptian court to make sure he was not being deceived. This man duly returned with a second message from the queen: 'Why do you say "They are deceiving me"? If I had a son, would I write to a foreigner to publish my distress and that of my country? You have insulted me in speaking thus. He who was my husband is dead and I have no son. I will never take one of my subjects and marry him. I have written to no one but you. Everyone says you have many sons; give me one of them that he may become my husband.' The Egyptian queen who sent these messages was almost certainly Ankhesenamun, the third daughter of the 'heretic' King Akhenaten and, though still a young girl, widow of the boy-king Tutankhamun, who died when hardly eighteen years of age. Having no children, she would have had, in theory at least, the right to choose her second husband and so to determine the successor to the throne of Egypt. Suppiluliumas was not the man to miss so unusual an opportunity, and one of his sons was duly dispatched. But the plan miscarried. We are told that the Hittite prince was put to death on his arrival in Egypt, presumably by agents of the priest and courtier Ai, who became the next king of Egypt and appears to have married Ankhesenamun, thus legitimating his usurpation of the throne. Doubtless this was the marriage from which Ankhesenamun thought to save herself by her appeal to the Hittite king.

Shortly after this the son of the murdered Tushratta of Mitanni, having barely escaped with his life, presented himself as a suppliant before Suppiluliumas. Here was an opportunity to form a buffer-state against the rising menace of Assyria which the shrewd Hittite king was not slow to seize. The young man was commended to Piyassilis, King of Carchemish, and together they advanced across the Euphrates with strong forces and re-entered Wassukkanni, the Mitannian capital. A new vassal kingdom of Mitanni was brought into being, but proved in the end to be too weak to resist the onslaught of Assur-uballit, who shortly after the death of Suppiluliumas was able to incorporate the territory in his dominions, and so faced the Hittites across the Euphrates.

However, the Hittite control of Syria was never again seriously disturbed. When Suppiluliumas and shortly afterwards his eldest son Arnuwandas II were carried off by a pestilence, and the throne descended to the young and inexperienced Mursilis II, the princes of Aleppo and Carchemish remained loyal, and it was mainly from the western provinces of the Empire that the challenge came. Here much is uncertain owing to the difficulty of locating the many places named. The powerful kingdom of Arzawa, which, as we have seen, had once been subdued by Labarnas himself, had asserted its independence during the period of Hittite decline, and its king had even corresponded on friendly terms with the King of Egypt. It had been re-conquered by Suppiluliumas, but now again, with its satellites Mira, Kuwaliya, Hapalla, and the Land of the River Seha, it rose in revolt.

The young Mursilis, however, was a true son of his father. By a great campaign which lasted two years, and of which we have a very detailed account, Arzawa was completely crushed, its king was slain, and Hittite nominees were installed as rulers of the several kingdoms. One at least of these chieftains was already bound to the Hittite throne by marriage to a Hittite princess. The settlement lasted the lifetime of Mursilis, but the Hittite Empire was never very secure on this flank, and each succeeding king had to quell a rebellion there.

The northern border was also a perpetual cause of anxiety, though for another reason. Here was no powerful rival like Arzawa in the west; the difficulty was that there was no settled government at all with which a treaty could be made. Hittite garrisons were posted in the main centres, but they do not seem to have been strong enough to hold down the turbulent Kaska-folk who inhabited these remote valleys. There is no hint whatever that the tribesmen were receiving help from beyond the borders of the Hittite world; yet the king was obliged every few years to lead his imperial army up into the northern hills to pacify the country. Mursilis records such campaigns (again in great detail) for years 1, 2, 5, 6, 7, 9, 19, 24, 25, 26 of his reign. Each campaign seems to have been successful, yet no finality was achieved; the tribes were always ready to break out afresh at the slightest sign of weakness. Thus it is difficult to avoid the suspicion that the causes of unrest lay deeper than the Hittites themselves knew.

Farther east the kingdom of Azzi-Hayasa gave trouble in the seventh year of the reign and had to be entirely re-conquered. This campaign was at first entrusted to one of the king's generals, the king being obliged to attend to his religious duties in Kummanni (the classical Comana).

Meanwhile even Syria broke out in revolt, apparently at the instigation of Egypt, which was beginning to exert itself again under the rule of the general Haremhab. The king of Carchemish, the king's brother Shar-Kushukh, who had exercised effective control over his territories for some ten years, happened to join his brother at Kummanni for the festival, and while there he fell ill and died. During the absence of its king Carchemish was apparently captured, though by whom is uncertain. The king's personal intervention was imperative, and accordingly in his ninth year he descended into Syria. The mere presence of the imperial army seems to have been enough to reduce the Syrian princes to submission. The son of Shar-Kushukh was duly installed as King of Carchemish, and within the year Mursilis was able to proceed north to conclude the operations against Azzi-Hayasa.

The remainder of the king's campaigns cannot be located exactly. There is strangely no mention of Kizzuwatna, although the country was said to have revolted at the beginning of the reign. As no king of Kizzuwatna is mentioned after the time of Suppiluliumas, and it seems to have become a province of Hatti during the reign of Mursilis, its re-conquest must have been described in a portion of the text that is now missing.

Mursilis left to his son and successor Muwatallis an empire firmly established and surrounded by a network of vassal kingdoms. No serious trouble occurred on the new king's accession. A show of force was necessary in the west, but the name of the opponent is not preserved. The vassal princes of the lands of Arzawa were confirmed in their positions, and a new treaty was drawn up with one Alaksandus, King of Wilusa, a country which is here named as one of the Arzawa lands, but is said to have remained consistently loyal to Hatti from the time of Labarnas. Secure on this flank, Muwatallis was free to devote his attentions to a new danger from the south. For the Egyptian colossus was at last astir. The kings of the Nineteenth Dynasty were ambitious to recover the territories in Syria formerly conquered by Tuthmosis III and lost again through the apathy of the religious reformer Akhenaten. About 1300 B.C. Sethos I led his army up into Canaan, where he restored law and order, and pushed on as far as Kadesh on the Orontes. Apparently the Hittites reacted energetically, and throughout the rest of the reign of Sethos I the peace was preserved. But on the accession of Ramesses II in 1290 B.C. it became clear that a trial of strength between the two rival empires could no longer be avoided, and to this purpose Muwatallis summoned contingents from each of his allies. A list of them is given by the Egyptian scribes (the Hittite records of this reign have not been found), and here we find for the first time mention of the Dardanians, familiar from Homer's Iliad, and the Philistines, as well as the Sherden, who appear frequently in Egyptian inscriptions. None of these peoples is mentioned in extant Hittite documents, however, and in the absence of contemporary Hittite records the reason for their presence among the Hittite forces in this struggle remains a matter for speculation. The imperial armies met at Kadesh in the fifth year of Ramesses, 1286/5 B.C., and though the Pharaoh vaunted his prowess on the Egyptian temple walls, the Hittite ascendancy in Syria was maintained. Muwatallis was even able to advance and conquer the district of Aba, or Abina, near Damascus. Thus in fact there can be no question that the battle of Kadesh resulted in a decisive victory for the Hittites. Some details of the battle are given below, p. 110.

During the reign of Muwatallis the north-eastern provinces of the realm had been organized as a distinct principality with its capital at Hakpis, under the king's able and ambitious brother Hattusilis, the king himself residing at a more southerly city named Dattassa, in order to be nearer to the scene of operations in Syria. Hattusilis thus held a position of great power, and it is little wonder that Urhi-Teshub,[1] the young son of Muwatallis who succeeded him about 1282 B.C., attempted to reduce his territories. Perhaps he suspected that his uncle already had designs on the

1. He appears to have taken the throne name Mursilis (III).

throne. But he himself has left no inscriptions, and the details of his short reign are entirely unknown except in so far as we learn them from the tendentious account of Hattusilis. The latter tells how he suffered the insults of Urhi-Teshub for seven years, but finally declared open war on his nephew and drove him from the throne. That he succeeded so easily in this *coup d'état* suggests that the government of Urhi-Teshub had not been altogether popular or wise. Urhi-Teshub himself was taken prisoner in the city of Samuha (near Malatya), but was treated leniently and sent into honourable exile in the distant Syrian province of Nuhassi.

With the accession in 1275 B.C. of Hattusilis III, already an experienced field commander and a man of nearly fifty years of age, there began for the Hittite Empire a period of comparative peace and prosperity. At the beginning of the reign there was some friction with Egypt, the cause of which is unknown, and the Kassite King of Babylon, Kadashman-Turgu, promised military assistance to Hattusilis in the event of war. But the matter was settled peaceably. It may have been the rising power of Assyria that served to draw together the rival empires of Hatti and Egypt. Relations between them became increasingly friendly, until in 1269 B.C. there was concluded the famous treaty which guaranteed peace and security throughout the lands of the Levant. Not only the kings but also the queens of the two countries exchanged congratulatory messages, one of which is preserved. Finally, thirteen years later the treaty was cemented by the marriage of a Hittite princess to the Pharaoh Ramesses. That Hattusilis at the age of sixty-nine had a marriageable daughter is explained by the fact that he married his queen, Puduhepa, a daughter of a priest of Kizzuwatna, on his return from his brother's Egyptian campaign, only twenty-nine years before.

Under Hattusilis the capital was moved back to Hattusas,

which had apparently been sacked by the Kaskan tribesmen during the absence of his brother Muwatallis in the south. The city was rebuilt and the archives re-copied. An impression of order and prosperity is created by the large number of religious and administrative decrees issued by this king and his queen, Puduhepa.

The small fragment which is all that survives of the annals of Hattusilis suggests that all was not so well in the west. Probably some military operations became necessary against the old enemy Arzawa in order to restore the situation, but no details are known. Relations with Babylonia also deteriorated upon the death of Kadashman-Turgu c. 1274 B.C., and there is a letter addressed by Hattusilis to the young Kadashman-Enlil complaining that since his accession the latter had ceased to send messengers to Hatti. The banished Urhi-Teshub probably had a hand in this, for Hattusilis tells us that Urhi-Teshub, while residing in Nuhassi, was found to be intriguing with the Babylonians, and was therefore removed from Nuhassi and sent 'aside to the sea', an obscure phrase, which may be a way of referring to the island of Cyprus. That he was later living in a foreign country is known from another document, and this may well have been Cyprus. From here he seems to have approached the King of Egypt. But if his purpose in these activities was to obtain the help of a foreign power in order to recover his throne, he evidently met with no success.

King Hattusilis is the author of a remarkable document which is described fully in Chapter VIII. Its main object seems to have been to justify him for his seizure of the throne and his expulsion of the legitimate king. The case which he presents is that he acted thus under great provocation and also at the direct bidding of the goddess Ishtar of Samuha. Obviously the account is tendentious and cannot altogether be trusted; but as evidence of a highly developed political conscience it is unique in the ancient world.

In view of his age the death of Hattusilis must have occurred not long after the marriage of his daughter to the King of Egypt. His son and successor, Tudhaliyas IV, seems to have taken a special interest in his religious duties and to have instituted a number of reforms relating to festivals and other ceremonies. It may have been he who ordered the carving of the reliefs at Yazilikaya (see below pp. 134, 144, 199), for a King Tudhaliyas is shown in the main gallery carrying his 'monogram' (Fig. 8, no. 64) and again in the side gallery in the embrace of his god (Plate 15). All this suggests that the earlier part of the reign at least was peaceful and prosperous. There was some campaigning in the west, apparently with success, for the land of Assuwa (later the Roman province of Asia, the name of which has now been extended to the whole continent) was incorporated in the Hittite dominions.

However, before the end of the reign a cloud appeared on the western horizon. The King of Ahhiyawā (possibly an Achaean ruler – see below) and an individual named Attarissiyas, of the same country, began to interfere in the most westerly Hittite dependencies. One Madduwattas, whose name has been compared with those of the early kings of Lydia, Alyattes and Sadyattes, driven out of his country by Attarissiyas, presented himself before the Hittite king and was given a small vassal kingdom somewhere in the west of Asia Minor. Thereafter Tudhaliyas was apparently still strong enough to repulse further attacks.

But the days of the Hittite Empire were already numbered. Under the next king, Arnuwandas III, the situation in the west rapidly deteriorated. Madduwattas made common cause with Attarissiyas, and though the Hittite king in a lengthy rescript addresses him as nothing more than a disloyal vassal, we sense an entirely new situation in that area. In particular, we are told that Madduwattas 'took the whole land of Arzawa'. At the same time another adventurer named Mitas was active in the eastern hills where had formerly been the kingdom of Hayasa; the identity of his name with that of the king of the Mushki of the eighth century B.C., who is usually equated with the Phrygian Midas of Greek tradition, may be no more than coincidence, but it is possible that the Mushki (classical Moschi) were already in this region and that Mitas was a dynastic name. Be that as it may, we know that great mass-movements of population were afoot which the brittle Hittite confederacy was utterly unable to withstand. The edicts of Arnuwandas contain no hint of the approaching doom. He was succeeded by his brother, a second Suppiluliumas, but the reign of the latter was probably short, for we know of it only from the oaths of fealty sworn by certain dignitaries and officials. The records of Ramesses III tell how the isles were disturbed and the Hittites with other peoples fled into Syria in a great invasion which, in conjunction with the 'Peoples of the Sea', menaced Egypt and left the Philistines settled on the coast of Palestine (which thus acquired its modern name). In Asia Minor, to judge from Homeric legend, the Phrygians soon replaced the Hittites as the dominant power.

4. THE NEO-HITTITE KINGDOMS

Yet in the south-eastern provinces of the Hittite Empire Hittite culture had a strange afterglow which lasted for no less than five centuries. Assyrian records continue to refer to Syria and the Taurus area as the 'Land of Hatti' and speak of kings bearing names like Sapalulme, Mutallu, Katuzili, and Lubarna (cf. Suppiluliumas, Muwatallis, Hattusilis or Kantuzzilis, Labarnas); similarly, these kings of Syrian principalities appear in the Old Testament as 'Kings of the Hittites' (2 Kings vii. 6; 2 Chron. i. 17), and many of them assiduously erected stone monuments bearing long inscriptions in Hittite hieroglyphics. All this proves that the traditions of Hittite culture were perpetuated from Malatya to the borders of Palestine down to the time when all that area became part of the empire of Assyria.

Yet the language and the religion of these 'Neo-Hittite' inscriptions are not those of the Hittites of Hattusas, nor are they those of the common people who had inhabited Syria under the Hittite Empire (for they were Hurrians). It seems that Syria must have been overrun by another people coming from one of the Hittite provinces, who had adopted the Hittite civilization: the question is discussed in Chapter VI, where it is suggested that the province in question was that of Kizzuwatna. This was no organized invasion under a single leader, for it resulted in the emergence during the twelfth century B.C. of a large number of independent petty 'kingdoms', the names of which, in so far as they can be made out from the scanty evidence, were as follows.

In the Taurus Mountains and on the southern edge of the central plateau Tuwana (classical Tyana), Tunna (classical Tynna), Hupisna (classical Kybistra), Shinukhtu, and Ishtunda were scarcely more than city-states; somewhere in this region, or to the north or east of it, is to be localized the confederacy called Tabal (the Biblical Tubal), and it is possible, though by no means certain, that the city-states of the Tyanitis mentioned above were included in the latter. The modern Malatya now appears for the first time in history as Milid, and the modern Marash as Marqasi, the districts of which these were the capital cities, being called respectively Kammanu and Gurgum. South of Milid was the district of Kummukhi (the classical Commagene) extending down the Euphrates, and south of this again lay the important city and kingdom of Carchemish. The area between Carchemish and Gurgum comprised the kingdom of Arpad, to the west of which, and reaching to the gulf of Alexandretta, was the state later known as Sam'al but at first probably as

Ya'diya, with its capital at the city now well known to archaeologists as the site called Zinjirli (Sinjerli). The Amuq plain appears in the latter part of the period as Unqi, but at first under the name of Hattina, with its capital Kinalua (the Biblical Calneh). The district of Aleppo formed another kingdom, the name of which seems to fluctuate; probably the district was called Luhuti and the capital, at first situated at Aleppo itself, was later moved to Hatarikka (the Biblical Hadrach of Zech. ix. 1). Most southerly of all was the powerful kingdom of Hamath, with several dependencies along the western seaboard. Finally, east of the Euphrates was a kingdom centred on Til-Barsip, now Tell Ahmar, a short distance downstream from Carchemish.

It will be seen from these names that there can be no question of a mere survival of the old Hittite vassal-kingdoms of Syria when the capital was overrun. The only common factors between the two epochs are Carchemish and the three cities of the Tyanitis (Hittite Tuwanuwa, Tunna, and Hupisna). Aleppo, one of the key-positions of imperial Hatti, appears as Halman and is of less importance than the upstart Arpad, its near neighbour to the north. All the other names are new, and many of these towns were probably new foundations.

The history of these kingdoms can be traced only in the barest outline from the records of the neighbouring states – Assyria, Urartu (Ararat), and Israel. The Hittite hieroglyphic inscriptions provide the names of kings, but decipherment has now advanced far enough to show that they are for the most part dedications and their historical content is disappointingly meagre.

The first Assyrian king to reach the Euphrates after the downfall of Hattusas was Tiglath-pileser I, who in 1110 B.C. encountered at Milid a kingdom which he calls 'Great Hatti'. This may well mean that the King of Milid exercised a form of suzerainty over the princelings of the neighbouring region. Later in his reign Tiglath-pileser reached the Mediterranean, and on his return received homage from another king of 'Great Hatti', presumably a king of Carchemish, which would be on his route home. Thus the two great cities of the Euphrates crossings were apparently the first to establish a hegemony in northern Syria.

The Assyrian armies, however, retired, and it was many years before an Assyrian king again reached or crossed the Euphrates. During this period of Assyrian weakness the Aramean nomads pressed in from the east and founded kingdoms and dynasties in Syria in their turn. The first and most powerful of these was Damascus, which was south of the line of Hittite penetration. Farther north the Arameans must have come into conflict with the newly established Hittite principalities. The Hittite dynasties of Til-Barsip, Ya'diya, and Arpad were overthrown and replaced by Arameans; Ya'diya was renamed Sam'al (or alternatively Bît Gabbari, 'House of Gabbar', after the name of the founder of the new dynasty); Til-Barsip and Arpad in the same way became the capitals of new kingdoms known as Bît Adini and Bît Agusi. These Aramean kings wrote inscriptions either in literary Phoenician or in their own Aramean language. The other Hittite dynasties succeeded in maintaining themselves and continued to erect inscriptions in hieroglyphs.

The history of Cilicia during this period was entirely unknown until the discovery of the inscriptions of Karatepe, and it is not yet certain how these should be interpreted. The author of the inscriptions, Asitawandas, appears to be not himself a king but the vassal or lieutenant of the King of Adana. In the Phoenician version the latter is described not as King of Adana (as in the Hittite text) but as King of the *Dnnym*, an ethnic term which has been vocalized and translated 'the Danunians'. The parallelism of the two versions apparently shows that the name of the Danunians is derived from that of the city Adana; but this does not preclude a connexion with the Daniuna, who appear among the 'Peoples of the Sea' in Egyptian inscriptions of the twelfth century, and who may equally well have come from the ancient city of Adana (Hittite Ataniya). The suggested connexion with the Homeric Danaoi, however, seems more problematical. There was then in the eighth century B.C. (this seems to be the most likely date for the inscriptions) a kingdom whose capital was Adana and which appears to have comprised most of the Cilician plain. The 'people of Adana' (Hittite *adanawanai*, Phoenician *dnnym*) would have been the survivors of a migration which took many of the Luwians of Kizzuwatna across the Amanus into Syria at the time of Ramesses III. Cilicia was known to the Assyrians from the time of Shalmaneser III onwards as Que or Qawe, a name for which no explanation has yet been found.

Once these changes were effected, the Neo-Hittite kingdoms and their Aramean neighbours quickly settled down to a brief period of prosperity and affluence. This is to be inferred from the large sums of gold and silver which the Assyrian kings were able to exact from them as tribute. Hittite culture penetrated southwards into Palestine; Hittite mercenaries such as Uriah (2 Sam. xi. 3 ff.) and Ahimelech (1 Sam. xxvi. 6) served in the Hebrew armies, and Solomon introduced Hittite ladies into his harem.

The recovery of Assyria began during the reign of Adad-nirari II (912–891 B.C.) and was continued under his successor Tukulti-Ninurta II (891–884 B.C.), but the Syrian kingdoms failed to heed the warning. Assur-nasir-pal (884–859 B.C.) rapidly consolidated his predecessors' conquests, and in his first seven years regained control of most of the country east of the Euphrates. When in 876 B.C. the Assyrian king appeared before Carchemish and demanded passage, the king of that city offered no resistance and submitted to the payment of a heavy tribute, including 20 talents (about 1,000 lb) of silver. The Assyrian army crossed the Euphrates and passed right through Syria to the coast, the other Hittite kingdoms following the example set by Carchemish. This failure of the Hittite states to combine against the invader is presumably evidence of internecine rivalries among themselves, of which we have no further information. Some attempt at combination was made when eighteen years later Shalmaneser III crossed the Euphrates farther north and was confronted by the forces of Carchemish, Hattina, Bît Adini, and Sam'al. But the resistance of four of these small states was ineffectual. North Syria again fell to the Assyrians, and in the following year Carchemish itself was besieged and captured. The first effective opposition encountered by the Assyrians was that of the kings of Hamath and Damascus, who, by calling on the contingents of twelve subject princes, mainly from the Phoenician coastlands, were able to meet Shalmaneser at Qarqar in 853 B.C. with a force of 63,000 infantry, 2,000 light cavalry, 4,000 chariots, and 1,000 camels. The battle that ensued caused very heavy losses to the allies, but resulted in the abandonment of the Assyrian campaign. Evidently an alliance of all the Syrian kingdoms could have kept the Assyrians at bay. As it was, Shalmaneser renewed the attack on Damascus in the following years and so weakened that kingdom that about 804 B.C. Adad-nirari III, aided by Zakir, an Aramean who a few years earlier had gained control of the Hittite city of Hamath, was able to reduce it to subjection and to claim mastery of the whole of 'Hatti, Amurru, and Palashtu'.

But now for about half a century the Assyrian control again relaxed, owing to the appearance of a new rival in the northern mountains – the kingdom of Urartu (Ararat) – which drew off the main effort of the Assyrian kings. The North Syrian Hittite states (South Syria was now entirely

Aramean) may have felt a certain racial or cultural affinity
with Urartu, and first Milid, then Gurgum, Sam'al, Unqi
(Hattina), Arpad, Carchemish, Kummukhi, and Que, all
became adherents of its kings Argistis I and Sarduris II.
Syria was thus split in two, and the trade from the interior,
which formerly reached the coast at the southern Phoenician ports of Tyre, Sidon, and Byblos, was necessarily
diverted to the mouth of the Orontes, where it was handled
by a newly founded Greek settlement, the town of Posei-
deion, recently identified by Sir Leonard Woolley with the
ancient site called Al Mina.

This situation came to an abrupt end with the resurgence
of Assyria under Tiglath-pileser III (745–727 B.C.). Already
in the third (full) year of his reign, 742 B.C., this king was
able to advance westwards to settle affairs once and for all
in Syria. Sarduris himself came to the assistance of his Syrian
vassals, and a great pitched battle was fought in which the
forces of Urartu were utterly routed, Sarduris himself
escaping ignominiously on a mare. A further three years
were needed to reduce the city of Arpad to submission, but
by 740 B.C. all the Syrian states had returned to their Assyrian allegiance. Yet only two years later Tiglath-pileser
was recalled to Syria to quell another rebellion. The now
irresistible Assyrian power could no longer tolerate such instability on the part of its vassals, and so in the year 738 B.C.
the policy of direct annexation was extended into Syria.
The first Hittite state to become an Assyrian province seems
to have been Unqi, and it was not long before the same fate
overtook most of its neighbours. For the policy of Tiglath-
pileser was followed even more ruthlessly by his successors
Shalmaneser V and Sargon II. Of the more important states
Sam'al and Que were probably annexed about 724 B.C.,
then Hamath in 720, Carchemish in 717, Tabal in 713, Gurgum perhaps in 711, Kummukhi (which had become united
with Milid) in 709.

Thus ended the history of the Hittite states of North Syria. When Greek travellers penetrated into these territories, they found only provinces of the Assyrian Empire. The very name of Hatti was already forgotten.

5. THE ACHAEANS AND TROJANS IN THE HITTITE TEXTS

E. Forrer's sensational announcement that he had found the Homeric Achaeans and even particular personalities such as Atreus, Eteocles, and Andreus in the Hittite texts has been briefly mentioned in the Introduction, together with the subsequent reaction against his views. Some of the facts and arguments may now be presented.

The controversy concerns the country called in the Hittite texts *Ahhiyawā* or occasionally *Ahhiyā*. The earliest appearance of the name occurs in the time of Suppiluliumas, who sent somebody – possibly, but not certainly, his wife – into banishment there. Forrer drew from this passage the conclusion that Suppiluliumas had married an Achaean princess. Quite apart from the question (which will be discussed below) of the identity of Ahhiyawā with the country of the Achaeans, i.e., Mycenean Greece, this conclusion rests on a rather bold assumption about the procedure of banishment, namely that a person, in particular the queen, would not be banished to a foreign country unless he or she happened to be a native of that country. It may be thought that the argument has some force in the case of a queen; but since King Urhi-Teshub was certainly banished to a foreign country, perhaps Cyprus (see above, p. 37), one cannot argue that exile was a punishment reserved for persons of foreign origin. The most that can be said with certainty is that the country chosen for the banishment would be one with which the Hittite king had friendly relations and which could therefore be relied on not to allow the exile to stir up trouble. We should therefore infer that during the reign of Suppiluliumas relations between Hatti and Ahhiyawā were of a friendly nature.

In the Annals of Mursilis II, year three, we first hear of a connexion between Ahhiyawā and the city (here the 'country') of Millawanda; but the passage is so badly broken that several totally different restorations are equally possible and probable. The same is true of another passage in the fourth year. This is particularly unfortunate, as there is mention of a ship, and the passage might have decided the question whether Ahhiyawā was 'overseas'.

Some time during his reign King Mursilis fell ill, and the divination priests instituted an inquiry about the cause of the divine anger (see below, p. 159). There exists a large tablet inscribed with the questions and answers which they put to the oracle. In the course of this inquiry we learn that the god of Ahhiyawā and the god of Lazpa(s) have been fetched in the hope that they will be able to effect a cure, and the inquiry is directed to finding out the proper ritual for these gods. This again is evidence of friendly relations between Hatti and Ahhiyawā. The name Lazpas has been compared with Lesbos.

The most important document of all, the so-called Tawagalawas Letter, is a communication addressed to the King of Ahhiyawā by a Hittite king whose name is not preserved, but who was already advanced in years. It covered at least three tablets, of which we have the third and perhaps a fragment of the first or second. It is full of allusions which are difficult to understand, and is also badly mutilated, but is none the less of great interest. It seems that a certain Piyamaradus, formerly a Hittite subject of high rank, had turned freebooter and was carrying out raids and causing disaffection in the Lukka Lands, perhaps Lycia, part of which, but probably not the whole, was a province of the Hittite empire. The base of his operations was the neighbouring city of Millawanda (elsewhere Milawata), but this place was outside the Hittite dominions and under the indirect control of the King of Ahhiyawā. The main purpose of the letter was to prevail upon the King of Ahhiyawā to extradite Piyama-radus, and so put an end to the disturbances in the Lukka Lands. But the interpretation is complicated by the introduction of an incident concerning one Tawagalawas (or Tawakalawas), who seems to have been a relative of the King of Ahhiyawā (though not his brother, as has been asserted) and resident in Millawanda or somewhere near by. The people of the Lukka Lands had first appealed for assistance to this Tawagalawas, probably because he was near at hand; later when the city of Attarimma was attacked (by whom is not clear – the name is broken but is not Piyama-radus) they called in the Hittite king. This seems to imply that the Lukka Lands were a no-man's-land between the two powers, Ahhiyawā and Hatti, and that the frontier was ill-defined. Tawagalawas, having presumably established himself in part of the Lukka Lands, sent a message to the Hittite king demanding recognition as a vassal. The Hittite king, apparently not unwilling, sent his son, a high-ranking military officer, to conduct Tawagalawas to his presence, but Tawagalawas took offence because the envoy was not the commander-in-chief himself and withdrew in anger. This incident seems to be included because the Hittite king thought Tawagalawas and his friends would have misrepresented the facts, and he wished to show that his own behaviour had been correct. After suppressing the revolt in the Lukka Lands the Hittite king received a message from the King of Ahhiyawā telling him that he had ordered his agent in Millawanda, whose name was Atpas, to hand over Piyama-radus. The king therefore proceeded into Millawanda, but only to find that Piyama-radus had been allowed to escape by ship. This is made the subject of a further complaint. It will be noted that Millawanda is hereby shown to be a coastal town. The rest of the letter is largely concerned with various arguments and suggestions intended to persuade the King of Ahhiyawā to hand over Piyama-radus. One such suggestion is of special interest here, namely that the messenger who brought the letter should be retained as a hostage for the safety of Piyama-radus, 'for', says the Hittite king, ' this messenger is a man of some importance; he is the groom who has ridden with me in my chariot from my youth up, and not only with me, but also with your brother and with Tawagalawas'. Here is evidence of a very close, even intimate, relationship at one time between Hatti and Ahhiyawā, or at least between their royal families. Indeed, the whole tenor of the letter is friendly and respectful. It is implied that the King of Ahhiyawā cannot be fully aware of the situation and is likely to comply as soon as it is properly explained to him. But at the same time it is clear that the Ahhiyawans at Millawanda enjoy considerable independence of action, and one has the impression that the king of Ahhiyawā is a somewhat remote figure and is not in complete control of affairs at Millawanda.

Forrer's assertion that Tawagalawas is described as an 'Aeolian' king is based on a misunderstanding of the text; but there was never any other reason, beyond the slight resemblance of the name, for identifying Tawagalawas with Eteocles (originally Ἐτεϝοκλέϝης, i.e., Etewoclewês) son of Andreus, King of Orchomenos, nor is Forrer's alleged discovery of Andreus himself in the above-mentioned divination text any better founded.

The problem of the authorship of the Tawagalawas Letter depends on another document in which Piyama-radus and Atpas are mentioned together and which must therefore be approximately contemporary with it. This is a letter written to an unknown Hittite king by Manapa-Dattas, who was ruler of the Land of the Seha River from the fourth year of Mursilis II till some time in the reign of Muwatallis. Either Mursilis or Muwatallis must therefore be the author of the Tawagalawas Letter. It is true that Piyamaradus alone is also mentioned in a fragment of the time of Hattusilis. But the fragment is so small that it is not even clear whether the episode of Piyama-radus is contemporary with the document or is cited as a precedent.

Later, though how much later we do not know, the ruler of Millawanda became a vassal of the Hittite king, and there is a much-mutilated letter dealing with various points at issue between them (the so-called Milawata Letter). The case of Piyama-radus is here cited as a precedent, and it seems to be implied that in the sequel the King of Ahhiyawā had in fact complied with the Hittite king's request and handed over the marauder.

Probably from the time of Hattusilis we have a letter replying to a request for a share in a consignment of gifts sent to the King of Hatti by the King of Ahhiyawā; the nature of these gifts is not specified. Another fragment, which refers to the events connected with the *coup d'état* of Hattusilis, links the name of Ahhiyawā with that of Urhi-Teshub, but the context is destroyed.

For the status of Ahhiyawā among the powers of the Near Eastern world of that time a passage from the treaty between Tudhaliyas IV and a King of Amurru is important. The passage refers to 'the kings who are of equal rank to me, the King of Egypt, the King of Babylon, the King of Assyria, and the King of Ahhiyawā', but the words 'and the King of Ahhiyawā' have been erased (though the signs are still legible). It would hardly have occurred to the scribe to insert the name of the King of Ahhiyawā unless the latter had in fact been one of the great powers of the time; but the erasure seems to indicate that the Hittite chancery did not wish to recognize the fact officially. The treaty goes on to lay down regulations for Amurru in dealing with these powers. Unfortunately the passage dealing with Ahhiyawā is (as in so many instances) badly broken, but it is at least clear that the contact between Amurru and Ahhiyawā would probably be in the form of an Ahhiyawan ship putting in on the Syrian coast.

Another fragmentary text, probably of the time of Tudhaliyas IV, refers to the King of Ahhiyawā in connexion with the Land of the Seha River and states that he 'withdrew'. It is evident that on this occasion at least the King of Ahhiyawā was present in person in Asia Minor. The Seha River-Land was an outlying dependency of the Hittite empire, and the text suggests a situation resembling that described in the Tawagalawas Letter, where Ahhiyawan leaders occupy parts of the Lukka Lands but subsequently withdraw in response to a peremptory message from the Hittite king. However, so little of the tablet is preserved that other interpretations are possible.

It was also during the reign of Tudhaliyas IV that the activities of Attarissiyas (or Attarsiyas) began. This man is described as a 'man of Ahhiyā', and Forrer suggested that he might be identified with Atreus; but he is nowhere said to be 'king' of Ahhiyā, and the phonetic resemblance of the names is not very close. The references occur in the letter of indictment addressed by Arnuwandas III to the rebellious vassal Madduwattas, one of the latest of all the Hittite documents (see above, p. 38). Madduwattas originally arrived at the Hittite court as a fugitive from Attarissiyas, who had driven him out of his country (where this was is not stated), and Tudhaliyas IV gave him a principality in the 'Mountain-land of Zippasla', where he would be 'near the Land of Hatti'. There is no suggestion that this principality was on the coast. But here too Attarissiyas attacked him a second time. The Hittite king sent a detachment under one of his generals, and a battle was fought in which Attarissiyas

51

had 100 chariots and an unknown number of foot-soldiers under his command; Attarissiyas then withdrew and Madduwattas was reinstated. Later, however, Madduwattas seems to have joined forces with Attarissiyas and is involved with him in an attack on Alasiya, which King Arnuwandas claims to be a Hittite dependency. That Alasiya is Cyprus, or at least a part of Cyprus, though formerly questioned, has become a certainty since the discovery in 1961 of a Hittite text bearing the record of a naval victory over the ships of Alasiya. One wonders, none the less, by what right the land-locked Hittites should have claimed the island as one of their possessions.

Such in brief is the history of relations between Hatti and Ahhiyawā. The two countries were at first on such friendly terms that relatives of the King of Ahhiyawā were apparently sent to Hatti for lessons in chariot-driving, and Ahhiyawan gods were brought to Hatti to cure the illness of the king. Later we hear of increasingly unfriendly acts committed by Ahhiyawan agents on the borders of the Hittite dominions, culminating in the attacks of Attarissiyas by land and sea during the reigns of Tudhaliyas IV and Arnuwandas III. But although these activities begin during the reign of Mursilis, official relations with the King of Ahhiyawā appear to have remained outwardly friendly at least until the end of the reign of Hattusilis. After this the only reference to the King of Ahhiyawā reveals him as interfering in person, possibly in a hostile manner, in the territory of a Hittite vassal-kingdom, and evidence of good official relations ceases.

The Ahhiyawans were clearly a powerful sea-faring people, whose ships reached as far as the coast of Syria (Amurru). An individual leader such as Attarissiyas could also operate with a considerable military force in the interior of Asia Minor. The activities of these people impinged on the Hittite empire at four points: the Lukka

Lands, the Land of the Seha River, the Land of Zippasla, and Alasiya. But these facts do not help much towards the localization of Ahhiyawā itself; for contact with Alasiya was undoubtedly by sea, and none of the other Hittite provinces in question can be located definitely. Even the identification of the Lukka Lands with the later Lycia is uncertain. One city, and one only, is mentioned as belonging in some way to the King of Ahhiyawā: Millawanda. But Millawanda is not an integral part of the kingdom of Ahhiyawā. It forms a distinct 'land', and though in the 'Tawagalawas Letter' its ruler obeys the orders of the King of Ahhiyawā, in the later 'Milawata Letter' he is a vassal of the Hittite king. The whole correspondence suggests that the King of Ahhiyawā is not in close contact with affairs in Millawanda and is receiving distorted reports about them from his underlings.

Now it is known that from the downfall of Knossos about 1400 B.C. until the Dorian invasion in the twelfth century the command of the seas was firmly in the hands of the Mycenean Greeks, who are the Homeric *Achaioi* – originally Ἀχαιϝοι (i.e., *Achaiwoi*). The well-known products of their workshops are found in abundance in the islands, especially in Cyprus, Crete, and Rhodes, in each of which there must have been important Achaean settlements; they are also plentiful at certain sites in Syria and Cilicia, and are found sporadically at various points along the southern and western coasts of Asia Minor, especially at Miletus. Further, the archaic dialect spoken later in Pamphylia has suggested to some that there was an Achaean settlement in that area, though this is unsupported by archaeology. Forrer therefore did not hesitate to equate Ahhiyawā with a hypothetical Ἀχαιϝα (*Achaiwa*) and placed Millawanda at Milyas in Pamphylia. However, it seems that the original form of the classical *Achaïa* (Ionic *Achaïē*) would have been not *Achaiwā* but *Achaiwiā*. The argument of F. Sommer, that since Homer, our earliest authority, uses *Achaiis*, not *Achaiia*, we have no right to assume the existence of this form before the seventh century B.C., can be discounted, for Homer's usage was clearly due to the demands of the metre in which he wrote. Achaiwia, then, may be safely postulated as the name of the 'Land of the Achaeans' in the language of the Mycenaeans, especially since the decipherment of the Mycenean script has proved that they spoke an early form of Greek. Now *Achaiwiā* and *Ahhiyawā* are indeed similar but not identical. The Hittites were in contact with Ahhiyawā over a period of some two centuries, and it is not obvious why they should have substituted *hh* for *ch* (which was not the Scottish or German *ch* but a hard *k* sound with aspiration), *iya* for *ai* (a diphthong which was quite familiar to them) or *a* for *ia* in the termination. The late form Ahhiyā is even more difficult to explain.

It is therefore held by Sommer and other scholars that the resemblance of the names is mere coincidence and that the facts can be adequately explained on the assumption that Ahhiyawā was a country situated on the coast of Asia Minor. Forrer's approach to the problem has been stigmatized as prejudiced, in so far as he was avowedly sustained throughout his study of the texts by the hope of finding there references to the Greeks and Trojans. But the grounds for this 'prejudice' remain: in Cilicia at least, and probably also on the Aegean coast, the Myceneans cannot have failed to come into contact with the Hittites, and the few facts that we can glean from the texts about the people of Ahhiyawā tally very well with what is known of the Myceneans. Much depends on the general problem of Hittite political geography, which is still far from an agreed solution. But it is difficult to dispute that the Lukka Lands, the Seha River Land, the Land of Zippasla, and Millawanda, wherever their precise situation may have been, were all among the most westerly provinces of the Hittite empire. If, then, Ahhiyawā were a country in Asia Minor, it must be placed somewhere in the extreme west of the peninsula, and the maritime contacts of the Ahhiyawans with Amurru and Alasiya cannot be explained away as a matter of minor importance. The Ahhiyawans, like the Myceneans, must have held command of the seas; but the Greek tradition of successive 'thalassocracies' shows that there was never room for more than one ruler of the seas in the eastern Mediterranean at the same time. It is to be hoped that agreement will soon be reached on the map of Hittite Asia Minor, and that it will then be clear whether there is room there for a country of the importance of Ahhiyawā. If there is not, the historical grounds for identifying the people of Ahhiyawā with the Achaeans will have become so strong that the linguistic objections will have to be overruled. Indeed, many philologists feel that this situation has already been reached and have made suggestions for explaining the discrepancies between the Hittite and Greek forms of the name.

If the identity of the Ahhiyawā folk with the Achaeans be assumed at least as a working hypothesis, there is room for much speculation on matters of detail. The Hittites appear to have known a single kingdom of Ahhiyawā; and the evidence of archaeology suggests that in the fourteenth and early thirteenth centuries B.C. mainland Greece at least was united under the kings of Mycenae. Was Ahhiyawā the kingdom of Mycenae itself? Or was it one of the island kingdoms of Crete, Rhodes, or Cyprus, which may well have exercised a considerable degree of independence? All these would have had ships; but it is perhaps easier to imagine the ruler of one of the island principalities taking part in a campaign, or in a political manoeuvre, on the mainland of Asia Minor than the king of one of the states of the Greek mainland. The strongest case can probably be made for the kingdom of the younger 'Minos' in Crete (for the Homeric poems show that Minos, son of Zeus, was an Achaean, ancestor of the hero Idomeneus, and not the ruler of the earlier 'Minoan' kingdom of Knossos). According to tradition, Minos had a powerful navy, with which he suppressed the Carian pirates in the islands (cf. Piyama-radus), and his brothers Sarpedon and Rhadamanthys colonized the coastal areas of Caria and Lycia. He also had a son Deucalion, whose name bears a striking resemblance in its essential elements to that of Tawakalawas, though the tradition did not connect him with Asia Minor. As for Millawanda, the account of the Hittite king's approach to that city points plainly to Miletus, where there was undoubtedly an Achaean colony, rather than to Milyas, which was not easily accessible from the plateau. However, a full discussion of all the possibilities which present themselves would be beyond the scope of this book.

A few words must be added on the alleged occurrence of the city of Troy and of the Trojan Alexandros-Paris in the Hittite texts. The name for which the identification with Troy (Greek Τροία) has been proposed is written in Hittite *Ta-ru-(u-)i-ša*, which is capable of several different pronunciations, viz., Tarūwisa, Tarōwisa, Tarwisa, Trūisa, or Trōisa. The name occurs only once, in a list of towns and districts of the Land of Assuwa, which itself is not mentioned elsewhere. But a few of the towns and districts of Assuwa included in this list are not unknown, and there is fairly general agreement that the list as a whole extends from the 'Lukka Lands' in the opposite direction from the countries and places with which the other Hittite texts make us familiar. Briefly, this means that Assuwa is most probably to be located on the west coast of Asia Minor, and it has been suggested that the name is actually the original form of the word Asia, for the Roman province of Asia was precisely in this region. The text in question is part of the much mutilated annals of Tudhaliyas IV, who seems to have been the first Hittite king to visit those parts. Now the name *Ta-ru-(u-)i-ša* is the last, and therefore presumably the

most northerly, of the districts of Assuwa; that the place
was somewhere in the vicinity of the Troad is therefore
highly probable. But beyond this there is nothing to support the identification of the names. According to the rules
of Greek phonology it is actually impossible for Troisa to
develop into Troia, nor is there any reason to suppose that
an exception to the rule would occur in this particular case.
The only way out of this difficulty is to suppose that *Ta-ru-
(u-)i-ša* is a derivative from a primary form *Ta-ru-i-ya*,
which has not yet been found in the texts (cf. Karkisa and
Karkiya).

Immediately before *Ta-ru-(u-)i-ša* in this text there occurs a name written *U-i-lu-ši-ia*, to be pronounced Wilusiya, which recalls the Homeric Ilios, originally Fίλιος. This
leads at once to a comparison with the name of the vassal
kingdom of *U-i-lu-ša* (Wilusa), the king of which at the
time of Muwatallis (*c.* 1300 B.C.) was Alaksandus. The
reader cannot fail to be struck by the resemblance of this
name to Alexandros (alias Paris) the prince of Ilios (Troy).
Lastly, we have the legend preserved by Stephanus of By-
zantium that the town of Samylia in Caria had been founded by one Motylos 'who received Helen and Paris' (presumably on their voyage from Sparta to Troy); here we
seem to have a reminiscence of the historical treaty of vassalage between Muwatallis and Alaksandus.

Phonetically none of these equations is altogether impossible, provided we are willing to accept the hypothetical
Ta-ru-i-ya, and provided also the name Alexander is regarded as a Grecized form of the Anatolian Alaksandus and
not as a genuinely Greek name. If it were certain, or even
probable, on other grounds that the Hittites never penetrated as far to the west as the Troad, one would not hesitate to abandon the whole tissue of hypotheses. On the contrary, however, we have the evidence of the Egyptian text
that the *Drdny* (Dardanians – no other similar name is

known) fought as allies of the Hittites at the battle of Kadesh. It is true that most scholars have distinguished Wilusa from Wilusiya and have placed the former on the south coast of Asia Minor; for Wilusa was part of the confederacy of Arzawa, and its location is inseparable from that of the Arzawan complex as a whole. But so long as the greater problem of Hittite geography remains unsolved, the arguments for the location of Wilusa cannot be regarded as conclusive.

There is indeed a serious chronological objection to the identification of Alaksandus with Alexandros-Paris. According to the traditional chronology, which is based mainly on genealogies, the Trojan war took place about 1190 B.C. Archaeologically this is the date of the fall of Troy VIIa, which perished in a conflagration. This would separate Paris from Alaksandus by a whole century. However, Alaksandus is contemporary with the end of the great city Troy VI, which corresponds most closely with Homer's description of the city, but is said to have perished by earthquake. If the genealogies may be ignored and the Trojan war dated about 1300 B.C. instead of 1190, Alaksandus could be Paris himself; we might suppose that he succeeded to a much-reduced kingdom after the departure of the Greeks and thereupon entered into treaty relations with the Hittite king. That an earthquake should provide the opportunity for the capture of a beleaguered city is by no means improbable, and the 'wooden horse' might have been brought as an offering to Poseidon *ennosigaios*.[1] In this way it is possible to combine all the tenuous traces cited above into a composite picture. But it must be emphasized that this is not history.

1. I owe these suggestions to Canon W. J. Phythian Adams.

6. THE HITTITES IN PALESTINE

We have now to deal with the paradoxical fact that, whereas the Hittites appear in the Old Testament as a Palestinian
tribe, increasing knowledge of the history of the ancient
people of Hatti has led us ever farther from Palestine, until
their homeland has been discovered in the heart of the Anatolian plateau. Moreover, the preceding outline of Hittite
history will have shown that before the reign of Suppiluliumas there was no Hittite state south of the Taurus; that
the Syrian vassal states of the Hittite Empire were confined
to the area north of Kadesh on the Orontes; and that,
although Hittite armies reached Damascus, they never
entered Palestine itself. Of the neo-Hittite states there was
none south of Hamath, and the latter did not include any
part of Palestine within its territories, being separated from
it by the Aramean kingdom of Damascus.

The presence of Hittites in Palestine before the Israelite
conquest thus presents a curious problem. So far from explaining it, all our accumulated knowledge of the people of
Hatti has only made it more perplexing. The stories of
Abraham's purchase of the cave of Machpelah (Gen. xxiii.)
and of Esau's Hittite wives (Gen. xxvi. 34, xxxvi. 1–3)
have, it is true, been ascribed by critics to the post-
exilic 'Priestly' writer, and are therefore not of much value
as historical evidence; nor are the various lists of Canaanite
tribes thought to be very much earlier in their date of composition. But the important passage Numbers xiii. 29 cannot be explained away. Here it is stated quite definitely that
the Hittites occupied the hill country, with Amorites in the
coastal plain and the Jordan valley, and Amalekites in the
south. This passage has been attributed to the early writer
E, and since the location of the Hittites agrees with the story
about the purchase of the cave of Machpelah near Hebron

from a Hittite, we may assume that the latter is based on an early source.

We must also consider the passage Joshua i. 2–4, where Yahweh says to Joshua: 'Arise, go over this Jordan, thou, and all this people, unto the land which I do give to them, even to the children of Israel. ... From the wilderness, and this Lebanon, even unto the great river, the river Euphrates, all the land of the Hittites, and unto the great sea toward the going down of the sun, shall be your border.' This command does not make sense. The country between the Lebanon and the Euphrates was not across the Jordan for the Israelites at that time – their tents were pitched in the plains of Moab – nor was it ever occupied by them. In fact, they crossed the Jordan and occupied the hill-country of Judaea – precisely the country attributed to the Hittites in Numbers xiii. 29. If we omit the words 'From the wilderness, and this Lebanon, even unto the great river, the river Euphrates' the passage at once becomes intelligible. The addition of these words is easily explained as a gloss by a late writer to whom the name Hittites meant the Neo-Hittite kingdoms of Syria, the Hittites of the Judaean hills having long since disappeared.

Who, then, were these Hittites of the Palestinian hills? A very ingenious answer has been put forward by E. Forrer.[1] When the Land of Hatti was suffering from the pestilence at the beginning of the reign of Mursilis II (c. 1330 B.C.[2]) the king searched the archives for a possible reason for the god's anger and came across two tablets which seemed to provide a clue. The first of these tablets showed that a certain festival had been neglected and is of no interest in this connexion. The second, however, which concerned the city of Kurustamma, is described as follows:

---

1. *Palestine Exploration Quarterly*, 1936, pp. 190–203, and 1937, pp. 100–15.
2. The pestilence began at the end of the reign of Suppiluliumas, and in the prayer here quoted it is said to have lasted already twenty years.

When the Weather-god of Hatti brought the men of Kurustamma into the land of Egypt, and the Weather-god of Hatti
bound them[1] by a treaty to the people of Hatti, and they were
sworn in by the Weather-god of Hatti, whereas the people of
Hatti and the people of Egypt had (thus) been placed under
oath by the Weather-god of Hatti, then the people of Hatti
committed a *volte-face*(?) and there and then they violated the
oath of the god, and my father sent infantry and chariotry,
and they invaded the border land of Egypt, the land of Amka,[2]
and again he sent them and again they invaded. ...

This invasion was successful, and many prisoners were
taken, but it was among these prisoners that the pestilence
first broke out, and it was they who introduced it into the
land of Hatti. Here, it seemed to Mursilis, was an obvious
case of retribution for an affront to the Weather-god by the
violation of his oath.

The city of Kurustamma was situated in the northern or
north-eastern sector of the Hittite kingdom; it was the
boundary city towards Hatti of the territory allocated by
Muwatallis to his brother Hattusilis (see above, p. 35).
However surprising it may seem, the text here quoted states
explicitly that during the reign of Suppiluliumas some men
from this obscure northern city entered the 'land of
Egypt', a term which would include all territory under
Egyptian rule. The text leaves the circumstances under
which this occurred obscure, but the reference to the
Weather-god of Hatti as the instigator of the move is in
favour of a deliberate act of state rather than a flight of
fugitives from the Hittite conquest, as suggested by Forrer.
However that may be, we have here one certain instance of
a group of Hittites (i.e., subjects of the King of Hatti) entering Egyptian territory, and the possibility of their having
settled in the sparsely populated Palestinian hills is not to be

1. 'Them' here is probably intended to refer to the people of Egypt.
2. The Biqā' valley between Lebanon and Antilebanon.

61

ignored. That they did so is, of course, a bare conjecture. There may have been other settlers from the lands ruled by the Hittites; though one might expect settlers from the nearest 'Hittite' territories in Syria, which had only recently been conquered by Suppiluliumas, to be known by some other name than Hittite. Emigration of Anatolian Hittites to Palestine cannot have been a frequent occurrence.

There is one other possible solution to this enigma. We have seen that the earliest inhabitants of Anatolia were a people whom we call Hattians because they spoke a language which is called *hattili* in the Hittite texts.[1] There are no written documents in this part of the world earlier than 2000 B.C., and we do not know how widely this language was spoken in the third millennium. Nor indeed do we know whether its speakers called themselves by this name. Linguistic groups do not usually possess a common name for themselves, and the word *hattili* may have been coined by the incoming Indo-European 'Hittites' from the ancient name of the country Hatti and its capital Hattus(as).[2] However, we may at least mention the possibility, which in the nature of the evidence is not susceptible of proof, that 'Hattian' was once spoken over a very wide area which included Palestine, and that the Hittites of the Judaean hills were a remnant of this people who had remained isolated when northern Palestine and Syria were occupied by Semitic and Hurrian peoples towards the end of the third millennium. If this is the truth, it is unlikely that any further evidence will ever be forthcoming. If, on the other hand, these 'sons of Heth' were emigrants from the Hittite Empire with whom the Hittite king made a treaty, there is some hope that further excavation among the archives of Boghazköy will bring enlightenment.

1. See above, pp. 17–18, and below, p. 122.
2. See above, p. 18.

CHAPTER II

Hittite State and Society

I. THE KING

THE position of the king in the early Hittite state seems not to have been very secure. One of the first recorded events in the history of Hattusas is the nomination by the nobles (or grandees) of a rival king in opposition to Labarnas I, whose father had designated him as his successor; and the subsequent history of the kingdom is fraught with revolts and rebellions on the part of the king's kinsmen, with the king constantly struggling to preserve the internal harmony of the realm. The death of a king seems generally to have caused a constitutional crisis, which the wise monarch sought to avert during his lifetime by the public designation of his successor. These facts have been held to indicate that the Hittite monarchy was originally elective, on the supposition that the designation of the heir before the assembled nobility should be interpreted as a formal request for the assembly's assent to the appointment, without which it would not be legally valid. This theory is of great interest, since elective monarchies are known to have existed among the Anglo-Saxons and other Germanic peoples. It is not in fact supported by the speech of Hattusilis I (the only extant record of a royal act of 'designation'), for there is no suggestion in this text that the king recognized the slightest limitation of his right to appoint his successor. But it is still possible to interpret the insecurity of the monarchy in early times as due to a conflict of will between the nobles, with their ancient rights, and the king, who was striving to establish the principle of hereditary succession. On this view the

63

absence in the king's speeches of references to the traditional rights of the nobility is not difficult to understand.

The royal succession was finally regulated by King Telipinus, who enacted the following law:

> Let a prince, the son of a wife of the first rank, be king. If there is no prince of the first rank, let one who is a son of the second rank become king. If, however, there is no prince, let them take a husband for a daughter of the first rank and let him become king.

This act of legislation marked a turning-point in Hittite history. Before it the kingdom was subject to a series of recurrent crises: after it there was an assurance of stability, and we never again find the authority of the king challenged by ambitious noblemen. Indeed, such was its success that some two hundred years later, when King Muwatallis died without leaving a legitimate heir, the throne passed without interference to Urhi-Teshub, the son of a concubine, and it was only after seven years that this youth's insolence and incompetence forced his powerful uncle Hattusilis to carry out a *coup d'état*.

The kings of the Old Kingdom style themselves 'Great King, *tabarna*'. The title 'Great King' belongs to the language of diplomacy and denotes the Hittite king's claim to be one of the great powers of the time, with dominion over lesser kings. *Tabarna* is probably nothing but the name of the ancient forebear Labarnas in a disguised form. The title is borne only by living monarchs, and it is thought that each reigning king was regarded by the Hittites as the incarnation of the founder of the royal line. The variation in the initial letter would indicate that the original (Hattian?) form of the name contained a peculiar consonant which the Indo-European Hittites were unable to pronounce.

During the later Empire *tabarna* is usually replaced by a title meaning 'My Sun'. This must have been properly a form of address used by the king's subjects, and was certainly borrowed from the contemporary kingdoms of Mitanni and Egypt together with the winged sun as a symbol of royalty (see pp. 211–12). The oriental conception of a king endowed with superhuman powers also makes its appearance during the imperial age. It expresses itself in the phrase 'Hero, beloved of the god (or goddess) ...', which follows the name of all the later kings, and in a passage such as the following from the autobiography of Hattusilis III: 'The goddess, my lady, always held me by the hand; and since I was a divinely favoured man, and walked in the favour of the gods, I never committed the evil deeds of mankind.' From the same period we have numerous texts describing the elaborate rituals observed at the Court and designed to protect the king from the slightest defilement.

The Hittite king was never actually deified during his lifetime. But there was a recognized cult of the spirits of former kings, and so the death of a king is regularly expressed euphemistically by the phrase 'he became a god'.

The king was at the same time supreme commander of the army, supreme judicial authority, and chief priest; he would also, as head of the state, naturally be responsible for all diplomatic dealings with foreign powers. Only his judicial duties seem normally to have been delegated to subordinates; his military and religious ones he was expected to perform in person, and if the latter were sometimes neglected through preoccupation with distant military operations, this was regarded as a sin which would bring down the anger of the gods upon the nation. Occasionally we even hear that important campaigns were entrusted to generals because the king was obliged to hasten back to the capital for the celebration of a festival. But normally he would be found during the summer months at the head of his troops in the field, and would devote the winter to the celebration of festivals and other religious duties at home.

These involved his personal attendance at each of the main cult-centres of the realm, and there are texts describing the tours which he used to make, often in the company of the queen and the crown prince. Such texts are indeed an important source of information about the location of these cities, for they state the exact time needed for the journey from place to place.

It is in his capacity as priest that we most often find the Hittite king represented on the monuments. We see him at Alaja Hüyük (Plate 16) worshipping with hands raised in greeting before the image of a bull (the symbol of the Weather-god), or at Malatya pouring libations before the great Weather-god of Hatti himself. On these and all other monuments he wears a special costume consisting of a long garment reaching to the ankles, and over it an elaborate shawl draped over one arm and under the other, with the end hanging down freely over the front of the body; his head-dress is apparently a close-fitting cap and he carries a long crook resembling the *lituus* of the Roman augurs. (See Plates 15, 16, fig. 8 no. 64 and fig. 17.) This was the costume of the Sun-god (fig. 8 no. 34).

2. THE QUEEN

Another peculiar feature of the Hittite monarchy is the strongly independent position of the queen. Her title, Tawannannas, derived from the name of her ancestor, the wife of King Labarnas, was inherited only on the death of her predecessor. Thus so long as the Queen Mother lived, the wife of the reigning king could only be styled 'the king's wife'.

A strong and not always amiable personality seems to have been characteristic of the Hittite queens. The widow of King Suppiluliumas especially caused so much trouble to her son Mursilis II that he was obliged to expel her from the palace and so to become the cause of her death – a *cause célèbre* which we still find weighing on the conscience of Hattusilis III, nearly half a century later. The latter's queen, Puduhepa, played a prominent part in affairs of state, and is regularly associated with her husband in all state documents. She even conducted an independent correspondence with the Queen of Egypt. She is shown sacrificing to the great goddess of the Hittites at Ferahettin (Fraktin), and the text of the treaty with Egypt testifies that she possessed her own official seal depicting her in the embrace of the same goddess.

3. SOCIAL CLASSES

On two known occasions an early Hittite king summoned his citizens for the purpose of making an important pronouncement, namely on the adoption of Mursilis I as heir to the throne, and on the promulgation of the edict of Telipinus regarding the law of succession and the reform of the judicial system. These two royal addresses afford us precious information about the composition of the Hittite nation in the earliest times.

It is clear that the king's kinsmen, called the 'Great Family', enjoyed special privileges, which they constantly abused. The highest offices of state were generally reserved for them. Their titles are significant: chief of the bodyguard, chief of the courtiers, chief of the wine-pourers, chief of the treasurers, chief of the sceptre-bearers, chief of the 'overseers of 1,000', 'father of the house'. The names of most of these functionaries show them to belong in origin to the staff of the palace, and if we find (as we do) that the holding of these appointments often carried with it a high military command, it is evident that the Hittites had a long tradition of settled Court life and that their military expansion was a comparatively recent development. In fact, we know that kings and palaces were already in existence in many Anatolian cities as early as the time of the Assyrian colonists, and it seems probable that the conditions found in the early kingdom of Hattusas were originally repeated in other places.

The departments of the palace over which these 'dignitaries' presided apparently had their own personnel, though we cannot always identify each class of person mentioned in the text with its respective officer. These underlings are addressed by King Telipinus as 'Courtiers, bodyguard, golden-grooms, cup-bearers, table-men, cooks, sceptremen, overseers of 1,000, and chamberlains', and it is of them as a body that he explicitly uses the word *pankus*, meaning probably, in this context, 'whole community'. Thus when we find the assembly convened by Hattusilis described as the 'fighting men of the *pankus* and the dignitaries', and later as 'fighting men, servants, and grandees', it is evident that the same classes are there intended and that these classes constitute the entire community in so far as it is concerned in affairs of state.

Yet we learn incidentally in the course of the speech of Hattusilis that the greater part of the population of the country was regarded as outside this community. For in addressing his son he remarks: 'The elders of Hatti shall not speak to thee, neither shall a man of ... nor a man of Hemmuwa nor a man of Tamalkiya, nor a man of ..., nor indeed any of the people of the country speak to thee.' Obviously these persons are not present in the assembly. What is particularly striking is the reference to the 'elders', for the elders are the governing body of a city, the town council, with whom provincial governors on tour are required to collaborate in judicial and other affairs. The conclusion seems to be clear: the Hittite state was the creation of an exclusive caste superimposed on the indigenous population of the country, which had originally been loosely organized in a number of independent townships, each governed by a body of Elders. This conclusion agrees well with the linguistic evidence, according to which a group of Indo-European immigrants became dominant over an aboriginal race of 'Hattians'.

This assembly of the 'whole body of citizens' seems to have functioned in the early Hittite state as a court of law, for Telipinus alludes to a case in which he ordered the reprieve of three junior officials who had been convicted by the *pankus* of the assassination of two former kings, and condemned to death. It appears that these men were acting under the orders of more important personages, and Telipinus, in his anxiety to curb the power of the nobles, ordained that the *pankus* must in future ensure that the instigator of a crime should suffer punishment in his own person, even though he be a high-ranking dignitary or even the king himself. It is not clear whether this represents a deliberate extension of the powers of the *pankus* or whether the king was merely recalling the assembly to duties which it had always possessed but which it had often feared to perform.

From the time of Telipinus we hear no more of this assembly. For the period immediately following his reign there are, it is true, no texts; but for the last two centuries of the empire, for which we have ample documentation, this absence of any reference to the *pankus* can hardly be fortuitous. Perhaps its sphere of activity decreased in importance as the kingdom became more stable and the city-state developed into an empire, until finally it fell into abeyance. As a result of the disappearance of this most characteristically Hittite institution, the later Empire appears to conform more closely to the pattern of absolute oriental monarchies governing through officials appointed by the king. It is possible, though not certain, that the class from which these officials were drawn became gradually less exclusive. The nobility, however, remained till the end a class apart. Many of them were the possessors of large estates, held as fiefs conferred by the king. No doubt it was they who provided the chariotry, on which the strength of the Hittite army so largely depended, for only a man of substance could afford so expensive an equipment.

Of the common people we know comparatively little. The majority would be peasants working on the land; but there was also a well-defined class of craftsmen, who would be found mainly in the towns and are apparently termed 'men of the tool'. Builders, weavers, leather-workers, potters, and smiths are specifically mentioned. On certain large estates, detailed inventories of which have been preserved, both peasants and craftsmen appear as serfs bound to the soil; but such conditions were probably exceptional. The ordinary citizen was free, though liable at any time to be called on for forced labour (Hittite *luzzi*), and persons of the artisan class at least normally possessed land and other property.

The status of the servants who were attached to the households of the wealthier citizens is not entirely clear. In the societies of classical antiquity, and likewise in Babylonia, the slave was a chattel, the property of his master, and might be bought and sold like any other commodity. The position of the Hittite servant is rather fully described in two passages intended to illustrate the relation of man to the gods:

Is the disposition of men and of the gods at all different? No! Even in this matter somewhat different? No! But their disposition is quite the same. When a servant stands before his master, he is washed and wears clean clothes; and either he gives him something to eat or he gives him something to drink. And he, his master, eats and drinks something and he is relaxed in spirit and is favourably inclined(?) to him. If, however, he (the servant) is ever dilatory(?) or is not observant(?), there is a different disposition towards him. And if ever a servant vexes his master, either they kill him or they injure his nose, his eyes, or his ears; or he (the master) calls him to account (and also) his wife, his sons, his brother, his sister, his relatives by marriage, and his family, whether it be a male servant or a female servant. Then they revile him in public(?) and treat him as of no account. And if ever he dies, he does not die alone, but his family is included with him. If then anyone vexes the feelings of a god, does the god punish him alone for it? Does he not punish his wife, his children, his descendants, his family, his slaves male and female, his cattle, his sheep, and his harvest for it, and remove him utterly?

And secondly:

If a servant is in any way in trouble, he makes a petition to his master; and his master hears him and is [kindly disposed] towards him, and puts right what was troubling him. Or if the servant is in any way at fault, and confesses his fault before his master, then whatever his master wants to do with him he will do. But because he has confessed his fault before his master, his master's spirit is soothed and the master will not call that servant to account.

It is clear that the master was assumed to have unlimited right, even the power of life and death, to deal with his servant as he thought fit. This is slavery, even if (as we see from the second passage) the treatment would in practice be mitigated by reason, common sense, and morality.

It is therefore rather curious that the Law Code contains many clauses in which the servant is treated as a person whose life and bodily integrity are to be protected, but whose value, in terms of compensation for injury, is exactly half that of a freeman; and there is no mention in these clauses of the master, who would surely be exempt from these laws in dealing with his own slaves, and who in the case of injury by a third party might well be entitled to compensation himself for the damage done to his property. Conversely, punishments are laid down for slaves (servants) who commit offences – the penalty is usually just half the amount due from a freeman for the same offence, though it may include bodily mutilation. In only two instances is there any suggestion that the master bears any responsibility for his servant's offences. Thus the Hittite 'servant' apparently had both legal rights and duties. Further, it was evidently normal for him to possess property, and the laws contain clauses regulating marriages between 'servants' and free women, as if such a marriage were of frequent occurrence and quite in order provided the bridegroom had proffered the bridal gifts. A person with such rights is not a slave in the normal sense of the term; his status resembles rather that of the *muškênu* (plebeian) in the Babylonia of Hammurabi's time. This may be rather a textual or literary problem concerning the sources of the Hittite Law Code itself. On account of the absence of private documents we know nothing of the means by which these servants were obtained or of their origin. There is indeed a reference, in a fragment of a letter from the King of Egypt, to Negro slaves, but these were doubtless exceptional.

4. THE GOVERNMENT

The traditional civil organization of the country was essentially parochial, the scattered townships and valley-communities having each its local council of 'Elders'. These would normally deal with local administration, and in particular with the settlement of disputes. Only the great religious centres were organized on a different system. We know, from Strabo's account of the holy city Comana in the time of the Roman emperor Tiberius, how from time immemorial such cities had been entirely dependent on the temple, and the High Priest himself was at the same time the civil governor. There are only indirect allusions to these holy cities in the Hittite texts, but we can be sure that this type of institution was of very ancient origin.

The kings of Hattusas at first retained direct control of the new territories acquired by conquest by entrusting their administration to their own sons. We have seen how the sons of Labarnas used to go out to administer the provinces allotted to them on returning from the annual campaign. Later, we read of similar appointments conferred on generals, who were usually relatives of the king. This administration of a province involved such duties as the repair of roads, public buildings, and temples, the appointment of priests, the celebration of religious ceremonies, and the dispensation of justice. The appointment of such administrators seems often to have been informal and temporary, and the office did not necessarily carry any special title.

Such a system no doubt became unworkable as soon as the empire expanded beyond the limits of the Cappadocian plateau. Even before this the beginning of a different system may be seen in the creation of appanages for princes of the royal house, who in an early text are styled 'Prince' of such cities as Zalpa, Hupisna, Ussa, Sugziya, and Nenassa. But the difficulty of rapid communication through the mountain passes would necessitate the appointment of governors of a more permanent and independent kind, bound to the sovereign power by solemn and explicit oaths of fealty. Moreover, this expanding Hittite empire proved a powerful magnet to the smaller and weaker kingdoms on its periphery. The kingdoms of Syria in particular were placed in a precarious position between the two ambitious empires of Hatti and Egypt, and their rulers sought to preserve their thrones by a flexible policy of alignment with the power that appeared at any time to be the stronger. Amurru, the kingdom of the Amorites in the Lebanon, and Kizzuwatna in Cilicia were drawn into the orbit of the Hittite empire and were counted as vassal-kingdoms alongside those whose territories the Hittite kings had actually acquired by force of arms.

73

The status of the provinces acquired in these ways depended on many factors. Key positions such as Aleppo, Carchemish, and Dattassa were incorporated in the kingdom and reserved for royal princes, who ruled there as vassals of a specially intimate kind. Here the keynote is struck by a sentiment such as the following (quoted from the treaty with the prince of Aleppo): 'We, the sons of Suppiluliumas, and our whole house, shall be united.' The obligation to mutual assistance is general, and apparently admits of no exception; it was evidently considered unnecessary to lay down precise and detailed stipulations.

At the opposite extreme stand the 'protectorates', mainly kingdoms which had enjoyed considerable prestige in a fairly recent past and which it was felt necessary to conciliate by at least a semblance of independence. The typical case here is that of Kizzuwatna, the kingdom which controlled the Cilician plain: the weaning of this state from its allegiance to Mitanni is represented as an act of liberation, and almost every obligation undertaken by the king of Kizzuwatna is carefully matched by a reciprocal and identical obligation on the part of the Hittite king. But he is none the less under Hittite protection, has to appear annually at Hattusas to do homage, and undertakes to eschew all diplomatic intercourse with the king of the Hurri.

One might have expected that Aziru, the ruler of Amurru, who had likewise submitted voluntarily to Hittite suzerainty, would have been accorded similar privileges. But, unlike Kizzuwatna, Amurru had not recently been a great power, and in fact the terms accepted by Aziru are identical with those imposed on Nuhassi, a Syrian principality which had defied Suppiluliumas and might therefore have been expected to receive harsher treatment. In the same way the Land of the Seha River, which submitted voluntarily, was given the same terms as the conquered kingdoms of the Arzawa area.

Most of the subject kingdoms were ruled by vassals who were natives of the country, but who, either as refugees or as leaders of a pro-Hittite party, had been installed directly as liegemen of the Hittite overlord. The vassal king was the sovereign ruler within his territory; but he was forbidden to hold any intercourse with a foreign power, and it was a serious offence for him to entertain foreign ambassadors at his court. He was usually expected to provide a contingent for the Hittite army, whenever the campaign was directed against one of the major powers or against one in the vicinity of his own domains. He was obliged to hand over all refugees from the Land of Hatti, but could not claim a like favour in return (the Hittites well knew the usefulness of such refugees in the event of disaffection on the part of their vassals). His oath of fealty was made to the king and his successors in perpetuity. In return, the king usually guaranteed to protect the vassal against his enemies and to ensure the succession of his legitimate heirs.

The loyalty of the vassal was symbolized by the annual act of homage accompanied by the rendering of tribute. Later, apparently, the tribute was sent by messenger.

These terms represent in the main the interests of the overlord and reflect the actual power-relation between him and his vassal. At the moment of his installation, the former refugee is well content with his position. But the Hittites, like the Sumerians and Akkadians before them, appreciated that human power is a precarious sanction, inviting revolt as soon as the opportunity may offer. Hence arose the custom, known from the earliest times in Mesopotamia, of enlisting the aid of the gods as witnesses and guardians of the contract by means of the oath. In Mesopotamia the appeal to fear was sometimes enhanced by taking hostages, but this custom was repugnant to the Hittites, and was never adopted by them. For them the oath, with its solemn religious associations, was fundamental, and was evidently regarded as a powerful sanction. The gods of both parties were usually invoked, for the religious outlook of the time was strongly national.

But even the fear of the wrath of heaven was evidently felt by the Hittites to be an unsatisfactory basis for a permanent relationship. Diplomatic marriages were much favoured as a means of winning over the vassal to the interests of the central dynasty. A strong appeal was also regularly made to the vassal's feeling of gratitude by means of a long preamble describing the good services rendered to him in the past by the Hittite overlord, and thus representing the demands made in the treaty as the right and proper return due from him. This appeal to the vassal's better nature is rather typical of the essential humanity of the Hittite outlook.

The treaty itself was generally inscribed on a tablet of precious metal (silver, gold, and iron are attested) and impressed with the royal seal. These documents have perished. The clay tablets which have survived are copies made for the palace archives, and none of them bears the king's seal. The document was the charter from which the vassal derived his authority, and its loss was a serious matter to him. It is recorded that the treaty with the King of Aleppo was stolen from the temple where it was kept, and this ruler was at pains to obtain a new copy from the Hittite chancery.

The system so carefully built up was not allowed to bear fruit. The onslaught of Assyria in the east, the intrigues of Arzawa in the west, and the exploits of adventurers like Madduwattas and Mitas caused the loss of outlying provinces and in practice it was only by constant fighting that the frontiers could be maintained.

5. FOREIGN POLICY

Outside their frontiers the early Hittite kings saw only enemies. Whether a new approach is marked by the conclusion of a treaty with Kizzuwatna by King Telipinus is impossible to say, since the treaty is not preserved. By the time of Suppiluliumas the world of Western Asia had drawn together and was controlled by three Great Powers: Egypt (Misri, the Biblical Mizraim), Babylonia (called at this period Kar-Duniash), and Mitanni (the Hurrian kingdom ruled by an aristocracy of Indo-Iranian stock). These Powers had achieved a state of equilibrium, and their diplomatic correspondence found at Tell El Amarna shows that they were on excellent terms with one another. Embassies with elaborate gifts passed to and fro, the three monarchs addressed each other as brothers, and the friendships were regularly cemented by diplomatic marriages. The campaigns of Suppiluliumas brought the power of Mitanni to an end, and thereafter Hatti was perforce accepted as one of the three Great Powers of this ancient concert of nations.

When two 'Great Kings' made a treaty with one another it was on terms of absolute equality and reciprocity. The only surviving example of such a treaty is that between Hattusilis III and Ramesses II, concluded about 1269 B.C., but at least two previous treaties between Hatti and Egypt are known to have existed, and we may be sure that the friendly relations between Babylonia and these two powers rested on a similar contractual basis. The keynote of such treaties is the establishment of a relation of 'brotherhood'. This implies the impossibility of war between the two powers and an alliance for offence and defence. These themes are elaborated at some length. The contracting parties also undertake that on the death of either the other will ensure the accession of his legitimate heir. This reciprocal dynastic guarantee is, as we have seen, an equally essential clause in the treaties with vassals, for where the dynasty is identified with the state, a revolution would mean the destruction of the kingdom itself, whatever its status in the international world. The extradition of fugitives is also laid down in the

'treaty of brotherhood' on a completely reciprocal basis.
There are no other limitations on the sovereignty of the
allies, who are thus free to enter into whatever diplomatic
relations with third parties they may choose. Lastly, not
only is each clause repeated *verbatim* so as to create identical
obligations for both parties, but the whole treaty is drawn
up separately by each and sent to the other for ratification;
thus the Ramesses–Hattusilis treaty has been found in two
versions, one inscribed in Egyptian hieroglyphics on the
walls of the temple of Karnak, the other in Akkadian on a
cuneiform tablet from Boghazköy. As a compliment, the
same privilege was occasionally accorded to a vassal.

In their political manoeuvres the nations were careful to
avoid offending their powerful neighbours. This can be
illustrated by the treaty between Suppiluliumas and the
King of Kizzuwatna – one of the earliest of all the extant
Hittite treaties. The seduction of Kizzuwatna is presented as
a case of self-determination and is justified by reference to a
precedent in which the Mitannian king had himself made
this principle the basis of his case.

The people of Isuwa [says Suppiluliumas] fled before My
Majesty and descended to the Hurrian country. I, the Sun, sent
word to the Hurrian: 'Return my subjects to me!' But the Hurrian
sent word back to My Majesty as follows: 'No! Those cities had
previously ... come to the Hurri country and had settled there. It
is true they later went back to the Land of Hatti as fugitives; but
now finally the cattle have chosen their stable, they have definitely
come to my country.' So the Hurrian did not extradite my subjects to me.... And I, the Sun, sent word to the Hurrian as follows:
'If some country seceded from you and went over to the Land of
Hatti, how would that be?' The Hurrian sent word to me as
follows: 'Exactly the same.' Now the people of Kizzuwatna are
Hittite cattle and have chosen their stable, they have deserted the
Hurrian and gone over to My Majesty. ... The land of Kizzuwatna rejoices very much over its liberation.

This is a piece of propaganda, with a familiar ring in the twentieth century A.D. But it testifies to the existence of an international court of opinion before which the Hittite king felt it necessary to justify his actions.

CHAPTER III

Life and Economy

THE plateau of Asia Minor is in a sense a continuation of the Russian steppe, and its climate is hard. Bitter winds from the north bring heavy falls of snow during the winter months, and after the brief but delightful spring the country is scorched during the summer by a relentless sun. The rain-clouds spend themselves for the most part on the slopes of Taurus or on the hillsides bordering the Black Sea. Thus the central plateau is a wind-swept steppe-land, and it is only in the river-valleys that enough water and shelter can be found for human habitation. One may travel for hours over the bleak undulating plain until suddenly one is looking down into a well-watered valley many hundreds of feet below, while beyond there is a distant view of rounded hills similar to those over which one has been journeying. In the Hittite home-land to the north of the Cappadox River (Delije Irmak) the streams and valleys are more numerous and the country is somewhat less bleak. Here almost every acre is within reach of a village and is assiduously cultivated, but the absence of trees on the higher ground is striking, and there is no shelter there from the biting winds of winter. (See Plate 31.)

Conditions may have been more temperate in the Hittite period. That the people were, as to-day, mainly devoted to agriculture is confirmed by the texts. Our main source for the nature of Hittite society, the Law Code, presupposes an agrarian economy throughout. We also have lists of fields and elaborate title-deeds containing inventories of estates which were obviously of considerable size.

Following are some paragraphs of the Law Code which

illustrate the agricultural background of Hittite civilization:

75. If anyone borrows and yokes an ox, a horse, a mule, or an ass and it dies, or a wolf devours it, or it goes astray, he shall pay its full value; but if he says 'By the hand of a god it died', then he shall take the oath.

86. If a pig goes upon a threshing-floor or a field or a garden and the owner of the meadow, the field, or the garden smites it so that it die, he shall give it back to its owner; but if he does not give it back, he becomes a thief.

105. If anyone sets [brushwood(?)] on fire and [leaves] it there and the fire seizes a vineyard, if vines, apple-trees, pomegranates, and pear-trees(?) burn up, for one tree he shall give [six] shekels of silver and re-plant the plantation. If it be a slave, he shall give three shekels of silver.

151. If anyone hires a plough-ox, for one month its hire is one shekel of silver.

159. If anyone harnesses a yoke of oxen, its hire is one half-peck of barley.

91. If anyone steals bees in a swarm, formerly they used to give one mina of silver, (but) now he shall give five shekels of silver.

Following is a typical paragraph from a land-deed:

Estate of Tiwataparas: 1 man, Tiwataparas; 1 boy, Haruwandulis; 1 woman, Azzias; 2 girls, Anittis and Hantawiyas; (total) 5 persons; 2 oxen, 22 sheep, 6 draught-oxen ...; [18] ewes, and with the ewes 2 female lambs, and with the rams 2 male lambs; 18 goats, and with the goats 4 kids, and with the he-goat 1 kid; (total) 36 small cattle: 1 house. As pasture for oxen, 1 acre of meadow in the town Parkalla. $3\frac{1}{2}$ acres of vineyard, and in it 40 apple-trees(?), 42 pomegranate-trees(?), in the town Hanzusra, belonging to the estate of Hantapis.

From these quotations we have already learnt most of the domestic animals kept and many of the fruit-trees cultivated by the Hittites, and we see that they correspond largely with those of to-day.

The principal food-crops were barley and emmer-wheat, which were used not only for flour and bread but also for the brewing of beer. The vine is thought to be indigenous in Anatolia, and was certainly extensively cultivated in Hittite times. The olive, which can now be grown only in the coastal plains, is known to have flourished in the Roman period at a considerable altitude and is the normal source of oil in the Hittite texts. Corn, wine, and oil represent the staple products of the country on which in the standard rogation prayers the gods were implored to bestow their blessing. Peas and beans are also occasionally mentioned in the texts, and flax may have been grown locally as it is to-day.

The great mountain masses of Anatolia are rich in minerals, and these were certainly exploited from very ancient times. Copper was the principal export of the Assyrian traders in Cappadocia just before the foundation of the kingdom of Hatti, and silver was evidently plentiful from that time onwards, since it served as a currency. The ancient copper-mines cannot be located precisely, but doubtless Bolkar Maden in the Cilician Taurus was then, as now, a principal mining centre for silver and lead, since there are Neo-Hittite monuments in the vicinity. The Hittite and Assyro-Cappadocian texts give the actual names of the mountains and cities from which these metals were obtained, but unfortunately the places cannot be identified. Iron ores are also abundant in the Anatolian mountains, but throughout the second millennium iron was a precious metal in Anatolia, as elsewhere in the ancient Near East, owing to the fact that the technique of smelting the metal and producing the high temperature required for working it was not generally understood. Copper and bronze were the common metals, used extensively for the manufacture of weapons and utensils of all kinds. Only a few iron objects of the Hittite period have been found, and though iron swords, iron writing-tablets, even iron statues of gods and animals are mentioned in the Hittite texts, these were all special articles, either dedicated in the temples or intended as royal gifts. Ostensibly the earliest reference of this kind is in the inscription of Anittas (see above, p. 20), who records that he received as tribute from the city of Puruskhanda an iron sceptre and an iron throne, but in view of the doubtful authenticity of this document the passage is not good evidence for the manufacture of these large objects at such an early date, even though small iron objects, such as pins and small ornaments, have been found in much earlier contexts. It seems that the technique of iron-working was mastered during the Hittite period by a few skilled craftsmen who were able to charge a high price for their products.

The pre-eminence of the people of Asia Minor in iron-smelting, if not in iron-working, is confirmed for the thirteenth century by a famous passage from a letter of the Hittite king Hattusilis III to one of his contemporaries, probably the King of Assyria:

As for the good iron which you wrote about to me, good iron is not available in my seal-house in Kizzuwatna. That it is a bad time for producing iron I have written. They will produce good iron, but as yet they will not have finished. When they have finished I shall send it to you. To-day now I am dispatching an iron dagger-blade to you.

It would probably be a mistake to read too much into this passage. It does not, for instance, prove that the Hittite king was placing an embargo on the export of iron for military reasons. The reference to the 'bad time for producing iron' may be explained by the assumption, based on comparison with other societies, that the smelting was carried out by peasants in their homes during the winter season when there was no work to be done in the fields. So it might well occur that in the late summer or autumn the stocks of smelted iron were very low. The passage was also originally used to prove that Kizzuwatna was in the region of Pontus, later known to the Greeks as the home of the iron-working Chalybes. But we now know that Kizzuwatna was in the south, embracing Cataonia and part of Cilicia, and it is probable that either the store-house of this district was used as a depot for exports coming from elsewhere in the kingdom or that iron was mined somewhere in the Taurus Mountains, where it is known to exist.

The medium of exchange in the Hittite kingdom, and indeed throughout the Near Eastern world of that time, was silver (or for small denominations lead) in bars or rings, and measured by weight, though the more primitive method of reckoning in terms of measures of barley is also occasionally found. The unit of weight was the shekel, and 60 of these were equivalent to 1 mina, as in Babylonia; but it is not improbable that the actual weight of the shekel was less than that of the Babylonian shekel (8·4 grammes). For it is stipulated in a treaty that tribute should be weighed out 'by the weights of the merchants of Hatti', and many centuries later we know that the mina of Carchemish weighed 300 grammes as against the 505 grammes of the Babylonian mina. The Law Code contains a table of prices, of which an extract is given below.

1. Domestic Animals

Sheep	1 shekel
Goat	$\frac{2}{3}$ shekel
Cow	7 shekels
Horse	14 shekels
Horse 'for harnessing'	20 (or 30?) shekels
Ox 'for ploughing'	15 shekels
Bull (or full-grown ox?)	10 shekels
Mule	1 mina

The text states that the price of a stallion, of a mare for harnessing, of a male donkey, and of a female donkey for

harnessing is 'the same', but does not state the actual price.
It does not state the price of a pig.

2. Meat

Here the prices are given in terms of 'sheep', though since
a sheep costs 1 shekel the figures would be the same.

Meat of 1 sheep	$\frac{1}{10}$ sheep
,, ,, ox	$\frac{1}{2}$ sheep
,, ,, lamb	$\frac{1}{20}$ sheep
,, ,, kid	$\frac{1}{20}$ sheep
,, ,, calf	$\frac{1}{10}$ sheep

3. Skins

Skin of sheep with fleece	1 shekel
,, ,, shorn sheep	$\frac{1}{10}$ shekel
,, ,, goat	$\frac{1}{4}$ shekel
,, ,, shorn goat	$\frac{1}{15}$ shekel
,, ,, full-grown ox	1 shekel
,, ,, lamb	$\frac{1}{20}$ shekel
,, ,, kid	$\frac{1}{20}$ shekel
,, ,, calf	$\frac{1}{10}$ shekel

4. Agricultural Produce

The value of the measures has not been ascertained.

1 *parisu* of emmer-wheat	$\frac{1}{2}$ shekel
1 *zipittani* of oil	2 shekels
1 *zipittani* of butter	1 shekel
1 *parisu* of barley	$\frac{1}{4}$ shekel
1 *zipittani* of lard	1 shekel
1 *zipittani* of honey	1 shekel
1 *parisu* of wine	$\frac{1}{2}$ shekel
1 cheese	$\frac{1}{2}$ shekel

5. Land

1 acre of irrigated land	3 shekels
1 acre of *halani*-land	2 shekels
1 acre of vineyard	1 mina

The meaning of the term *halani* is unknown.

6. Garments and Cloth

Fine garment	30 shekels
Blue woollen garment	20 shekels
Head-band	1 shekel
Fine shirt	3 shekels
Large linen cloth	5 shekels

7. Metals

1 mina of copper	$\frac{1}{4}$ shekel

The existence of this silver currency and the use of the Babylonian names for units of weight is another instance of the debt owed by the Hittite civilization to its eastern neighbours. Hittite merchants are mentioned in the Law Code as travelling to the provinces of Luwiya and Pala, and there is no reason to doubt that they would trade their wares across the frontiers into the neighbouring countries. The tablets of the Assyrian colonists of the nineteenth century B.C. probably give a fairly reliable idea of the nature of this international trade, for the Assyrians were merely middle-men plying between Assur and the Anatolian principalities. Anatolian metals, especially copper, were exported in exchange for Mesopotamian woven materials and tin; the latter must therefore have been obtained somewhere to the east of the Hittite kingdom and imported (at that time at least) via Assur. However, we cannot be sure that conditions during the Hittite period were the same. It is possible that the tin deposits of the Caucasus region were becoming available through direct channels. Above all, we are told incidentally in a religious text that copper was brought from Alasiya, that is Cyprus, which contained the richest copper-mines in the ancient world. Does this mean that the copper-mines of Anatolia were becoming exhausted? If Alasiya was a foreign country it would appear to be so. But it must be remembered that the Hittite king, Arnuwandas

III, claimed Alasiya at least as part of his sphere of influence, if not as a province of his empire. If Alasiya was merely an additional source of copper within the empire, this would account for the low price of copper as against silver (1:240) in the price-list above, and there might still be a surplus for export, as in the earlier period. There is, however, very little direct evidence, either in the texts or from excavations, of the commercial dealings of the Hittites either with each other or with the world at large.

CHAPTER IV

Law and Institutions

I. THE CODE

IN the ruins of Boghazköy were found many fragments of clay tablets inscribed with laws. Two of these were almost complete, and their text has been largely restored from parallel fragments. Both contain one hundred clauses; and though the tablets themselves are not marked as parts of a single work, these two hundred laws are generally regarded by modern scholars as forming a continuous series and are numbered for reference purposes in sequence. The other fragmentary tablets are parts of similar texts, the original number of which cannot be exactly estimated. They evidently ranged from almost exact duplicates of the main series to selections in which the laws appear in a markedly different form. In some instances extra laws seem to have been added. But there is not the slightest trace of another independent series.

The Hittite archives thus contained several closely related but not identical collections of laws. Now in the main series it is often stated that 'formerly' a certain penalty was in force, but 'now' the king has ordained another, generally less severe. Evidently the Hittites avoided the tendency towards stagnation inherent in the process of codification, and did not hesitate to reform their laws in accordance with changing needs. Hittite law was a growing organism, and the different versions of the code probably represent successive stages in its development. But the tablets contain no indication of date, and there is another possibility, namely that the law varied in different parts of the land. This supposition is supported by the following passage from a text containing instructions to Hittite garrison-commanders:

As in the various countries the control of capital offences has been exercised in the past – in whatever city they used to execute him they shall execute him, but in whatever city they used to banish him they shall banish him.

However that may be, the internal arrangement of the code provides convincing evidence for its gradual growth. It may be summarized as follows:

Tablet I. 'If a man'

1–6	Homicide.
7–18	Assault and battery.
19–24	Ownership of slaves, including rules applying to slaves who have escaped.
25	Sanitation.
26–36	Marriage procedure (exceptional cases).
37–38	Justifiable homicide.
39–41	Feudal duties connected with land tenure.
42	Hiring for a campaign (responsibility and rate of pay).
43	Accidents at a river-crossing.
44A	Homicide (pushing a man into a fire).
44B	Magical contamination.
45	Finding property.
46–56	Conditions of land tenure.
57–92	Theft and other offences concerning cattle.
93–97	Theft.
98–100	Arson.

Tablet II. 'If a vine'

101–118	Offences in connexion with vineyards and orchards.
119–145	Theft and damage to various forms of property.
146–149	Irregularities in connexion with sale and purchase.
150–161	Rates of pay for various services.
162	Offences connected with canals.

We can see from the above summary that while certain subjects, particularly at the beginning of the first tablet, are treated with some semblance of system, isolated clauses relating to the same subjects are found later in the series and seem to be later additions. The subject of land-tenure is divided into two parts by the intrusion of five clauses concerned with totally different subjects. Further, two clauses, one in each tablet, contain the same case, but with a slightly different ruling (§§ 35 and 175), a fact which inevitably raises doubts as to the justification of treating the two tablets as a single composition.

It has been thought that the extant tablets cannot represent the complete Hittite code, on the ground that such chapters as that on marriage deal only with exceptional cases, and certain important subjects such as adoption, inheritance, and the laws of contract are omitted altogether. But it would be strange if, when so many recensions of this series of laws have survived, the remainder of the code had disappeared without trace, nor is there any evidence that the Hittites had at any time been governed by some other system of law, to which these might be merely amendments. We must, it seems, accept the fact that the Hittites did not consider it necessary to legislate about these subjects, presumably because they did not normally give rise to dispute, being regulated by the customary law of the people.

Can we assume that these laws give a true picture of the Hittite legal practice? Similar questions have been raised about the Mesopotamian codes. But whereas in Babylonia and Assyria innumerable private contracts and reports of cases have been recovered, from which we are able to see to what extent the laws were actually applied, not a single private Hittite document has yet been found, against which the laws of this people might be checked. We know from the texts that such documents existed, and it is quite possible that examples may yet be recovered. But until this occurs we have to rely entirely on internal evidence.

With a few exceptions these laws are framed in the form of hypothetical cases followed by an appropriate ruling, after the manner of the code of Hammurabi and other ancient codes. Many of them from their very singularity and the inclusion of irrelevant details can be seen at once to be derived from precedents that have actually occurred in the courts, and there can be little doubt that the greater part of the code is of this nature. One clause even contains a brief story of an actual case that had been brought before the king. There cannot therefore have been any very serious divergence between theory and practice, though, as we have seen, the law may have varied slightly in different parts of the country.

The clauses specifying the prices of commodities and the rates of wages present a rather special problem. It is difficult to believe that these ordinances had universal validity. Such prices necessarily vary according to the supply and demand, and their control would require a bureaucratic organization which cannot possibly have existed in those times. Similar rulings in the code of Hammurabi do not correspond with the facts as observable in the contracts. Possibly these may be intended as maximum prices, which should not be exceeded; but as approximations they no doubt present a fairly accurate picture of economic conditions.

We conclude then that most of these laws are compiled from the judgements of the courts. What do we know of the courts themselves?

2. THE COURTS

It must be admitted that, largely on account of the lack of private documents, our information about the Hittite tribunals and law-courts is very meagre.

Disputes would come in the first instance before the Elders or Aldermen, who, as we have seen, formed governing councils in most of the provincial cities of the country. They are mentioned only once in the code, as deciding the ownership of stray cattle. They would be a popular tribunal – an organ of the people – and as such the State was only indirectly concerned with them.

The representative of the State in judicial matters would normally be one of the king's officers, e.g., the garrison-commander, whose duties are fully set forth in a document which has survived in a comparatively good state of preservation. Following are some extracts from these instructions:

Into whatever city you return, summon forth all the people of the city. Whoever has a suit, decide it for him and satisfy him. If the slave of a man, or the maidservant of a man, or a bereaved woman has a suit, decide it for them and satisfy them.

Do not make the better case the worse or the worse case the better. Do what is just.

In exercising these functions the officer was expected to

cooperate with the local authority, as we see from the following passage:

> Now the commander of the garrison, the mayor, and the elders shall administer justice fairly, and the people shall bring their cases.

Another passage from the same text illustrates the position of the king as the ultimate authority:

> If anyone brings a case which is (provisionally) sealed upon a tablet, then the commander shall decide the case fairly and satisfy him. But if the case is too involved he shall refer it to the king.

The king's decision seems to have been required in cases of sorcery and in all cases involving the death penalty. A theft of more than two talents of timber also had to be referred to him.

The authority of the courts was upheld by the threat of the direst penalty against anyone who should violate a legal decision:

> If anyone oppose the judgement of the king, his house shall become a ruin(?)[1]. If anyone oppose the judgement of a dignitary his head shall be cut off. (§ 173.)

The term 'dignitary' seems to be a general title for the king's representative.

An outstanding feature of Hittite legal procedure is the immense trouble taken to ascertain the facts. We possess highly detailed minutes of courts of inquiry in cases of peculation and neglect of duty, which are unique in the

---

1. Possibly the word 'house' should be translated 'household' and the phrase may refer to a punishment such as that of Achan in Joshua vii. 16–26.

literature of oriental peoples and have quite a modern ring. The best-preserved text of this type opens as follows:

Regarding the stores which [the queen] entrusted to 'Great-is-the-Storm-God', son of Ukkuras the 'leader of ten' – to wit, [chariots], utensils of bronze and copper, garments and materials, bows, arrows, shields, [clubs], civilian captives(!), oxen, sheep, horses, and mules – the stores which he had issued to anybody he had not sealed, and he had no *dusdumis* and no *lalamis* (two words of unknown meaning). So the queen said: 'Let the "golden pages" and the chamberlains of the queen and Great-is-the-Storm-God and (?) Ukkuras the leader of ten go and swear solemn oaths in the temple of Lilwanis.'

The hearing opens with sworn statements from the defendant's father and another witness, which together occupy ninety-five lines. Great-is-the-Storm-God is then questioned:

Thus said Maruwas: 'One pair of mules you gave to Hillarizzi.' Great-is-the-Storm-God replied: 'The mules belong to Hillarizzi; I took them and gave them back safe and sound(?).'

Thus said Maruwas: 'You gave mules to Piha- ....'. Great-is-the-Storm-God replied: 'They were not from the stable.'

Thus said Yarrazalmas the 'golden page': 'Zuwappis sold a horse and got a talent of bronze.' Great-is-the-Storm-God replied: 'He told me it was dead!'

After various witnesses have given their evidence, the text ends abruptly; it was probably continued on a second tablet. Doubtless such cases were exceptional, being concerned with affairs at Court. But the text shows a spirit of careful and unbiased investigation which may perhaps be taken as typical of Hittite administration as a whole.

3. RETRIBUTION AND RESTITUTION

In a primitive society punishment is synonymous with revenge, and it is impossible to distinguish 'civil' from 'criminal' offences. The injured party will avenge himself as best he can upon the wrongdoer, or if he is dead, vengeance becomes the duty of his relatives, and there arises a blood-feud. The matter may, however, be settled by a payment of money if the parties can agree to this; such a payment is known as 'composition'.

The state is concerned primarily with the preservation of law and order, and must therefore at the outset endeavour to set a limit to private vengeance and eventually to eliminate it altogether. The law of 'talion' (an eye for an eye and a tooth for a tooth) probably represents the first step in this process: the injured party may not inflict a greater injury than he has himself suffered. A more enlightened law-giver will see that two wrongs do not make a right, and will consider the purpose of punishment; retribution is useful only in so far as it acts as a deterrent, whereas the wrong itself can be redressed only by restitution or compensation of the injured party. Finally, a third factor, reformation, may be introduced.

In this respect the Hittite law is comparatively advanced. Retribution plays an inconspicuous part in comparison with the principle of restitution. The only capital offences are rape, sexual intercourse with animals, and defiance of the authority of the state; also, if the offender is a slave, disobedience to his master and sorcery. Bodily mutilation – a normal punishment in the Assyrian laws – is here reserved for slaves. For all other offences by freemen, including assault, black magic, and homicide, as well as theft and all forms of damage to property, compensation or restitution is ordered; retribution enters in only in so far as the offender may be required to pay several times the value of the damage he has caused. Examples of reparation in kind are the rebuilding of a house damaged by fire, and the replacing of a damaged article by one in good condition; but normally the reparation is in terms of money (silver).

Following are some examples:

11. If anyone breaks a freeman's arm or leg, he pays him twenty shekels of silver and he (the plaintiff) lets him go home.[1]

12. If anyone breaks the arm or leg of a male or female slave he pays ten shekels of silver and he (the plaintiff) lets him go home.[1]

63. If anyone steals a plough-ox, formerly they used to give fifteen oxen, but now he gives ten oxen; he gives three oxen two years old, three yearling oxen, and four sucklings(?) and he (the plaintiff) lets him go home.[1]

170. If a freeman kills a serpent and speaks the name of another (a form of sorcery), he shall give one pound of silver; if a slave does it, he shall die.

25. If a man puts filth into a pot or a tank, formerly they paid six shekels of silver; he who put the filth in paid three shekels of silver (to the owner?), and into the palace they used to take three shekels of silver. But now the king has remitted the share of the palace; the one who put the filth in pays three shekels of silver only and he (the plaintiff) lets him go home.[1]

98. If a freeman sets a house on fire, he shall rebuild the house; but whatever perishes inside the house, be it a man, an ox, or a sheep, for these he shall not compensate.

It is interesting to compare the laws on homicide with those of other ancient codes. In all cases compensation is prescribed, the rate for a slave being always exactly half that for a freeman. The laws for freemen are as follows:

1. If anyone kills a man or a woman in a quarrel, he makes amends for him by giving four persons, men or women (respectively), and he (the victim's heir) lets him go home.[1]

3. If anyone strike a free man or woman and he (or she) die, if his hand (alone) is at fault, he makes amends for that one by giving two persons; and he (the victim's heir) lets him go home.[1]

1. This translation of this difficult phrase, involving a change of subject, has been suggested by Professor Sedat Alp and seems to make excellent sense.

5. If anyone kills a Hittite merchant, he pays 1½(?) pounds of silver and he (the heir) lets him go home; if (it happens) in the country of Luwiya or in the country of Palā he pays 1½(?) pounds of silver and makes good the loss of his goods; if it is in the land of Hatti, he (only) makes amends for the merchant.

6. If a person, male or female, is killed in another city, the man on whose land he dies cuts off 100 cubits of the field and he (i.e., the heir) takes it.

For the last two paragraphs the parallel text has a different version:

III. If anyone kills a Hittite merchant for the sake of his goods, he shall give . . . pounds of silver and compensate threefold for the goods. But if he has no goods with him, but kills him in a quarrel, he gives six pounds of silver. But if his hand (alone) is at fault, he gives two pounds of silver.

IV. If anyone is killed on strange ground, if it be a freeman, he (i.e., the owner of the land) shall give a field, a house, (and) one pound twenty shekels of silver; if it be a woman, he shall give three pounds of silver. But if it is not cultivated ground, the property of another man, (they shall take) a distance of three miles this way and that, and whatever village is found in (that area), he (the heir) shall take those same (compensations from there); if there is no village, he shall go away empty.

Both versions make a careful distinction between killing in anger and killing accidentally; but it is curious that the only case which we should describe as wilful murder is mentioned in connexion with a merchant, who seems to be treated rather in a class by himself, and is associated with the motive of robbery. The absence of a specific clause dealing with murder has been noticed also in both the code of Hammurabi and in the Assyrian laws. The crime is treated at length in the Israelite code, but we see from such passages as Deuteronomy xix. 12 that the Hebrew judicial authorities had nothing to do with the murderer except to hand him over to the vengeance of the gō'el, the 'redeemer', i.e., the next of kin. Hence it is thought that the silence of the other oriental codes on this matter is due to the fact that murder was still extra-judicial, a thing to be settled by private vengeance. That the blood-feud still survived in the Hittite Old Kingdom is clear from the following passage in the Edict of Telipinus:

The rule of blood is as follows. Whoever commits a deed of blood, whatever the 'lord of blood' (i.e., the Hebrew *gō'el*) says – if he says 'Let him die', he shall die; but if he says 'Let him make restitution', he shall make restitution: the king shall have no say in it.

The practice of giving 'persons' as part of the composition for manslaughter is remarkable. The expression is that generally used for slaves. Perhaps such slaves were slain at the tomb of the deceased, as in some other ancient societies. That the nearest village is responsible for compensating the victim's family if the murderer has escaped has always been a widespread custom in Eastern countries. There are parallels in the code of Hammurabi and in medieval Islam; and it has been reported that an Arab working on an excavation in the neighbourhood of Mosul expressed his intention of killing a man at random in a certain village because a relative of his had been murdered there. In Deuteronomy xxi. 1–10 the elders of the nearest village are enjoined to clear themselves of the blood-guilt by a ceremonial oath, and it is thus implied that there too the village would otherwise have been held responsible for the crime. The unique feature of the Hittite law is the three-mile limit, outside which responsibility ceases.

The sense of §5 is not clear. One would suppose that the death of a merchant in the distant countries of Luwiya and Palā would require a lower rate of composition than in the homeland of Hatti, on account of the greater risk taken by him in travelling so far from civilization; but it is difficult to get this meaning out of the words, largely owing to the doubt in the reading of the figures.

4. COLLECTIVE RESPONSIBILITY

We have seen that traces of the primitive blood-feud still survived in Hittite society. To that same custom belongs the belief that the guilt attaches to the whole family of a wrong-doer, and that its members may all be involved in his punishment.

In the Hittite laws the only trace of this principle is in §173, already quoted, in which it is stated that the punishment for disobeying the order of the king shall involve the offender's 'house', i.e., his whole household and family. Elsewhere throughout the code individual responsibility is the rule.

However, the passage quoted above in illustration of the position of slaves in Hittite society clearly shows that the principle of collective responsibility was still active in its application to slaves: 'If ever he dies, he does not die alone, but his family is included with him.' In the same text a close parallel is drawn between the relation of a slave to his master and that of man to the gods; we need not therefore be surprised to find that divine retribution is regularly conceived as affecting a man's whole family and all his descendants (cf. Exodus xx. 5). But outside the religious sphere it is extremely rare.

5. MARRIAGE AND THE FAMILY

The organization of the family implied throughout the Hittite laws is of the usual patriarchal type. The power of the man over his children is illustrated by the provision that he shall provide a son in place of a child whom he has killed (§ 44A), and by the fact that in marriage a father is able to 'give away' his daughter to the bridegroom. His power over his wife is implicit in the whole phraseology used at marriage: the bridegroom 'takes' his wife and thereafter 'possesses' her; if she is taken in adultery, he has the right to decide her fate.

We know that in parts of Asia Minor, notably among the Lycians, a matrilinear system was still in existence in the time of Herodotus, and it may be that certain privileges enjoyed by women among the Hittites represent vestiges of this more primitive system. Thus one rather obscure law (§171) provides for certain conditions under which a mother may disown her son, and in another (§§ 28–9) she is associated with the father in disposing of their daughter in marriage. Possibly also the very independent position of the Hittite queen may have a similar origin.

The marriage customs of the Hittites seem to have closely resembled those of Babylonia. The first stage was the betrothal, which was accompanied by some sort of present from the bridegroom. However, the betrothal had no binding force, for it was still open to the girl to marry another man, with or without her parents' consent, provided the original fiancé was indemnified by the return of his present. The marriage itself was normally accompanied by a symbolic gift (Hittite *kusata*) from the bridegroom to the family of the bride, corresponding exactly to the Babylonian *terhatu*; but for various reasons it is probably erroneous to regard this gift as a 'bride-price' and as evidence that the Hittite and Babylonian marriage had originally been of the type known as 'marriage by purchase'. At the same time the bride received a dowry (Hittite *iwaru*) from her father. If after this the consummation of the marriage was refused by the bridegroom or opposed by the bride's family this was tantamount to non-fulfilment of the contract: the engagement was annulled and the guilty party was penalized, the bridegroom by the forfeit of his *kusata*, the bride's family by a two- or three-fold compensation paid to the bridegroom. Normally the married pair would set up house together, but an alternative arrangement was recognized whereby the wife remained in her father's house – a custom found also among the Assyrians. After the consummation adultery by the wife was punishable by death.

On the death of the wife her dowry became the property of her husband if she was living in his house, but if she was living with her father this did not occur – the text is broken at this point, but it seems that the dowry passed to her children.

The law contained detailed regulations prohibiting marriage between near relatives. A man is forbidden to have intercourse with his mother or his daughter, with the mother, sister, or daughter (by a former marriage) of his wife, or with the wife of either his father or his brother during their lifetime. In the midst of these regulations §193 states that if a man die his widow shall be married first to his brother, then (i.e., presumably, if the brother die) to his father, and then, if the father die, to his nephew. In its context this clause appears simply to state an exception to the series of prohibitions, and accordingly one copy adds the words: 'It is not punishable'. But the law is remarkably similar to the Hebrew law of the levirate marriage, according to which if a man died childless it was the duty of his brother, or failing him, of his father or nearest surviving kinsman, to marry the widow, the offspring of this union taking the name and inheritance of the dead man. The custom is illustrated by the stories of Judah and Er (Gen. xxxviii) and of Ruth and Boaz (Ruth iv); its purpose seems to have been to perpetuate the family of the deceased 'that his name be not blotted out of Israel' (Deut. xxv. 6). The Babylonians and Assyrians attained this end by other means, and had no need of the levirate; but §193 proves the existence of the custom among the Hittites, although the section is inserted in its context for another purpose, and is evidently not intended as a full statement of the law. Similarly, § 190 says that there is no punishment for intercourse with a stepmother after the death of the father; but this again probably indicates the existence of a custom, widespread among ancient peoples, whereby sons inherit their fathers' wives (with the exception of their own mothers).[1] It is noteworthy that marriage between brother and sister is not forbidden in the Hittite laws, and indeed it appears that King Arnuwandas I himself was married to his sister.

Marriages in which either party was a slave were recognized by the Hittites as valid. There are no less than six laws regulating such marriages, but the different versions are curiously inconsistent in this matter.

6. LAND TENURE

Land-ownership among the Hittites was bound up with a complicated system of feudal dues and services, the details of which are by no means clear. From the fact that the code includes no less than fourteen clauses on this subject, we may perhaps infer that it was a frequent source of litigation.

Two classes of holding are distinguished – that of the 'liegeman' or fief-holder and that of the 'man of the tool (or weapon)'. The latter might be freely bought and sold, but it seems that the former was entailed, and so could change hands only under the legal fiction of an adoption. Much has been written about this subject on the assumption that the 'man of the weapon' was a soldier who received the holding on terms of military service, on the analogy of the system known to have been instituted by Hammurabi at Larsa. But more recent research has thrown a rather differ-

1. On the levirate marriage see Driver and Miles, *The Assyrian Laws*, pp. 240–50.

ent light on the matter. It appears that the 'weapon-man' is really a 'tool-man', i.e., a member of the artisan class. The main difference between these two kinds of holding is that the 'liegeman' derives his title from the king, the 'artisan' from the local authority; for on the disappearance of a liegeman the fief reverts to the palace, whereas the land of a missing artisan is taken over by the village. In principle, it seems, the liegeman held his estate under specific terms of service (Hittite *sahhan*), which was, however, frequently converted into a form of ground-rent; while the artisan shared the liability of most ordinary citizens to the corvée (Hittite *luzzi*). But the two conceptions seem to have become somewhat confused, and in practice either class of person could take over the holding of the other, provided he undertook to perform the appropriate duties. The artisan's holding could even, in the event of his disappearance, be allotted to a 'civilian captive', one of the numerous body of persons deported from conquered territory and held at the disposal of the king (see below, p. 115). Such a person would then assume the status of an 'artisan'.

The royal domains must have been of vast extent, for many of the fiefs held by individuals were very large. Among the largest landowners also must be counted the temples, some of which formed, as it were, small states within the State; they too let out their estates to farmers who paid a ground-rent in kind.

CHAPTER V

Warfare

I. THE ARMY

THE strength of the Hittite Empire, as of other contemporary kingdoms, lay in the intensive development of a new weapon, which had made its appearance throughout Western Asia shortly after 1600 B.C. – the light horse-drawn chariot.

The war-chariot as such was not new. The Sumerians possessed two types of chariot, one with two and the other with four wheels, but the wheels were solid, the chariots were heavy, and the animals that drew them appear to have been wild asses. The Sumerians always relied mainly upon their phalanx of infantry. For the period of the Amorite kingdoms that followed we are not well informed in this respect, but although the horse was known, it does not seem to have been put to any military use. The Assyrian merchants of Cappadocia seem to have used horses as draught-animals, but their chariot was still the old Sumerian type with four wheels. The light horse-drawn chariot with spoked wheels belongs to the world which succeeded the downfall of the Amorites, and makes its appearance at about the same time in Kassite Babylonia, in the Egypt of the eighteenth dynasty, and in the new kingdom of Mitanni in the north. It created a revolution in the nature of warfare: henceforward speed was to be the determining factor in the battle.

The archives of Boghazköy provide the clue which explains this sudden development; for they contained an elaborate work in four tablets on the training and acclima-

tization of horses by a certain Kikkuli of the land of Mitanni, and in this work are found certain technical terms belonging to a language akin to Sanskrit, the ancient speech
of the Aryans of Northern India. Now we know from other
texts that the rulers of Mitanni worshipped Indo-Aryan
deities such as Indra, Varuna, and the Nasatya twins, and
their personal names betray a similar origin. Hence we must
conclude that this Aryan clan, moving westwards, brought
with them their special knowledge of horse-breeding, and
that it was from them that the art was learnt by the peoples
of Western Asia. It is significant that the names of Indian
deities are found to form an element in the names of the
Kassite rulers of Babylonia, though in other respects the
Kassite language is of a totally different kind.

The Hittite Empire under Suppiluliumas and his successors certainly shared in this development. The Hittite army
of this period is vividly portrayed for us in the Egyptian reliefs depicting the great battle of Kadesh, and it is clear that
its chariotry was second to none. But it is questionable
whether this arm was equally well developed under the Old
Kingdom. It is true that at the siege of Urshu, which, as
we have seen, formed an incident in the campaign of one of
the early kings, eighty chariots are said to have taken part
in the battle. But the text containing this reference is a literary composition, possibly of a later date. The treatise of Kikkuli is certainly later, and it is unlikely that the Hittites
would have employed this Mitannian as their instructor if
they were already familiar with the science of horse-training. However that may be, in describing the army of the
Hittites we refer exclusively to the period of the Empire,
for which the Egyptian reliefs provide such striking evidence.

The Hittite chariot differs little in design from that of the
Egyptians. Both have wheels with six spokes. But whereas
the Egyptian chariots hold two men – driver and fighter –

those of the Hittites appear somewhat heavier and have a crew of three, the functions of attack and defence being differentiated. The weapons of attack are the lance and the bow; the shield is either rectangular or cut into a shape resembling a broad double-axe held vertically (see Plate 3). The larger crew of the Hittite chariot would have the added advantage of ensuring superiority of numbers in the close fighting that might follow the initial charge.

The infantry of the Hittite army were no doubt more numerous than the charioteers, but in the open battle which the Hittites generally sought they played a subordinate part. On the Egyptian reliefs they are not seen in action, but are shown clustered round the fortress of Kadesh to protect the king and the baggage-train.

These were the main arms of the Hittite forces. There was no cavalry, though occasionally messengers appear to have been mounted on horseback. Troops of 'Sutu' – probably light auxiliaries armed with bow and arrow – were sometimes employed for surprise attacks necessitating swift movement. We hear also of pioneers or sappers in connexion with the construction of fortifications. The baggage-train, as shown on the Egyptian reliefs, consisted of heavy four-wheeled vehicles drawn by bullocks, and heavily laden asses. There was no Hittite fleet, and we do not know what ships were used for intercourse with the island of Cyprus, which the Hittites appear to have controlled.

With regard to the clothing and armament of the Hittite infantry there is a strange discrepancy between the Egyptian reliefs and their own monuments. On the former the Hittites are shown wearing a long gown with short sleeves. But on the Anatolian monuments warriors (and warrior deities) are clad in a short tunic, clasped round the waist by a belt and ending above the knee; sometimes this is reduced to a mere kilt, the trunk being bare. It has been suggested that the long robe shown on the Egyptian monuments was a kind of tropical uniform for use in the hot plains of Syria; but this is pure conjecture.

The most remarkable representation of a Hittite warrior is the figure carved in high relief on the inner face of the great monolith which formed the jamb of the so-called King's Gate of the Hittite capital. This guardian of the gate (see Plate 4) apparently wears only a belted kilt and helmet, and carries a short sword and a battle-axe. The kilt shown on this and other monuments is simply a piece of material wrapped round the loins, the edge forming an oblique line in front of the body; it is here adorned with horizontal bands of alternating oblique lines and spirals. The helmet has ear-pieces and a plume, with an extension hanging down behind the nape of the neck like a pig-tail. The sword has a crescental hilt, a slightly curving blade, and a scabbard with an acutely curved tip. The battle-axe is shaped like a human hand, grasping the haft between the thumb and forefinger; the cutting edge forms an almost circular swelling added above the 'wrist'. From its very position this figure must surely represent a regular type of Hittite warrior in battle array.[1] A close parallel to it is a bronze statuette of uncertain provenance (see Plate 5a); the kilt is very similar, the trunk is bare, and it is clear that the head was once surmounted by a helmet; there is a suggestion of boots on the feet, but the feet of the King's Gate figure seem to be bare. An axe and a sword similar to those carried by the King's Gate figure have been excavated at Beisan in Palestine, and parallels to the axe are known from the Persian province of Luristan.

By contrast, the long-robed Hittites of the Egyptian sculptures are armed with a long spear. This weapon is also known from Anatolian monuments, but chiefly from those belonging to the Neo-Hittite period following the downfall of the Hittite Empire. The explanation of these

[1]. On this figure see also below, p. 200.

discrepancies probably lies in the heterogeneous nature of the Hittite confederacy.

In fact, the army which fought against the Egyptians at Kadesh was the strongest force ever mustered by the Hittite kings. For this greatest of all campaigns King Muwatallis had summoned contingents from every possible ally and vassal in accordance with the terms of their various treaties. For normal campaigns the forces of the homelands and of countries contiguous to the scene of operations would naturally suffice.

For garrison duties there must have been a small standing army containing a certain proportion of mercenary troops, but we know little about its method of recruitment. Desertion was a serious crime, and the garrison-commander had explicit orders to report all cases to the Palace.

2. MILITARY OPERATIONS

The active campaigning season was limited to the spring and summer months, for the heavy snowfall on the Anatolian plateau prevented operations during the winter. Every year at the beginning of spring the omens would be taken, and if they were favourable the order for mobilization was sent out, a rendezvous was named, and at the appointed time and place the king himself held a review of his forces and took over the command in person. The campaign usually lasted throughout the summer. As the autumn drew on, the king was often advised by his officers that 'the year was too short' for anything more than minor operations, and when these were accomplished the army would withdraw into its winter quarters.

The Hittite kings were masters of strategy and tactics. The object of the campaign was always to catch the enemy's army in the open, where the invincible Hittite chariotry might be used to full effect. The enemy's best hope was to avoid a pitched battle, disperse his troops, and wage a guerilla warfare. In this sense the great strategic march of Suppiluliumas into northern Mesopotamia at the beginning of his reign failed in its main objective, for he passed right through the Mitannian capital and down into the Syrian plain without encountering the Mitannian forces. Here, however, is a brief account of a successful stratagem from the annals of Mursilis II:

As soon as I heard such words (i.e., a reported plot by one Pitaggatallis to prevent the entry of the Hittite army into the city of Sapidduwa), I made Altanna into a depot and left the baggage there; but the army I ordered to advance in battle order. And because (the enemy) had outposts, if I had tried to surround Pitaggatallis, the outposts would have seen me, and so he would not have waited for me and would have slipped away before me. So I turned my face in the opposite direction towards Pittaparas. But when night fell, I turned about and advanced against Pitaggatallis. I marched the whole night through, and daybreak found me on the outskirts of Sapidduwa. And as soon as the sun rose I advanced to battle against him; and those 9,000 men whom Pitaggatallis had brought with him joined battle with me, and I fought with them. And the gods stood by me, the proud Storm-god, my lord, the Sun-goddess of Arinna, my lady, ... and I destroyed the enemy.

If the Hittites failed to achieve surprise, it often happened that the enemy ensconced himself in a stronghold or on the top of a mountain peak, and a prolonged siege was necessary to reduce him to submission.

Of Hittite siegecraft we know comparatively little, but it was clearly effective, for so strong a city as Carchemish surrendered to King Suppiluliumas after a siege of only eight days. The only reference to the technique is in the account of the siege of Urshu, in which there is mention of the battering-ram and the 'mountain' – doubtless the 'agger' of the Romans up which the siege-engines had to be hauled.

The tactical genius of the Hittite kings is best known from the battle of Kadesh, which is described in great detail in an Egyptian text. The Hittite army based on Kadesh succeeded in completely concealing its position from the Egyptian scouts; and as the unsuspecting Egyptians advanced in marching order towards the city and started to pitch their camp, a strong detachment of Hittite chariotry passed round unnoticed behind the city, crossed the river Orontes, and fell upon the centre of the Egyptian column with shattering force. The Egyptian army would have been annihilated, had not a detached Egyptian regiment arrived most opportunely from another direction and caught the Hittites unawares as they were pillaging the camp. This lucky chance enabled the Egyptian king to save the remainder of his forces and to represent the battle as a great victory; but the impartial student will scarcely allow him much credit for the result.

3. DEFENCE

In defence no less than in the attack the Hittites were masters of the military art. The material remains bear impressive testimony to the strength of the fortifications with which they surrounded their cities.

At Boghazköy the natural strength of the gorges and crags needed little reinforcement; but around the open sector on the crest of the hill to the south massive walls were constructed, remains of which still stand to-day. The lines are double, consisting of a main wall and a lower subsidiary one thrown out about 20 feet in front of it. The main wall consists of an inner and outer shell of masonry with cross-walls between, forming a series of rectangular spaces filled with rubble – a method of construction which is characteristic of Hittite defensive walls wherever they are found. The outer shell of this wall is especially strong; it is constructed of massive stones of irregular shape, but with a preference for an approximately rectangular or five-sided form, from 1 to 5 feet in length and dressed so as to fit together, without mortar. Above this there would have been a superstructure of brickwork, but this is not preserved. Both walls are reinforced by projecting rectangular towers at intervals of

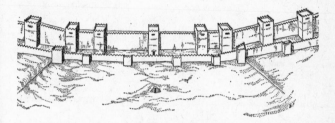

Fig. 3 – Reconstruction of defensive walls, Boghazköy, showing end of tunnel

about 100 feet; and the three main gateways are each flanked by huge blocks of masonry extending from the outer to the inner side of the whole system. The two walls together stand on a high rampart, the face of which is revetted with stone. At each entrance access to the city was by way of a steep ramp alongside the outer wall, at the top of which the road turned abruptly into a lane about 20 feet wide between the enormous flanking towers; within this the first gate was set back about 14 feet from the front, and there was a second flush with the inner face of the defences. There was also a tunnel under the rampart, through which the defenders could make a surprise sortie. The defensive strength of this system of fortifications is obvious, and it is hard to understand how the city could have been

Fig. 4 – Plan of gate, Boghazköy

Fig. 5 – Reconstruction of a gate, inner side

Fig. 6 – Reconstruction of a gate, outer side

captured and sacked on more than one occasion by ill-organized barbarian tribes. (See Figs. 3–6 and Plate 7.)

The city wall unearthed at Alishar (a neighbouring site) was of similar construction, but in place of the bastion-towers a saw-tooth or step design was adopted, giving enfilade in one direction only – an arrangement which seems less satisfactory. The wall of the small fort on the summit of Yümük Tepe near Mersin in Cilicia resembled the great wall of Boghazköy very closely, though the masonry was naturally less massive.

As already mentioned, we possess the standing orders for the officer commanding the frontier-defences. His strictly military duties (his civil functions have been quoted in the previous chapter) included the posting of sentries to watch the roads, the closing of the gates by night, the upkeep of the fortifications, and the provision of food, water, and fire-wood. Unfortunately most of the paragraphs in question are in a bad state of preservation and cannot be quoted *verbatim*.

The frontiers on which a policy of static defence was adopted were mainly the north and the south-west – precisely the areas where fortress-cities have been discovered. These were the directions in which the Hittite kingdom faced rugged and difficult country inhabited by turbulent tribes, whom the Hittites seem to have preferred to keep at bay rather than incorporate in their dominions by conquest. Against their more civilized neighbours (Arzawa to the west, and Egypt to the south-east) the principalities of the vassal-kings formed buffer states which protected Hittite territory from direct attack.

4. THE LAWS OF WAR

For the early Hittite kings conquest and plunder needed no apology; but by the fourteenth century, as we have seen, there had developed a closer intercourse between the civilized nations, and the Hittite kings of the imperial age were always at pains to justify a declaration of war, even against the petty tribal rulers on their northern frontiers. The usual procedure was to dispatch a letter demanding the extradition of Hittite subjects who had taken refuge in the enemy's territory. If the demand was refused, a second letter would follow, charging the enemy with having committed the first act of aggression and referring the affair to the judgement of heaven, to be settled by the ordeal of war. Here is the account of the correspondence that preceded the attack on Hayasa in the seventh year of Mursilis II:

After I had conquered the land of Tipiya, I sent a letter to Anniyas, the King of Azzi, and wrote to him: 'My subjects who went over to you while my father was in the land of Mitanni [give them back to me].' (One copy breaks off here, but we continue with a parallel text, which contains a much mutilated but obviously different version of this message.)

But the king of the land of Azzi wrote back to me ... as follows: 'Regarding what you write to me, – if [I have any civilian captives,] or anyone else has come (or, is coming) over to me, [I will not give them back,] and if you demand [............].'

But I wrote back thus: 'I have come and have encamped before the frontier of your country, and have not attacked your country, and have not laid hands on it by seizing civilian captives, cattle or sheep. But you have provoked a quarrel(?) [with My Majesty], and you have come [and attacked] the land of Dankuwa [and depopulated it]. Therefore the gods shall take their stand on my side, and shall decide the case in my favour.'

The challenge sent to the King of Arzawa in the third year of Mursilis is on similar lines:

'My subjects who went over to you, when I demanded them back from you, you did not restore them to me; and you called me a child and made light of me. Up then! Let us fight, and let the Storm-god, my lord, decide our case!'

The most elaborate apologia of this kind is the 326-line document composed by King Hattusilis III after his successful revolt against Urhi-Teshub. This work is discussed in detail below, p. 175. It shows a highly developed political conscience.

The treatment of the enemy depended on whether he surrendered willingly or resisted to the last. A city conquered by force of arms was the legitimate prey of the victorious army and was generally looted and burned to the ground. The devastated site was sometimes declared forever accursed and dedicated to the Storm-god by a solemn ritual, as a result of which it was thought to become the grazing-ground of the divine bulls Seris and Hurris. Future settlers would defy this taboo at their peril. The inhabitants of such a conquered place would be transplanted, with their cattle, to Hattusas and distributed as serfs among the Hittite officers and dignitaries. But there is no evidence that they were otherwise ill-treated. There is a complete absence of that lust for torture and cruelty which characterizes the annals of the Assyrian kings in their victories.

In the event of an early surrender by the enemy the Hittite king was usually content to accept his oath of allegiance. The considerations which moved him on such occasions are shown by the case of Manapa-Dattas of the land of the River Seha, whose past record showed him to be untrustworthy:

As soon as Manapa-Dattas, the son of Muwa-the-lion, heard about me 'His Majesty is coming!' he sent a messenger to meet me and wrote to me as follows: '[My Lord,] slay me not, but take me into allegiance; and as for the people who came over to me, I will deliver them to my lord.' But I answered him as follows: 'Once upon a time, when your brothers drove you out of your land, I commended you to the people of Karkisa, I even sent presents to the people of Karkisa on your behalf. But in spite of that you did not follow me, but you followed Uhha-zitis my enemy. So now am I going to take you into allegiance?' I would have gone forth and destroyed him, but he sent his mother to meet me; and she came and fell at my feet and spoke as follows: 'Our lord, do not destroy us, but take us, our lord, into allegiance!' And because a woman came to meet me and fell at my feet, I showed kindness to the woman and for that reason I did not proceed into the land of the River Seha.

If the surrender was accepted, no further action would be taken against the suppliant's territory, he would receive back his kingdom as a vassal, a treaty would be drawn up, and he would undertake to perform all the specific duties required of him. In such circumstances the people were said to be 'subjected in their place'. The standardized terminology may be seen in the summary which concludes the account of the conquest of Arzawa:

So I conquered the land of Arzawa. And one part I brought back to Hattusas, but the other part I subjected in its place and imposed on it a contribution of troops; and from then on they contributed troops regularly to me. And when I had conquered the whole land of Arzawa, the total of civilian captives that I, My Majesty, brought back to the royal palace was altogether 66,000 civilian captives; but what the lords, the soldiers, and the charioteers of Hattusas brought back in the way of civilian captives, oxen, and sheep – there was no counting it. And when I had conquered the whole land of Arzawa, I returned home to Hattusas.

CHAPTER VI

Languages and Races

A. THE WRITTEN LANGUAGES

IN 1919 E. Forrer announced his discovery that among the cuneiform texts from Boghazköy it was possible to distinguish eight different languages, and since that date there have been many allusions to the polyglot nature of the Hittite Empire. This is true up to a point, but Forrer's statement must not be taken to mean that all the eight languages were spoken within the Empire or were employed equally in the composition of inscriptions. Two languages only – Hittite and Akkadian – were used by the Hittite kings for their official documents; the only other language in which whole texts were occasionally written is that which we call Hurrian. Of the remainder, three are met with only in the form of short passages scattered among the Hittite religious texts, and one can be identified only by a few technical terms in a single document. The eighth language is Sumerian, and is included only because the Hittite scribes for their own purposes compiled vocabularies based on Sumerian sign-lists.

The main characteristics of these languages are as follows.

1. *Hittite*

The discovery that Hittite had affinities with the Indo-European languages was made by the Czech scholar B. Hrozný and published in 1915. The suggestion that an Indo-European language was spoken by the population of Asia Minor in the second millennium before Christ was so startling that it was at first received with great scepticism; but the connexion has been proved beyond all doubt and for more than twenty years has been accepted by all those who have studied the subject.

The relationship is most obvious in the inflexion of the noun. There are six cases (nominative, accusative, genitive, dative, ablative, and instrumental); personal names also exhibit a vocative consisting of the bare stem-form. The following table illustrates the close relation of the case-endings to those of Greek and Latin:

Case		Ending	Example and spelling	Greek and Latin
Nom.	s.	-s	humant-s (hu-ma-an-za)	λόγο-s, νύξ, mon-s
Acc.	s.	-(a)n[1]	humant-an (hu-ma-an-ta-an)	λόγο-ν, νύκτ-α, mont-em
Gen.	s.	-as	humant-as (hu-ma-an-ta-aš)	(λόγου), νυκτ-ός, mont-is
Dat.	s.	-i	humant-i (hu-ma-an-ti)	λόγῳ, νυκτ-ί, mont-i
Abl.	s.	-ts[2]	humant-a-ts (hu-ma-an-ta-az)	ἐκ-τός, fundi-tus
Inst.	s.	-it	humant-it (hu-ma-an-ti-it)	? ?

1. This arises from -ṃ (vocalic m); hence Latin -em and Gk. -a.
2. Written -z.

Unlike Greek and Latin, the Hittite noun has only two genders – animate and inanimate; adjectives in the inanimate gender have the bare stem form in the nominative and accusative singular, but are otherwise declined as above. The plural shows a less close resemblance to the Indo-European declension. There is no dual.

The enclitic personal pronouns -mu 'to me', -ta 'to thee', and -si 'to him' contain the same consonants as the corresponding Latin pronouns me 'me', te 'thee', and se 'himself'.

The verb has two voices – active and medio-passive. In the active the resemblance to the conjugation of the -μι verbs in Greek is very striking:

Sing.	1	-mi	ya-mi (i-ya-mi)	τίθημι
	2	-si	ya-si (i-ya-si)	τίθης
	3	-tsi	ya-tsi (i-ya-zi)	τίθητι (Doric)
Pl.	1	-weni	ya-weni (i-ya-u-e-ni)	τίθεμεν
	2	-teni	ya-teni (i-ya-at-te-ni)	τίθετε
	3	-ntsi	ya-ntsi (i-ya-an-zi)	τίθεντι (Doric)

There is also another active conjugation which seems to correspond rather to that of the perfect in other languages, but the resemblance is less obvious, and there is no trace of a difference in meaning.

In the vocabulary, on the other hand, the Indo-European element is comparatively small. The following are a few words which have Indo-European etymologies:

wātar 'water'; Greek ὕδωρ ' water '.
akw-anzi 'they drink'; Latin *aqua* 'water'.
genu 'knee'; Latin *genu* 'knee'.
kwis 'who'; Latin *quis* 'who'.

However, the greater part of the vocabulary is of non-Indo-European origin. Obvious examples are *tanduki-* 'mankind', *tītita-* 'nose', *kunna-* 'right (hand)', *taptappa-* 'nest', *amiyara-* 'canal'.

Increasing knowledge of the language has led to much discussion regarding the exact position of Hittite within the Indo-European family. It was very soon observed that the main features of the so-called 'satem' languages, especially Indo-Iranian (change of original *k* to *s*, *qu* to *k*, and *e* and *o* to *a*) are not shared by Hittite, and the conclusion was drawn that Hittite belonged to the 'centum' group (comprising Latin, Greek, Celtic, and the various Germanic languages). It is generally agreed, however, that this classification is somewhat misleading, and that in fact Hittite represents a distinct branch of the Indo-European family, beside the ten other branches already recognized. Many scholars would go further, and maintain that it can be shown from traces of archaic forms in Hittite, where all other languages have a common innovation, that Hittite was the first of the eleven branches to diverge from the parent stem. Others, however, dispute this, and the question is indeed highly controversial.

In one respect Hittite has rendered unexpected service to

Indo-European philology. It has long been maintained that the different forms under which certain words appear in the various languages can be satisfactorily explained only by the assumption that all these languages had lost certain guttural sounds (technically called laryngeals) which had originally been present in the parent speech. Now in Hittite the letter *ḫ* is frequently found in positions corresponding exactly to those where, in other languages, a laryngeal was supposed to have been lost, and this fact, however it may be interpreted in detail (the pronunciation of this *ḫ*, as well as many other points, is hotly debated), has strikingly vindicated the so-called 'laryngeal theory' in the broadest sense. Following are some examples of words containing this *ḫ*:

paḫḫur 'fire'; Greek πῦρ, English *pyre*.
laḫḫu- 'to pour'; Latin *lavit* 'he washed', English *lave*.
ḫastai 'bone'; Greek ὀστέον, cf. English *osteo-(pathy)*.
ḫanti 'over against'; Greek ἀντί, English *anti-*.

The true nature of the language was not at first appreciated by the early decipherers on account of the method of writing. The cuneiform script as adopted by the Hittites is a syllabary, in which each sign is read as a syllable consisting of either vowel+consonant, or consonant+vowel, or consonant+vowel+consonant. Such a script is well suited to a Semitic language, which avoids groups of more than two consonants, or of more than one at the beginning and end of the word, but in Hittite (as in other Indo-European languages) such groups were common, and in order to write them the Hittites were obliged to use syllables as if they were simple consonants, by ignoring the vowel in pronunciation. Another complication is caused by the fact that the voiced and unvoiced consonants (e.g., *d* and *t*, *b* and *p*, *g* and *k*) were distinguished in writing not by the appropriate signs, as in Akkadian – these are used by the Hittites indiscriminately – but by the convention of writing the unvoiced consonants as double letters. As a result, many words contain so many extra vowels and consonants that they appear deformed out of all recognition.

A further peculiarity of the Hittite method of writing may be mentioned here, namely 'allography', the practice of writing a different word from that which was actually pronounced. Hittite texts are liberally interspersed with purely Akkadian and Sumerian words, the latter usually written by single signs, the use of which as 'ideograms' (or better, 'Sumerograms') can often be recognized only by means of the context, for they may be the same signs that are normally used for mere syllables. But these 'foreign' words were probably (the Sumerian words certainly) not pronounced in reading; they merely conceal the corresponding Hittite word, which the reader was expected to substitute for them. This was undoubtedly intended as a kind of shorthand by the scribes. For us it has had both advantages and disadvantages. On the one hand, texts in which Akkadian words are frequent could be to some extent understood before ever a single word of Hittite was known; but on the other, the rules of 'allography' seem to have been so rigid that many common Hittite words (e.g., woman, sheep, copper, etc.) were never written phonetically at all and are therefore still unknown to us.

Other 'foreign' words which are intended to be read as they stand are preceded in the texts by a sign which corresponds to our inverted commas. All such words are found to belong to a language closely akin to Luwian (see below).

The name 'Hittite' was given to this language by modern scholars as being the official language of the Land of Hatti, and has been universally accepted; but it is strictly speaking incorrect. For the word *ḫattili* – properly 'in Hittite' – is used in the texts to introduce passages in a totally different language, to be described in the next section. When this was discovered, scholars searched the texts for the true name of the official language; but while Hrozný adopted the name 'Nésite' (i.e., the language of the city Nesa), Forrer preferred 'Kanisisch' (i.e., the language of Kanesh). It is now generally agreed that 'Nésite' or 'Nesian' (derived from the Hittite adverb *našili* or *nešumnili*) is indeed the true name of the language, but despite this the name 'Hittite' is now so well established that it will probably never be abandoned. The meaning of the term 'Kanesian' or 'Kaneshite' (Hittite *kanešumnili*) is somewhat controversial; if, however, Kanesh and Nesa are merely alternative forms of the same name (p. 19), the linguistic terms derived from them must be synonymous.

2. *Proto-Hittite, or Hattian*

This language is used for utterances by the priest in quite a number of cults, many of them those of the leading deities of the Hittite pantheon; but these utterances are all very brief, and the material is insufficient for us to gain at all a clear picture of the structure or vocabulary of the language. It seems to be characterized by an extensive use of prefixes; for example, the word *binu* 'child' forms a plural by means of the prefix *lē-*, i.e., *lēbinu*. Scholars have hitherto failed to find any linguistic group with which it can be even remotely connected.

As mentioned above, passages in this language are introduced by the word *ḫattili*. The name Proto-Hittite has been widely adopted in order to avoid confusion with the official Hittite, but is somewhat misleading, since it suggests an earlier stage of Hittite, whereas it is a language totally unrelated to the latter. The name Hattian is preferable, being derived from the adverb *ḫattili* as Luwian is from *luwili* (see next section).

3. *Luwian*

This language is closely related to Hittite. It differs from it, among other things, in forming the plural of nouns, pronouns, and adjectives in -*nzi* (possibly representing -*nts* in pronunciation) instead of the Hittite -*es*, and in a certain preference for the vowel *a*. But its chief peculiarity is that the dependence of one noun upon another is expressed not by a genitive case, as in other Indo-European languages, but by means of an adjective in -*assis* or -*assas*. This formation is productive of place-names; thus we find (omitting the case-ending -*s*) Dattassa and Tarhuntassa, meaning 'belonging to (the gods) Dattas and Tarhund', and light is thus thrown on the many place-names ending in -*assos* known from the Greek period. This language is also found for the most part in short passages, introduced by the adverb *luwili*, though the material is fuller than in the case of Hattian. Luwian was subdivided into several dialects, of which one was the 'hieroglyphic' language (see below) and another developed into the Lycian of the classical epoch.

4. *Palaic*

Still less is known of this language, which is attested only in the cult of one deity, Ziparwa. The name is given by the adverb *palaumnili*, from which we may form either 'Palaic' or 'Palaite'. Recent researches have at least proved that, like Hittite and Luwian, it belongs to the Indo-European family.

5. *Hurrian*

The material for the study of Hurrian is much more abundant than for Proto-Hittite, Luwian, and Palaic. In the Boghazköy texts Hurrian passages in rituals are very numerous, and even a few completely Hurrian texts have been found – among them fragments of a translation of the Epic of Gilgamesh, the greatest literary achievement of the Babylonian civilization. However, the principal source for the study of Hurrian is still the letter written by Tushratta, King of Mitanni, to Amenophis III of Egypt about 1400 B.C., and found among the ruins of the Egyptian capital at Tell el Amarna more than fifty years ago, for this text alone contains some 500 lines in reasonably good preservation. Other Hurrian texts have been found recently at Tell Hariri, the ancient Mari, on the Middle Euphrates, dating from about 1750 B.C., and at Ras Shamra (Ugarit) on the Syrian coast, where the language is written in a consonantal script. A direct descendant of Hurrian is the language of the kingdom of Urartu, sometimes called Vannic or Khaldian, which is known to us from royal inscriptions written in Assyrian cuneiform and dating from the seventh century B.C. The wider affinities of Hurrian are obscure. It is characterized by a prolific use of suffixes, and thus differs fundamentally from the other language of unknown affinities, Proto-Hittite. It seems possible that a connexion with the little-known languages of the Caucasus may eventually be established.

The name of the language is provided by the Hittite texts in which Hurrian passages are usually introduced by a formula such as 'the singer of the Land of Hurri sings as follows', or alternatively 'the singer sings as follows *hurlili*' (the reason for the addition of the letter *l* in the adverb is unknown).

6. *The Aryan Language of the Rulers of Mitanni*

In the treatise on horse-training by Kikkuli of Mitanni (see above, pp. 104–5) certain technical terms occur which, when analysed, are seen to contain elements closely akin to Sanskrit numerals, viz.:

aika-wartanna 'one turn'. Cf. Sanskrit *eka vártana-m* 'one turning'.

tēra-wartanna 'three turns'. Cf. Sanskrit *tri vártana-m* 'three turnings'.

panza-wartanna 'five turns'. Cf. Sanskrit *pañca vártana-m* 'five turnings'.

satta-wartanna 'seven turns'. Cf. Sanskrit *sapta vártana-m* 'seven turnings'.

navartanna 'nine turns'. Cf. Sanskrit *nava vártana-m* 'nine turnings'.

There are no texts written in this language, but these few words are evidence that it was spoken in Hittite times. That it was the language of the rulers of Mitanni will be shown below. We might therefore call it 'Mitannian', but this would be confusing, since this name has often in the past been given to the Hurrian language. Forrer, who identified the rulers of Mitanni with the *Umman Manda* of certain Babylonian and Assyrian texts, invented the name 'Mandaic', but this has never been generally accepted. In fact, no satisfactory name for the language has yet been found.

7. *Akkadian*

This is the name now universally given to the well-known Semitic language of Babylonia and Assyria; to the Hittites, however, it was known as 'Babylonian'. It was widely used in the Near East for diplomatic correspondence and documents of an international character, and the Hittite kings followed this custom when dealing with their southern and eastern neighbours. Many Hittite treaties and letters are therefore wholly in Akkadian and were available in translation long before the great bulk of the archive of Boghazköy had been deciphered. In addition, as mentioned above, Akkadian words are common in texts written in Hittite, but it is generally held that this is a form of allography.

8. *Sumerian*

This, the oldest language of lower Mesopotamia, though no longer spoken, was intensively studied in Hattusas as in

Babylonia, and Sumerian–Hittite vocabularies have been found there. Most Sumerian words are monosyllabic, and many of the syllables associated with the cuneiform signs in the Hittite period are really Sumerian words of which the meaning had been forgotten when the language ceased to be spoken. It was thus possible for the student of Sumerian to make use of single signs as 'ideograms', i.e., to signify the meaning or idea which they would have conveyed in Sumerian, and thus to save the extra time which he would have spent in writing the much longer Hittite or Akkadian word. In this way Sumerian served as a kind of shorthand, and this form of allography was much used by the learned Hittite scribes.

Such are the eight languages written in cuneiform on clay tablets at Boghazköy-Hattusas. To conclude our survey of the written Hittite languages we must now add one more.

9. *Hieroglyphic Hittite, or Tabalic*

The story of the discovery of the hieroglyphic inscriptions has been told in the introduction. Nearly all of them are on rock-carvings or stone monuments, the favourite material for the latter being basalt. The only exceptions are those on seals and the seven letters in the form of rolled-up strips of lead excavated at Assur and published in 1924. The earlier monumental form of the script has the signs raised in relief; later a cursive form arose in which they were incised. The signs themselves are pictograms, the objects which they represent being in many cases clearly recognizable. Parts of the body form a large class, such as hands in various positions, faces (always in profile), legs, and feet; there are heads of animals, such as oxen, horses, dogs, pigs, lions, stags, hares, birds, and fishes, also articles of furniture, such as chairs and tables, and parts of buildings, including a carefully drawn front view of a two-storied house. The order of the signs is 'boustrophedon',[1] i.e., the lines are read alternately right to left and left to right, a feature which is characteristic also of the early Greek inscriptions from the Ionian coast. The signs face the beginning of the line, as in Egyptian. The script was certainly an independent invention of the Hittites, stimulated in the most general way by acquaintance with the Egyptian hieroglyphs. It is one of several new scripts (including that which gave rise to our own alphabet) of hieroglyphic or cuneiform type which were invented in the middle of the second millennium under the stimulus of increasing international contacts in the lands of the Levant, where the cultures of the Nile and the Euphrates met and mingled. (See Plate 26.)

Very little progress was made in the decipherment until recent years; but now it has become clear that the language of these monuments is virtually a dialect of Luwian, though it differs, *inter alia*, in forming the plural of nouns by means of the ending -*ai*. Like Luwian, it is closely related to the Lycian language known from inscriptions of the Greek period. The fact that it shows *s* instead of *k* in combination with *u* does not prove it to be a *satem* language, as has been claimed.

The majority of the monuments in question were inscribed after the downfall of the Hittite Empire. Before that event, however, the script was already in use. Only a few of the longer inscriptions seem to belong to the classical Hittite period, and it is not entirely certain whether the language of these is the same as that of the later monuments; but recent researches seem to make this probable, and it thus follows that Hieroglyphic Hittite must also be included among the languages written by the scribes of the Hittite Empire. Apart from the longer inscriptions the script was regularly used both on stone monuments and on seals as a way of writing the names of the Hittite kings, somewhat in

1. A Greek word meaning 'in the manner of an ox ploughing'.

the manner of a monogram. But it is probable that it was in fact used much more extensively than would appear from the existing evidence, namely for all the administrative records of the Hittite kingdom, which have entirely perished because they were inscribed on tablets of wood.

No ancient name for the language is attested. Forrer has called it 'Tabalic', because the district where most of the inscriptions have been found bore the name Tabal (the Tubal of the Old Testament) in Assyrian times, but most other scholars have adopted the rather cumbrous expressions 'Hieroglyphic Hittite' or 'Hieroglyphic Luwian'.

B. THE SPOKEN LANGUAGES

We have now to ask the question: where, when, and by whom were these languages actually spoken?

No difficulty is presented by the use of Akkadian and Sumerian; they were purely literary languages at Hattusas, and we know their homeland and their history.

Nor is there any problem in the case of Hurrian and the Aryan formulas of the horse-training texts, whose author was a Hurrian from Mitanni. For the Hurrian people are known to have spread gradually southward and westward from their home in the mountainous region south of the Caspian Sea from about 2300 B.C. onwards, and to have become organized during the second millennium into several powerful kingdoms situated near the upper waters of the Euphrates and the Habur. One of these kingdoms, Mitanni, which, as we have seen, employed the Hurrian language for its diplomatic correspondence, was ruled by a dynasty of kings whose names have an Aryan etymology, and Indian deities, such as Indra and Varuna, figure prominently in its pantheon. It is thus clear that in Mitanni a population of Hurrians was dominated by a ruling caste of Indo-Aryans.

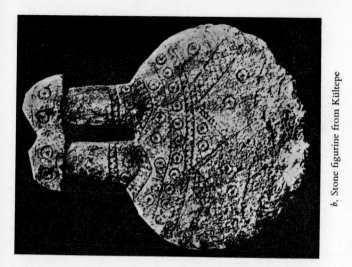

b. Stone figurine from Kültepe

a. Bronze statuette from Boghazköy

Hittite prisoners on Egyptian monuments

Hittite charioteers as represented by Egyptians

'King's Gate' figure, Boghazköy

b. Gold statuette in British Museum

a. Bronze statuette in Berlin Museum

c. Lead figurine from Kültepe

Boghazköy, view showing remains of Lower Temple. *Photo by Professor J. Garstang*

Boghazköy, southern wall and rampart

Boghazköy, lion gate

8

Alaja Hüyük, sphinxes

Boghazköy, sphinx from Yerkapu

Boghazköy, postern gate and tunnel

Yazilikaya, view of main gallery

a. Yazilikaya, central group

b. Yazilikaya, procession of gods

13

Yazilikaya, part of side gallery

Yazilikaya, bas-relief in side gallery

Alaja Hüyük, king and queen worshipping bull. *Photo by Professor J. Garstang*

Both languages are comparatively late intruders into the Hittite area, and the prominence of Hurrian in the archive of Hattusas is due to the great extension of Mitannian power in the period preceding the reign of Suppiluliumas.

The position is different with the other five languages: Hattian stands over against four closely related Indo-European languages – Hittite, Luwian, Palaic, and 'Hieroglyphic Hittite'. There is good reason to suppose that Hattian was a dead language at the time when the texts were written; for Hattian passages are often provided with an interlinear version in Hittite for the assistance of the functionaries who have to speak them. The name ḫattili suggests that its home-land was the Land of Hatti in the narrower sense, and the ancient place-names of this region seem to confirm this conclusion. But this, if anywhere, must have been the area where the Hittite language itself was spoken, and it is legitimate to conclude that it was the invasion of the Indo-Europeans that drove Hattian out of current use.

It has recently been suggested that by the time the texts were written Hittite had become a literary language which was no longer spoken, having been superseded as a vernacular by Hieroglyphic Hittite (or, less probably, by Luwian), rather as Akkadian later gave way before the more flexible Aramaic. For the period of the later Empire there is much to recommend this view, though the language must have been alive down to the reign of Suppiluliumas, since it shows a clearly marked development. That the later kings and princes should have erected public monuments all over the kingdom in the script and language of one of their less cultured provinces is difficult to imagine; the practice is more easily intelligible if Hieroglyphic Hittite had become the spoken dialect of their own people or was actually their own language. The theory has, however, been vigorously disputed, and would indeed be untenable if, as has been claimed, there is evidence for a continued development in the Hittite language during the later centuries. Further investigation of this point must therefore be awaited.

The original home of Hieroglyphic Hittite seems on present evidence most likely to have been Cilicia, for the earliest example of the hieroglyphic script is the seal of Isputakhsus, King of Kizzuwatna, an impression of which on a clay bulla was found at Tarsus by Miss Goldman's expedition in 1935, and the location of Kizzuwatna in Cilicia is virtually certain. If the theory mentioned in the previous paragraph is true, the language, though not the people themselves, would have spread northwards across the Taurus ranges during the time of the later kings of Hattusas. In the turmoil of the twelfth century the 'people of Adana' (Hittite *adanawanai*, Egyptian *daniuna*) appear to have joined the marauders known to the Egyptians as 'Peoples of the Sea' (see above, p. 43), and large numbers of them may well have settled subsequently in Syria and founded the 'Neo-Hittite' kingdoms described above (pp. 39 ff.). The Karatepe inscription, however, is evidence that the migration did not involve the whole population of the Cilician plain. The 'Land of Que' mentioned in Assyrian royal annals is none other than the kingdom of Adana to which the author of the Karatepe inscription owed allegiance.

Luwian is the language of the area called Luwiya, which included the state of Arzawa, and we know that the latter must have been somewhere on the western or southwestern coast of Asia Minor. In this area too the place-names ending in -*assa* are most common, and we have seen that these names are derivable from the Luwian language. Kizzuwatna was a Luwian border-land, for the gods Tarhund and Santas (Sandon) are the typical deities of the Luwian pantheon, and a man of Kizzuwatna is cited as the author of a Luwian ritual; this fact would be reflected in the close relationship between the Luwian and Hieroglyphic Hittite languages.

For the land of Palā, where Palaic was spoken, a location in northern Cappadocia between modern Kayseri and Sivas seems to be most probable, but this is one of the most vexed questions of Hittite geography. Some scholars have identified the name with classical Blaene in the far north-west.

CHAPTER VII

Religion

I. GENERAL REMARKS

W E have seen how the isolated city-communities of Anatolia were gradually welded into a semblance of unity by the genius of the kings of Hattusas but yet preserved to the end their local councils and many of their local rights. In religion also each little community seems to have maintained its independence, for the centralization of power at Hattusas was primarily a civil and military matter. The local shrines remained, their cults unimpaired. The policy of the kings seems to have been to enhance rather than to diminish their importance, while at the same time assuming in their own person the office of supreme high priest of the realm. In this capacity the king instituted an annual 'progress', in the course of which he visited the most important cult-centres and himself celebrated the main festivals. The upkeep of the temples was one of the chief tasks of the local commanders and provincial governors, and these shrines must have benefited greatly from the increasing stability and prosperity of the kingdom.

At the same time the centralization of the government made a certain synthesis inevitable. High acts of State must be placed under the solemn guarantee of all the gods and goddesses of the realm; and so the Hittite scribes compiled lists of all the local deities for invocation in the treaties and royal decrees. By a process of syncretism similar deities were grouped together or treated as identical, and there was some attempt to evolve an orderly pantheon. At the same time the state and the monarchy were placed under the protection of a particular group of great national divinities, who were worshipped at the capital with an elaborate ritual.

Now we possess among the tablets from Boghazköy abundant evidence for this State cult, and the religious conceptions on which it was based are revealed in the prayers of various members of the royal family and in the elaborate instructions issued to the priests and temple servants. There are also mythological poems of great interest which illuminate vividly the characters of the deities mentioned in them, but these are not for the most part the same deities as those of the State religion, or if they are the same there are strange inconsistencies between their roles in the different contexts. It seems therefore that these myths are derived from the local cults; but their place of origin is nowhere stated, nor do we know anything of the rites and ceremonies associated with them. Of the other popular local deities and their cult-centres we know little beside their names.

It is here that the monuments are of some assistance. Unlike the tablets, the monuments are distributed widely throughout the country and provide some direct evidence for local cults. Whereas the tablets give us the bare names of deities and of their cult-centres, the monuments portray divine types associated with particular localities. The deities are usually distinguished: (*a*) by a weapon or other implement held in the right hand; (*b*) by a symbol carried in the left hand; (*c*) by wings or other adjuncts; and (*d*) by a sacred animal on which they frequently stand. The main disadvantage of the monuments as evidence is that they date for the most part from after the end of the Hittite Empire, when syncretizing tendencies had affected most of the local cults as well as those of the capital; such monuments have to be used with caution. Of the few which belong certainly to the period of the empire, by far the most important is the great rock-sanctuary of Yazilikaya (Turkish for 'inscribed rock') about two miles from Boghazköy. Here a natural outcrop of rock forms an enclosed recess, on the walls of which the gods and goddesses of the Hittite kingdom are shown, carved in bas-relief, in two processions which converge on a central point on the wall facing the entrance (Plates 12, 13). This is a monument of the state religion. Many of the deities carry symbols, and though the weathering of the rock makes their recognition extremely difficult, recent advances in our knowledge of the hieroglyphic writing have revealed the astonishing fact that in the thirteenth century B.C. the theologians of the Hittite capital had adopted a Hurrian pantheon. The circumstances and nature of this development are discussed below, p. 144.

2. LOCAL CULTS

The characteristic god of Hittite Anatolia is the Weather-god, for in contrast to the torrid plains of Mesopotamia this is a land of clouds and storms. There are many local monuments illustrating the various types of this deity, and in the texts we find his cult associated with a very large number of cities. In Syrian art he often stands alone, wielding an axe and a symbolic flash of lightning; in Anatolia itself he drives in a primitive kind of chariot drawn by bulls over the heads of personified mountains. The bull is his sacred animal, and may stand alone on an altar as his cult-symbol, a usage illustrated by the orthostats of Alaja Hüyük (Fig. 11, p. 149). The Weather-god standing on the bull, who became well known throughout the Roman Empire under the name of Jupiter Dolichenus, seems to have been a later development.

In mythology the Weather-god figures as the slayer of the dragon Illuyankas. The myth is discussed below, p. 181.

The most famous temples of the Weather-god were to

be found in the Taurus region and the plain of North Syria. Now this was the part of the Hittite empire in which the Hurrians formed the predominant element in the population, and accordingly we find that throughout this area the cult is that of the Hurrian Weather-god Teshub and his consort Hebat.

In the Hurrian pantheon the goddess Hebat (or Hepit) is of almost equal importance with her husband Teshub. The two were worshipped together at Aleppo, Samuha (perhaps Malatya), Kummanni (probably the classical Comana Cappadociae), Uda (the classical Hyde), Hurma, and Apzisna. She appears in art as a matronly figure, sometimes standing on a lion, her sacred animal, but without other special attributes. At Kummanni she takes first place; and it is significant that Comana was the city of the War-goddess Ma-Bellona. But the goddess of Kummanni in the Hittite texts has apparently no warlike characteristics. Perhaps she acquired these subsequently as a result of syncretism.

Within the Hurrian milieu this divine pair have a son named Sharruma or Sharma. This god has been plausibly identified with the deity whose symbol in art is a pair of human legs and who is twice represented at Yazilikaya, once following immediately behind his mother Hebat in the procession of goddesses, and again in the small gallery at the side of the main shrine, in heroic proportions, holding King Tudhaliyas IV in his embrace (Plate 15). The texts mention him chiefly in connexion with Uda and Kummanni.

Another prominent Hurrian deity was the goddess Shaushka, identified with Ishtar and usually so written in the texts. The Hurrian Ishtar was worshipped at Samuha and at a number of other cities in the Taurus region. She was adopted by King Hattusilis III as his patron goddess, and this king's so-called autobiography is dedicated to her. She was visualized as a winged figure standing on a lion, and so may be recognized in the winged goddess on certain seal-impressions and other monuments. She has two female attendants called Ninatta and Kulitta.

There are many other Hurrian deities whose cult-centres were outside the Hittite orbit and who were never admitted into the Hittite pantheon. Mesopotamian deities, such as Anu and Antu, Enlil and Ninlil, Ea and Damkina, were introduced to the Hittites through the medium of the Hurrian religion, and are often mentioned in the texts, but they seem to have been recognized as foreign to the country.

To the west of the Hurrian country, between the southern edge of the salt basin and the foot-hills of Taurus, lay a group of important cities of which the best known is Tuwanuwa, the classical Tyana. Here the Weather-god was venerated, probably under another name which we do not know, for his consort appears no longer as Hebat, but under such names as Sahassaras, Huwassanas, Tasimis. This region seems to have been the centre of the worship of the Hattian god Wurunkatti (meaning 'King of the Land'), who appears in the texts under the name of the Sumerian war god Zababa.

Travelling north from Tuwanuwa, we enter the heart of the Hittite kingdom, the homeland of the Hattians. Here the great religious centre was Arinna, a holy city which has not been located but is said to have been within a single day's journey from the capital, Hattusas. At Arinna the principal deity was apparently the Sun-goddess, Wurusemu; the Weather-god takes second place as her consort, and there are daughters named Mezulla and Hulla and even a granddaughter Zintuhi. Farther east probably was another important centre of the worship of the Weather-god, the city of Nerik. The god Telipinu, whose name is inseparable from the Myth of the Missing God (see below, p. 183), is associated with four cities in this region. He was evidently a god of agriculture, since his father, the Weather-god, says of him: 'This son of mine is mighty; he harrows and ploughs, he irrigates the fields and makes the crops grow.' Since he plays the chief role in the myth which describes the paralysis of life caused by his withdrawal, he may have been a typical 'dying god' like Adonis, Attis, and Osiris, representing the vital forces of nature which appear to die in winter and revive in the spring. But since the Weather-god and the Sun-god also play the same role in the mythology, it is perhaps more probable that this was

Fig. 7 – The god on the stag. Steatite relief from Yeniköy

nothing more than a role which any god might play, and that the different versions of the myth arose separately in the different cult-centres of the gods concerned.

At Sarissa and Karakhna, and probably elsewhere, there was a cult of the god who appears in the texts under a title which seems to mean 'Protective Genius' or 'Providence'. But if this god has been correctly identified on the monuments, he was a god of the countryside, and indeed in one text he is described as 'a child of the open country'. His sacred animal was the stag, and he is represented standing on this animal and holding in his hand a hare and a falcon. This cult was very widespread and was evidently an ancient one, for models of stags have been found in tombs dating back to the third millennium B.C.

There are many other Hattian deities, but they are little more than names to us. Mountain-gods seem to have been numerous.

Of the Luwian pantheon we know little. Santas, the 'king', identified by the Hittites with Marduk, seems to have been a Luwian deity, though his attributes are uncertain. Dattas was the Luwian Weather-god. Numerous divine names ending in -assas, -assis, and -imis must be attributed to the Luwian language, but they are probably mere titles. Santas survived into the Greek period as Sandon, whose cult was celebrated at Tarsus.

The god Tarhund, to be identified with the Etruscan Tarchon, whose name is the basis of the personal name Tarquinius, was a Weather-god, but it is uncertain to which element of the population he belongs. He was the chief deity of the Neo-Hittite kingdoms, and one is inclined therefore to associate him with the speakers of the 'hieroglyphic Hittite' language; but, as we have seen, the original home of these people is itself uncertain. Tarhund does not appear at all in Hittite religious texts, but his name forms an element in many personal names which have a Luwian appearance. The goddess Kubaba is another deity who must be mentioned here, although she plays a very small part in the texts and her place of origin is uncertain; for she is undoubtedly the prototype of the Phrygian Cybebe-Cybele.

In this brief sketch only the main deities of the chief cult-centres have been mentioned, in order to avoid confusion. The texts teem with divine names, and we must suppose that at each shrine the high gods were surrounded by a host of minor gods and goddesses, of whose functions and attributes we have only the vaguest conception.

3. THE STATE RELIGION

Out of the diversity of the local cults the theologians of Hattusas created an official pantheon, the nucleus of which was the cult of the neighbouring shrine of Arinna. The Sun-goddess of Arinna was exalted as 'Queen of the Land of Hatti, Queen of Heaven and Earth, mistress of the kings and queens of the Land of Hatti, directing the government of the King and Queen of Hatti'. She became the supreme patroness of the Hittite state and monarchy, and the king always turned first to her for aid in battle or in time of national danger.

Her position *vis-à-vis* the Sun-god seems never to have been clearly defined. This god appears in mythology as the king of the gods, and in most of the lists attached to the treaties he takes first place. Like his Babylonian counterpart, he was regarded as the god of right and justice, a natural conception, since the sun in his daily course surveys from an impartial height all the deeds of men. King Muwatallis prays to him in the following words:

> Sun-god of heaven, my lord, shepherd of mankind! Thou risest, O Sun-god of heaven, from the sea and goest up to heaven. O Sun-god of heaven, my lord, daily thou sittest in judgement upon man, dog, pig, and the wild beasts of the field.

The same conception is found in a hymn addressed ostensibly to the Sun of Arinna, but as a masculine deity: 'The inspired lord of justice art thou, and in the place of justice thou art untiring.' Why is the Sun-god said to rise from the sea? It has been suggested that this sentence may indicate that the Hittite Sun-god is not indigenous in Anatolia but was brought there by a people dwelling on an eastern littoral. It is indeed a curious detail that one text describes the Sun-god as having fishes on his head, and there was a distinct type of Sun-god known as the 'Sun-god in the water'.

There was also a Sun-god (or perhaps rather a Sun-goddess) of the Underworld, through which the sun was supposed to pass on its way from west to east during the hours of darkness.

But according to the official theology the husband of the Sun-goddess of Arinna was not the Sun-god but the Weather-god of Hatti, sometimes called the Weather-god of Heaven. This great figure may have originated in the local cult of Arinna, of Hattusas or of Kussara (he is already the supreme divinity in the inscription of Anittas), but he is essentially the elder Weather-god whose cult, as we have already seen, was widespread throughout Anatolia. He is called 'King of Heaven, Lord of the Land of Hatti'. He also, like his consort, is a god of battle and is closely identified with the military fortunes of the nation. He alone may represent it in its dealing with foreign powers. Thus the treaty between Hattusilis III and Ramesses II of Egypt is said to be for the purpose of 'making eternal the relations which the Sun-god of Egypt and the Weather-god of Hatti have established for the land of Egypt and the Land of Hatti'.

In the later years of the Hittite Empire the state religion came under strong Hurrian influence. Doubtless that remarkable personality Queen Puduhepa played a great part in this movement, for she was a princess of Kummanni in Kizzuwatna, one of the chief cult-centres of Hebat, and her very name suggests that she was a devotee of this goddess.[1] It is in a prayer ascribed to this queen's husband King Hattusilis that the goddess Hebat is expressly identified with the Sun-goddess of Arinna, an act of syncretism of which there is no trace before this date. Conversely, on the royal seal whose impression is described in the Egyptian version of the treaty of Hattusilis with Egypt the queen was shown in the embrace of the Sun-goddess of Arinna: this intimate re-

1. The exact pronunciation of the name of the goddess is uncertain, as the spelling varies between Hebat and Hepat or even Hepit.

lationship can be understood on the assumption that the name of the Sun-goddess here stands for the Hurrian Hebat, the patron goddess of the queen's native town, though one ritual text suggests that a special relation between the Sun-goddess and the Queens of Hatti was recognized. Simultaneously perhaps, the Hurrian Teshub was identified with the Weather-god of Hatti and the divine Son Sharma with his counterpart the Weather-god of Nerik and Zippalanda.

Whether or not the reception of the Hurrian cults is thus correctly dated, the carving of the rock-sculptures of Yazilikaya must certainly have taken place when that process was already complete. For there the leading goddess of the pantheon bears the name Hepatu, written clearly in the hieroglyphic script, and there are reasons for supposing that the smaller figure of her son who stands behind her is designated as Sharma. The leading god opposite to her bears symbols meaning 'Weather-god of Heaven', but in view of the Hurrian name of his consort we may be sure he was intended to be known as Teshub. He is represented as a bearded man carrying in his right hand a club, his feet resting on the bowed necks of two figures whose bodies are drawn in a way which shows them to be deified mountains. The bull-drawn chariot in which on other monuments the god is shown driving over these mountains is missing at Yazilikaya, but the artist has shown the two bulls peering round the legs of the Weather-god and his consort. Now we know the names of these bulls and of the two mountains: the bulls are Seris and Hurris,[1] the mountains Namni and Hazzi. These are Hurrian names; in the Hurrian language Seri and Hurri mean respectively day and night; Hazzi is the Mons Casius near Antioch in North Syria (which was Hurrian country). It seems then that this conception of the Weather-god in his chariot is itself derived from a Hurrian source.

1. In the Song of Ullikummi they are called Serisu and Tella. See below, p. 193.

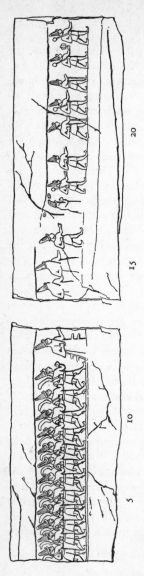

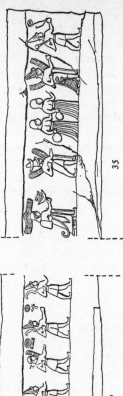

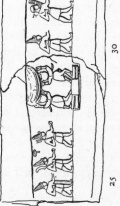

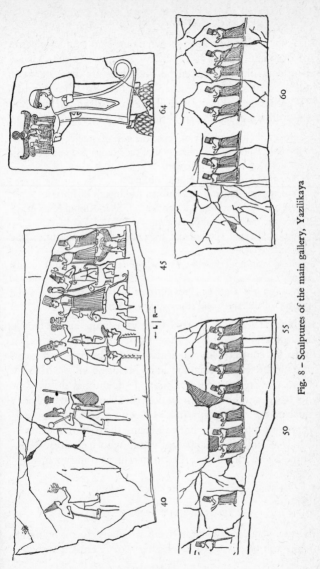

Fig. 8 – Sculptures of the main gallery, Yazilikaya

In fact, it has now been shown that the gods and goddesses of the main gallery at Yazilikaya are those of the Hurrian pantheon. Behind the central Teshub figure there stands an identical bearded Weather-god holding the symbols 'Weather-god of Hatti' (see above, p. 140), and behind him the following deities can be identified:

No. 40, holding an ear of corn: the god of grain.

No. 39, Ea (Mesopotamian god of the Nether Sea and a prominent deity among the Hurrians).

No. 38, Shaushka, the Hurrian Ishtar.

Nos. 37, 36: Ninatta and Kulitta, handmaids of Ishtar.

No. 35: the Moon-god, Kushukh (cf. Shar-Kushukh, p. 33).

No. 34: the Sun-god of Heaven.

No. 32, whose symbol has been identified as an antler: the 'Protective Genius'.

No. 30: an underworld deity, whose Hurrian name is possibly Hesui.

Nos. 29-28: a group showing two bull-men standing on the symbol of the Earth and supporting the Sky.

Behind Hebat and Sharma follows a long line of female figures whose symbols are largely obliterated and who can only be conjecturally identified with Hurrian goddesses. A sculptured block found in a neighbouring village has now filled the gap between nos. 55 and 56, and has shown that no. 56 is another representation of Shaushka, who had a dual nature. The king (no. 64) whose colossal figure is carved on a projecting buttress facing the back of the chamber is a Tudhaliyas, apparently one who had already 'become a god', since he is shown standing on mountains.

4. TEMPLES, CULTS, AND FESTIVALS

Hittite places of worship were of many forms, ranging from the open-air rock-sanctuary of Yazilikaya to the

Alaja Hüyük, boar hunt

Rock-relief at Gavur Kalesi

Rock-relief at Sirkeli by River Jeyhan. In background, medieval castle of Yilankale. *Photo by Professor J. Garstang*

a. Stone pedestal from Boghazköy

b. The 'Tarkondemos' seal

a. Cuboid seal

b. Lens-shaped seal

Hittite seals and their impressions

21

a. Impression of Hittite cylinder seal

b. Gold ring bought at Konya

b. Hittite rhyton from Karahüyük, Elbistan

a. Gold vessels from Alaja Hüyük. Pre-Hittite

Pottery vessels from Kültepe

Hittite cuneiform tablet

Hittite hieroglyphic inscription

Lion from Malatya

Figure of Weather-god from Zinjirli

Relief from Karatepe showing musicians and dancer

An Anatolian house under construction

The central Anatolian plain

Bulgar Maden and the Taurus Mountains. *Photo by Professor J. Garstang*

elaborate temples in Cyclopean masonry found at Boghaz-köy. In some cities, as already mentioned, the temple was at the same time the centre of the civil government and economic administration, and must have housed a very large staff of religious and civil functionaries. At the opposite extreme, as it appears from the texts, there were places where several shrines were together administered by a single priest; such shrines must have been of very modest dimensions.

Our knowledge of the lay-out of Hittite temples is derived from the five temples excavated at Boghazköy, which are strikingly similar in design (see Fig. 9). As in Babylonia and Crete, many small rooms are grouped around a paved court which varies from about 200 to 500 square metres in area. Here, however, the resemblance to the Babylonian temple ends. The cella, or holy of holies, of the Babylonian temple communicated directly with the court through an intervening antechapel, so that the congregation in the court would have a clear view of the god's statue in its niche in the middle of the farther wall of the cella through the two open doorways. In the Hittite temple, however, the entrance to the cella was not in the wall opposite to the cult-statue but in one of the adjacent sides, and was approached indirectly by way of two small rooms on the left, so that the worshipper would have to turn to his left on entering the shrine in order to face the statue at the farther end. In the temples of the upper city there is some indication that the deity was none the less visible from the court through interior windows in the intervening wall. But in the lower temple, even if such windows existed, the shrine is placed so far to one side of the building that there would in any case be no view of the cult-statue from the court, and we must conclude that there at least divine worship was the business of a select few who could be admitted to the cella itself and that a large congregation assembled in the court-yard could have only a remote part in such worship.

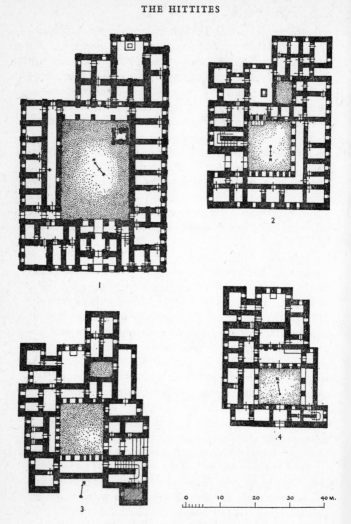

Fig. 9 – Plans of temples at Boghazköy

Another most characteristic feature of these Hittite temples, as reconstructed by the excavators, is the breaking up of the outer walls by deep windows reaching almost to floor level; Babylonian temples, on the other hand, looked inwards on to their own courtyards, and the rooms received the daylight only through small openings high up in the walls. In four of the Hittite temples the end of the cella, where the statue stood, projected beyond the outer wall of the adjoining rooms and was illuminated by two such windows on

Fig. 10 – Reconstruction of courtyard of Temple V, Boghazköy

either side (or by one, where only one side projects); a brilliant light would thus be thrown on the statue standing between them.

The function of the other rooms of the Hittite temples can only be surmised. In the great temple of the lower city (No. I) the cella is situated in a kind of annexe, which is out of alignment with the rest of the temple, and is further distinguished from it in being built of granite, whereas the main part of the building around the central court is of limestone. It seems probable here that the latter contained mainly civil offices of government and administration, especially in view of the fact that the whole temple was surrounded by a ring of irregular narrow chambers which contained large storage vessels and were evidently magazines. Whether the temples in the upper city also contained administrative offices it is difficult to say; their construction seems more homogeneous, and No. V at least contained a second shrine on the north side of the court.

There is no consistency in the orientation of these temples. No. I faces north-east, No. II south, No. III and No. IV north, and No. V east.

The deity was represented by a statue on a pedestal. The only object yet discovered which may possibly be regarded as such a cult-statue is the stone stele found abandoned on a hill-side near Fasillar and representing a bearded god standing upon two lions. But descriptions of such statues are numerous and show that they have mostly perished because they were made of precious metal or of wood plated with metal. The Weather-god of Heaven was represented by a golden statue holding in his right hand a club, in his left a golden symbol of 'good' (probably the triangle which appears in the centre of certain seals) and standing upon two male figures of mountain-gods (as on the rock-relief of Yazilikaya). Zababa was a silver statue of a standing man: 'in his right hand he holds a club, in his left he holds a shield, under him stands a lion, beneath the lion is a pedestal overlaid with silver'. 'Ishtar' (probably a special type of this goddess) was a sitting figure with wings coming out of her shoulder-blades, holding a golden cup in her right hand and in her left a symbol of 'good', standing on a pedestal which rested on the back of a winged lion or griffon, with figures of the attendant goddesses Ninatta and Kulitta on either side.

At the poorer shrines the deity was represented by a symbol or fetish. The Weather-god was often represented in the form of a bull, as illustrated in the relief found at Alaja Hüyük (Fig. 11), his attendant mountain-gods by a club, or other weapon, with a representation of the deity in some

way 'on' it (cf. the sword-deity in the small gallery at
Yazilikaya, Fig. 14). A very common cult-object was the
huwasi stone. This was a stele or *masseba* carved with an
inscription and sometimes with a figure of the god, and let
into a base such as Plate 20*a* (the inscription on which includes a representation of a base with two such *massebas*
upon it). Another regular piece of temple-furniture was the
istananas, which is equated textually with the Akkadian
aširtu, and has therefore been compared to the Canaanite

Fig. 11 – Bas-relief from Alaja Hüyük. King worshipping bull, as
symbol of the Weather-God. Cf. Plate 16

ashera; but it seems to function rather as a kind of stand or
altar. The furniture of the shrine and even the various parts
of the actual structure of the building were treated as divine,
and were associated with the presiding deity when sacrifices were offered.

The temple was the home of the god, and the priests were
his domestic staff. As far as we can see from the texts, this
simple conception underlies the whole of Hittite temple-
ritual. Every day it was the duty of the staff of the temple to
attend to the god's 'bodily needs' according to a fixed

routine; he must be washed, clothed, provided with food and drink, and entertained with dancing and music. This daily routine was taken for granted, and allusions to it are rare. 'They wash the god's person in the inner room, anoint him and dress him in a fine garment.' 'O Weather-god of Zippalanda, living self of the godhead, eat and be filled, drink and be satisfied.' One of the most valuable texts in this connexion is a tablet of disciplinary instruction for priests and temple-servants, though the emphasis is on the manner of performing ceremonies rather than on the ceremonies themselves. The ministrants must be perfectly clean and ritually pure. If they have come into contact with any form of pollution, or if they have slept with a woman, they must not approach the god until they have performed the necessary rite of purification. Food and drink that has been dedicated to the god must on no account be diverted or shared with laymen. Temple discipline demanded that every member of the staff should return to the temple at night, though he might spend the evening in the town; for spending the whole night with his wife the penalty was death. There are even regulations about fire-watching and nightly patrols.

But the god was not merely the householder of the temple, he was also the lord and master of his people, and as such entitled to offerings and tribute of many kinds as tokens of respect. Propitiatory offerings might be brought by any person at any time and often formed part of a magic ritual of healing. The first fruits of the land and yearling animals were especially dedicated to him, and it was believed that lavish offerings would win his favour. There is hardly any product of the land that might not be offered in this way, and it is often impossible to distinguish such offerings from the food and drink which constituted the god's regular meals. Animals must be without blemish and in good condition, and their value was greater if they were not yet mated. Subject to these restrictions even such normally 'unclean' animals as the dog and the pig were occasionally sacrificed, though oxen, sheep, and goats were naturally the more usual offerings. The animals were sacrificed by cutting the throat so that blood was shed, and for this reason the word used for sacrificing an animal was the same as that for making a drink-offering or libation, which was poured out on the ground. Bread and cheese were 'broken', though the exact implication of this term is uncertain.

It is surprising to find occasional instances of human sacrifice, e.g., in a ritual of purification following a military defeat which reminds one of the covenant in Gen. xv. 9–18:

If the troops have been beaten by the enemy they perform a ritual 'behind' the river, as follows: they 'cut through' a man, a goat, a puppy, and a little pig; they place half on this side and half on that side, and in front they make a gate of ..... wood and stretch a ..... over it, and in front of the gate they light fires on this side and on that, and the troops walk right through, and when they come to the river they sprinkle water over them.

In another broken passage a prisoner of war appears in a list of paraphernalia for sacrifice alongside a little pig and a dog. Such barbarous rituals belong to the 'popular' religion and are not part of the state cult; yet they are described and recorded in the archives without any sign of disapproval.

There are many references to the periodical religious festivals, of which there were evidently a large number and a great variety. The tablet of instructions already quoted mentions eighteen festivals, some named after seasons of the year, while others have names of unknown meaning. The priests are enjoined to 'celebrate the festivals at the time of the festivals' and not to perform the festival of the spring in the autumn and the festival of the autumn in the spring, or to put off a festival because the man who is performing it pleads that 'the harvest is upon me, or a journey, or some other business'. This list of festivals contains only those performed at Hattusas; comparison of the texts shows that each cult-centre had its own festival-calendar, but in most cases details are unknown.

One of the major festivals of the Hittite calendar was that called *purulliyas*, probably a Hattian word *purulli*, meaning 'of the earth', with Hittite genitival suffix. At this festival the Myth of the Slaying of the Dragon, discussed below, p. 181, was apparently recited. Its importance can be judged from the fact that King Mursilis II considered it necessary to return to Hattusas to celebrate it in the midst of a campaign.

When spring came round [he writes] because, although I had celebrated the *purulli*-festival in honour of the Weather-god of Hatti and the Weather-god of Zippalanda, I had not yet celebrated the *purulli*-festival – the great festival – in the mausoleum in honour of Lilwani, I came up to Hattusas and celebrated the *purulli*-festival – the great festival – in the mausoleum.

Such a spring festival, at which the combat of the god and the Dragon Illuyankas was acted or recited, would seem to belong to a well-known type of seasonal festival, the primitive purpose of which was to re-invigorate the earth after the stagnation of winter, the ritual combat symbolizing the triumph of life over death or good over evil. The chthonic character of the festival is evident not only in its name but also in its dedication to Lilwani, who was a goddess of the Earth, and in its association with the mausoleum.

There is a passing reference in a Hittite text to an assembly of the gods for the purpose of 'fixing the fates', and this strongly suggests that the Hittites had a New Year festival, similar to that at Babylon, at which such a gathering would be enacted in ritual form. Since the Hittite calendar year appears to have begun in the spring, this may have been the *purulli* festival itself, but there is no direct evidence.

When the king was to celebrate the festival in person, a

tablet of instructions was prepared in which the ceremony was described in the minutest detail. Many such tablets are preserved, as well as a few in which the king is not the central figure, but it is often impossible to identify the festival described because the title (or colophon) is broken off. One of these unidentified texts may well be the missing book of instructions for the *purulli*-festival, for a fragment exists containing the title of the ritual but nothing else. Those whose titles are preserved include the festivals of the cold weather (or winter), of the month, of the gate-house, of the *ḫuwasi*-stone of several gods, but above all that of the *andaḫšum* plant, again in honour of a number of gods. The *andaḫšum* is an edible plant, probably one which flourished in the spring, for this festival (if none other) was certainly celebrated in the spring-time. Its description occupied a whole series of large tablets, and exists in several slightly different copies. The essential part of the festival consists in sacrifices and libations to most of the gods and goddesses of the kingdom and to the various parts of the temple. These sacrifices are repeated at great length with numerous different forms of food, including the *andaḫšum* plant, and are of greater interest for the lists of deities which they contain than for the ceremonial procedure, which is very monotonous.

The rituals of most of these festivals seem to have been essentially similar, so that we may almost speak of a single 'royal ritual'. In all instances a large part of the book of instructions is devoted to preliminaries such as the king's toilet, the procession to the temple, and the ushering in of the royal pair and the other dignitaries to their respective places. The following excerpts will illustrate the style of these documents:

The king and queen come out of the *ḫalentuwa*-house. Two palace servants and one member of the bodyguard walk in front of the king, but the lords, the (rest of) the palace servants, and

the bodyguard walk behind the king. The 'statue-worshippers'
play the *arkammi*, the *huhupal*, and the *galgalturi* [three musical
instruments] behind and in front of the king. ... Other 'statue-
worshippers' wearing a yellow(?) garment stand beside the king;
they hold up their hands and turn round in their places. ...[1]

The king and queen go into the temple of Zababa. They kneel
once before the spear; the statue-worshipper speaks, the herald
calls. ...

The king and queen sit down on the throne. The palace-servant
brings in the cloth of the golden spear and the 'lituus'. He gives
the cloth of the golden spear to the king, but he puts the lituus by
the throne on the right of the king.

Two palace-servants bring the king and queen water for the
hands from a jar of gold. ... The king and queen wash their
hands. The chief of the palace-servants gives them a cloth and they
wipe their hands.

Two palace-servants place a knee-cloth for the king and queen.

The verger walking in front, the 'table-men' step forward.

The verger walks in front and shows the king's sons to their
seats.

The verger goes outside and walks in front of the chief cooks,
and the chief cooks step forward.

The verger again goes outside, walks in front of the 'pure
priest, the lord of Hatti, and the god's mother of Halki', and
shows them to their seats.

The Master of Ceremonies goes inside and announces to the
king. They bring forth the 'Ishtar' instruments – the king says,
'Let them bring them forth!'

The Master of Ceremonies goes outside to the courtyard and
says to the verger, 'They are ready, they are ready!' The verger
goes out to the gate and says to the singers, 'They are ready, they
are ready!' The singers pick up the 'Ishtar'-instruments. The
verger walking in front, the singers bring the 'Ishtar'-instruments
in, and take up their position.

The cooks place ready dishes of water and meat; they divide the
lean(?) from the fat(?).

1. This ritual dance is illustrated by the relief from Karatepe, Plate 29.

The verger goes in front of (various dignitaries) and shows them to their seats (one text here mentions the 'overseers of the meal').

The dishes are 'divided'.

After the dishes have been divided ... they give *marnuwan* (a drink) to the assembly.

The king then flings off the cloth (presumably that which covers the dishes). If he flings it to the palace-servants who are kneeling (there), then those palace-servants take it, but if he flings it to the bodyguard who are kneeling, the bodyguard take it, and they give it to the table-men. (At this point there was presumably a ceremonial meal, but not a single text refers explicitly to it.) The King makes a sign with his eyes and the sweeper sweeps the ground.

(After this follow the sacrifices.)

A unique ceremony was enacted apparently in the autumn at the city of Gursamassa (unidentified) in honour of the god Yarris. The cult-image was brought out to the *huwasi*-stone and there entertained with feasting and singing and with a piece of play-acting which is described as follows:

The young men are divided into two groups and receive names; the one group they call 'men of Hatti', the other group 'men of Masa'; and the men of Hatti carry weapons of copper, but the men of Masa carry weapons of reed. They fight with each other and the 'men of Hatti' win; and they seize a captive and devote him to the god.

It is supposed that this mock battle may perpetuate an historical battle which took place in the vicinity, but such ritual combats are not uncommon in folk-lore.

Another interesting ceremony is described in a fragmentary document.

In the morning a decorated chariot stands ready in front of the temple; three ribbons – one red, one white, and one blue – are tied on it. They harness the chariot and bring out the god from the temple and seat him in the chariot. The *burruti*-women, the *katru*-women, and the . . . . .-women go in front, also the dancers and the temple harlots go in front, and they hold lighted torches … and the god comes behind, and they take the god down through the Tawiniya Gate to the wood. And when the god comes to the *tarnawi*-house in the wood, the priest takes *muttis* and water and goes round the *tarnawi*-house, and the god enters the *tarnawi*-house. (Here follows a ritual the text of which is largely destroyed.)

One is reminded here of the Babylonian procession to the *akitu*-house at the New Year festival, but the resemblance is probably fortuitous.

Such rituals form a large proportion of the Hittite archive, but unfortunately many of them are fragmentary or only partly intelligible. These few examples must therefore suffice to give some idea of the variety of this class of text.

5. THEOLOGY AND DIVINATION

To a member of any of the ancient societies it was axiomatic that all phenomena in Nature, indeed all great matters that seemed to be beyond human control, were governed by mighty but man-like forces; and the division of the world into departments, each under the control of a separate divinity, was a conception which would easily arise out of experience of human affairs, assisted no doubt by the early discovery that no two communities worshipped quite the same deities. Every city had its temple, and in every temple lived a being who could not normally be seen and who had certainly lived in that same place since long before living memory. In the words of a Hittite story-teller:

> The Sun-god dwells in Sippar,
> the Moon-god dwells in Kuzina,

the Weather-god dwells in Kummiya,
Ishtar dwells in Nineveh,
Nanaia dwells in Kissina,
and in Babylon dwells Marduk.

The gods were therefore invisible and immortal. But in other respects, in their needs, their interests, and their relations to their worshippers, they were imagined as absolutely human. Beyond this theological speculation had not yet gone. The Hittites especially had no hesitation in attributing to their gods and goddesses behaviour which we should consider unseemly or at least undignified. The god was to his worshippers exactly what a master was to his slaves (see p. 70). He had to be fed, tended, appeased, and flattered. Even so, he could not be relied on to be always watching his servants' interests; part of his time would be spent in amusement or in travelling, sleeping, or attending to other business, and at such time his worshippers would call in vain for his help (as did the prophets of Baal at Mt Carmel). His actions, even when he attended to his duties, might not always be wise and might entail unforeseen consequences; it would then be the duty of his faithful servant to point this out to him, and he might be expected to correct his mistake. A Hittite king might acknowledge the incorrigible sinfulness of Man; but there was always a chance that misfortune might befall a man or the nation not as a result of punishment for sin but merely through divine negligence. There were always demons and evil spirits only too ready to take advantage of a lapse of vigilance on the part of the protector.

What is this, O gods, that you have done? (prays King Mursilis.) You have let in a plague and the land of Hatti, all of it, is dying, so no one prepares the offerings of food and drink. And you come to us, O gods, and for this matter you hold us guilty ... and there is nothing that we do aright in your eyes.

The king is here telling the gods frankly that such a lapse is ultimately to their own disadvantage, since it deprives them of the service of their worshippers.

If, however, misfortune comes as a punishment for sin, it will not be lifted until the sin has been confessed and atoned for. But the offender may be unconscious that any sin has been committed; indeed, it was believed by the Hittites that punishment was inflicted on the children for the sins of the fathers, and the offence in question might thus have occurred in a former generation. In such circumstances the god must inform the sufferer of the nature of the offence before penance could be rendered. This information could occasionally be obtained directly either through the mouth of an ecstatic or by means of a dream, for ecstasy and dreaming were believed to be forms of divine possession. But a more reliable, though more laborious, method of ascertaining the divine will was through divination, of which there were three kinds: extispicy (the examination of the entrails of the sacrificial victim), augury (divination from the movements of birds), and another which was perhaps some form of lottery and was the speciality of certain female soothsayers called simply the 'Old Women'. The science of divination was inherited by the Hittites from the traditional lore of the seers of Babylonia. It was believed that the gods sent warning to their worshippers of the fate that lay in store for them in the form of signs and portents (which meant in practice almost any unusual occurrence), but especially in the formation of the entrails of the sacrificial victim. Certain configurations of the liver and other viscera, certain movements of birds and other phenomena were regarded as favourable, others as unfavourable (in most cases the principles on which these ideas were based remain obscure). The Hittites, like the other ancient peoples, always consulted the omens before a military campaign or other important enterprise; but they also applied this traditional lore as a means of ascertaining the cause of a god's anger. A favourable omen was taken as the equivalent of a 'yes', an unfavourable one as a 'no' (or vice versa, according to the sense of the question). On this basis questions were put to the oracle, and by an enormously lengthy process of elimination it was possible to determine without fail the precise offence which required expiation. Following is an example of such an inquiry:

Whereas they have written to me (i.e., the officiating priest) from the palace (saying): 'The oracle has declared that Ishtar of Nineveh is angry in her temple', we consulted the priests and they said: 'A singer stole a golden jug, and it has not been replaced; the golden Amurru-tunic which the god wears is worn out; the chariot is broken; they used to present a .... from the palace, but it has not been presented; when the *ašrahitašši* festival is celebrated, they used to give the god one shekel of silver, red wool, blue wool, and one ...., but now they have celebrated the *ašrahitašši* festival but have not given the shekel of silver, the red wool, the blue wool and the ....; the *aiaru* festival used to be celebrated every year, but now it has been neglected.' Are these sins the cause of the god's anger? Then let the omen be unfavourable. (Here follow the details of the findings in technical language. Result:) unfavourable.

If this is the cause and there is nothing else, then let the omen be favourable. ... (Result:) favourable.

Had this omen been unfavourable, the inquiry would have continued indefinitely until a favourable answer was received.

On another occasion the god Hurianzipas was found to be angry. The priests were questioned and replied: 'The .... feast has been neglected; the *šittar* (sun-disc?) has not been decorated.' The oracle declared that the god was angry about this, but it was not the only thing. 'Since this has again turned out unfavourably, is the god angry because they have sacrificed too late to the god? If so, let the omens be unfavourable.' (Result:) unfavourable. If this ditto ditto (i.e., if this is the only thing), let the omens be favourable. (Result:) unfavourable. So we questioned the temple-servants again, and they said: 'A dog came into the temple and upset the table and threw down the sacrificial bread. Is the god angry about that?' (Result:) unfavourable.

And so on. The records of these acts of consultation of the 'oracle' are among the largest and most numerous (and worst-written) tablets of the Hittite archives and form a curious monument of misdirected ingenuity.

6. MAGIC

Magic is as old as man and as widespread. It is usually included under the heading of Religion, but is hardly worthy of the name, for it belongs to a more primitive level of thought. Early man, frustrated by the absence or inaccessibility of the object which he desired to control, instinctively went through the motions of the desired action in mimicry using a substitute for the object concerned. Out of this experience grew the belief in the efficacy of the 'analogical' methods which we call Magic, employing an elaborate symbolism, in which anything from the 'hair of the dog that bit him' to something sharing an entirely superficial quality with the object (such as chance resemblance of name) might be used as an effective substitute in the ritual. Negative results could always be readily explained by the effects of counter-magic. It would therefore be surprising if a belief in magic was not as much a part of the mental make-up of the peasant population of Anatolia in the second millennium B.C. as we know it to have been in contemporary Babylonia and Assyria.

In fact, magical rituals form a large proportion of the surviving Hittite literature; black magic was even recognized in the laws of the land as a crime in the same category as assault and battery. Magic was used to drive out disease and to restore impaired bodily functions, to banish every form of misfortune such as strife in the house, ghosts in the house, barrenness of crops and vineyards, or pestilence in the army, to curse one's enemies and to bring good luck to one's friends, to reinforce oaths by pronouncing curses on the potential violator, to attract those who were absent or in-attentive (including gods). It would be tedious to attempt to enumerate in detail the many ingenious devices employ-ed in these rituals, all of which are based on the principle of analogy. A few examples must suffice.

The following are excerpts from rituals for restoring the sexual functions to a man or woman in whom they are im-paired:

(The patient) stops his (or her) ears with black wool ... and puts on black clothes. ... (Then after various rites have been performed) the Old Woman tears from top to bottom the black shirt that he (or she) has put on and draws off from his (or her) legs the black gaiters(?) and takes out of his (or her) ears the black woollen stuffing, and says: 'I am now taking away from him (or her) darkness and stiffness caused by the matter of un-cleanness, on account of which matter of uncleanness he (or she) became dark and stiff; I am taking away sin.' Then she takes away the black clothes that he (or she) has put on and puts them in one place.

Afterwards she throws the black shirt, gaiters, and any-thing else that has been in contact with the patient into the river. In other texts the paraphernalia are buried in a hole in the ground and fixed down with pegs.

I put a mirror and a spindle into the hand of the patient and he passes under a 'gate', and when he steps out from under the gate I take away from him the mirror and the spindle and give him a bow, and I say to him: 'Behold! I have taken away from you womanhood and have given you back manhood; you have cast away the manners of woman and [you have taken] up the manners of man.'

(The Old Woman) grasps the horn of a fertile cow and says, 'Sun-god, my lord, as this cow is fertile and is in a fertile pen and is filling the pen with bulls and cows, so let this patient be fertile, let her fill her house with sons and daughters, grandchildren and great grandchildren, descendants in successive generations.'

She lifts figures of wax and mutton-fat over him (or her) and says, 'Whatever persons were making this person unclean, I am now holding two magic figures.' ... Then she squashes them and says, 'Whatever wicked persons were making him (or her) unclean, let them be squashed in the same way.'

A curse similar to the last passage is pronounced upon the oath-breaker in the following:

He puts wax and mutton-fat into their hands, then he casts it into the fire-place and says: 'As this wax has flattened, as this mutton-fat has perished, so shall he who breaks the oath and performs treason(?) against the King of Hatti be flattened like wax and perish like mutton-fat.'

The following example of the 'scapegoat' rite is taken from a ritual against pestilence in the camp:

They bring in a donkey and drive it towards the enemy's country and speak as follows: 'Thou, O Yarris, hast inflicted evil on this country and its camp; but let this donkey lift it and carry it into the enemy's country.'

It will be seen from these passages how magic tends to merge with religion; the spell, originally effective in itself, is reinforced by a prayer to a god, who may be the Sun-god as god of purification, or in the case of pestilence the god Yarris, to whose agency pestilences were ascribed.

Conversely, magic might be brought in as an accessory to religion, when it was feared that the god might be away from home and so prayer alone might not reach him. This is common with rogations of the *mugessar* type. The god is first besought to return home and bless his people; then 'paths' are laid for him, and honey, oil and other pleasant substances are placed upon them to attract him. Incense is burned for the same purpose. In some instances he is then 'pulled' along the paths, perhaps physically in the form of an image, though the sense is uncertain. The 'Myth of the Missing God' (pp. 183–9) forms part of a similar ritual, the whole story being apparently told in order to bring about the events which it describes, in particular the return of the god; the text continues immediately with the laying of 'paths' and other magic rituals.

The opposite of this magic of attraction is apotropaic magic, in which figures of fierce animals are buried in the foundation of houses (or otherwise disposed) to scare away evil. Thus in a ritual to expel evil spirits from the royal palace :

they make a little dog of tallow and place it on the threshold of the house and say 'You are the little dog of the table of the royal pair. Just as by day you do not allow other men into the courtyard, so do not let in the Evil Thing during the night.'

Such magic is not something mysterious and occult; it is merely primitive superstition surviving into a more enlightened age. Each ritual is the special formula of a particular individual, often from some outlying part of the empire, and the magical literature of the Hittites thus has the character of a national collection of folk-lore rather than that of a systematic corpus. The 'Old Women' (a homely term, surely drawn from the language of country villagers) are the exponents of the simplest formulae; only when religious elements are combined with the magic ritual do priests, augurs, or seers (i.e., persons trained in a special discipline) appear as practitioners. We do not know whether there was any college of magicians or incantation-priests associated with the state cult and the temples of Hattusas, and enjoying a special prestige; possibly the purpose of the collection of texts was to form the material for the foundation of such a college. But be this as it may, the efficacy of magic was not doubted, and in this respect the Hittites were children of their age.

7. BURIAL CUSTOMS

Among the tablets from Boghazköy are a number of fragments of a series describing the funerary ritual of a king or a queen. The ceremonial lasted for no less than thirteen days, possibly longer, but the disposal of the body was probably completed in the first two days, and for the second day a well-preserved text was discovered in the excavations of 1936. This text clearly implies that during the preceding day or night the body had been cremated, and indeed the fragment of the text for the first day refers to 'fire' and 'burning'. The text for the second day continues as follows:

On the second day as soon as it is light the women go [to?] the *ukturi*[1] to collect the bones; they extinguish the fire with ten jugs of beer, ten [jugs of wine], and ten jugs of *walhi*.[2]

A silver jar of half a mina and twenty shekels weight is filled with fine oil. They take up the bones with a silver *lappa*[3] and put them into the fine oil in the silver jar, then they take them out of the fine oil and lay them on a linen *gazzarnulli*, under which lies a 'fine garment'.

1. The context suggests 'pyre', but the word itself means 'firm, fixed, permanent', with a derived sense of 'remains, relics'. The use of the plural below seems to be against the rendering 'pyre'.
2. A drink often mentioned in rituals.
3. Possibly a kind of spoon.

Now when they have finished collecting the bones, they wrap them up together with the linen cloth in the 'fine garment' and place them on a chair; but if it is a woman, they place them on a stool.

Around the *ukturiyas*[1] (on? at?) which the body is burnt they put 12 loaves, and on the loaves they put a tallow-cake. The fire has already been quenched with beer and wine. Before the chair on which the bones are lying they place a table and they offer hot loaves, ... loaves and sweet loaves for breaking. The cooks and 'table-men' set the dishes at the first opportunity and at the first opportunity they take them up. And to all who have come to collect the bones they offer food to eat.

Then they give them three times to drink and even three times they give his soul to drink. There are no loaves or musical instruments of Ishtar.

There follow some magical operations performed by the 'Old Woman' and her 'companion', but these are obscure and difficult to follow on account of the bad state of the tablet at this point. Afterwards the text continues as follows:

[Now] two oxen and two lots of nine sheep have (meanwhile) been brought from the palace. One [ox and nine sheep] they sacrifice to the Sun-goddess [of Earth], but one ox and nine sheep (they sacrifice) [to the soul of] the deceased. [Then] they take up the bones and [carry them away] from the *ukturi* and bring them into his 'stone-house'. In the 'stone-house' in the inner chamber they lay out a bed, take the bones from the chair and lay them on the bed; a lamp [...........] [and? ...... of ..] shekels in weight with fine oil they place in front of the bones; then they sacrifice an ox and a sheep to the soul of the deceased.

The rest of this tablet is fragmentary, and the text for the following days is lost. The texts for the eighth, twelfth, and thirteenth days appear to be concerned with rituals and sacrifices of a general nature.

1. This form is plural. Cf. p. 164, n. 1.

In A.D. 1911 Dr Winckler found in a depression in the rock near the road to Yazilikaya a number of large pots (*pithoi*) laid in pairs mouth to mouth, and within these several smaller vessels containing cremation-ashes. These, however, are the only cremations yet discovered at a Hittite site of the second millennium. On the other hand, both at Alishar and at Boghazköy numerous inhumations were found by the excavators, the body being laid either in a pair of *pithoi* placed mouth to mouth, as in the cremations just described, or simply in an earth grave; at Boghazköy the earth graves were usually in the houses themselves. All these burials, and indeed the cremations too, appeared to be those of the common people, whereas the ritual of the text refers to the funeral of a king or queen. Here then, it would seem, is an important cultural difference between the rulers and the ruled, attested towards the end of the Empire of Hattusas (for that is the date of the ritual text). Yet this cultural difference is apparently unconnected with the social cleavage between the two classes which we have seen to have been most marked in the Old Kingdom. For the kings of the Old Kingdom did not practise cremation, as may be seen from the closing sentences of the oration of Hattusilis I (see p. 171): 'Wash my body, as is seemly; hold me to thy bosom, and at thy bosom bury me in the earth.'

The interest of this matter is enhanced when we compare the ceremony described above with the funerals of Patroclus and Hector in the *Iliad* xxiii. 233 and xxiv. 782 to end:

Funeral of Patroclus

But they that were with the son of Atreus gathered in a throng and the noise and din of their oncoming aroused him (Achilles); and he sat upright and spoke to them saying: 'Son of Atreus and ye other princes of the hosts of Achaia, first quench ye with flaming wine the burning pyre, even all whereon the might of the fire hath come, and thereafter let us gather the bones of Patroclus,

Menoitius' son, singling them out well from the rest; and easy they are to discern, for he lay in the midst of the pyre, while the others burned apart on the edges thereof, horses and men mingled together. Then let us place the bones in a golden urn wrapped in a double layer of fat, until such time as I myself be hidden in Hades. Howbeit no huge barrow do I bid you rear with toil for him, but such a one only as beseemeth ye that shall be left amid the benched ships when I am gone.' So spake he, and they hearkened to the swift-footed son of Peleus. First they quenched with flaming wine the pyre, so far as the flame had come upon it and the ash had settled deep; and with weeping they gathered up the bones of their gentle comrade into a golden urn, and wrapped them in a double layer of fat, and placing the urn in the hut they covered it with a soft linen cloth. Then they traced the compass of the barrow and set forth the foundations thereof round about the pyre, and forthwith they piled the up-piled earth. And when they had piled the barrow they set them to go back again. But Achilles stayed the folk even where they were, and made them sit in a wide gathering; and from his ships he brought forth prizes, cauldrons and tripods and horses and mules and strong oxen and fair-girdled women and grey iron.

Funeral of Hector

So spake he, and they yoked oxen and mules to waggons, and speedily thereafter gathered together before the city. For nine days' space they brought in measureless store of wood, but when the tenth dawn arose, giving light unto mortals, then bare they forth bold Hector, shedding tears the while, and on the topmost pyre they laid the dead man and cast fire thereon. But soon as early dawn appeared, the rosy-fingered, then gathered the folk about the pyre of glorious Hector. And when they were assembled and met together, first they quenched with flaming wine all the pyre, so far as the fire's might had come upon it, and thereafter his brethren and his comrades gathered the white bones, mourning, and big tears flowed ever down their cheeks. The bones they took and placed in a golden urn, covering them over with soft purple robes, and quickly laid the urn in a hollow grave, and covered it over with great close-set stones. Then with speed heaped they the mound, and round about were watchers set on every side, lest the well-greaved Achaeans should set upon them before the time. And when they had piled the barrow they went back, and gathering together duly feasted a glorious feast in the palace of Priam, the king fostered of Zeus.[1]

The Hittite and Homeric rituals have the following points in common: (1) the body is burnt; (2) the pyre is quenched with potable liquids; (3) the bones are dipped or wrapped in oil or fat; (4) the bones are wrapped in a linen cloth and a fine garment; (5) they are placed in a stone chamber (this does not apply to the funeral of Patroclus); (6) there is a feast.

On the other hand, they differ in the following respects: (1) the Homeric warriors place the bones, wrapped in fat, in a golden urn, which is not mentioned in the Hittite ritual; (2) in the Hittite ritual the bones are placed on a chair or a stool; (3) the Hittite 'stone-house' is apparently complete in itself, whereas the Homeric warriors raise a barrow over the grave; (4) the magical operations are peculiar to the Hittite ceremony, the athletic games to the Homeric.

It may be held that the points of similarity, when set against the differences, are not enough to prove borrowing or a common tradition. For if the body is once burnt, it would be necessary to deal with the bones by some sequence of operations of this kind. However, it does not seem very likely that the Hittite royal family would have suddenly adopted the practice of cremation unless they at least had some contact with a people who already cremated their dead, and it may be worth while to consider how this could have occurred.

It is a well-known archaeological fact that the Myceneans did not cremate their dead; cremation does not appear in

1. Translation by A. T. Murray (Loeb Classical Texts).

Greece until shortly after the end of the Mycenean civilization. In attributing the practice to the Achaean heroes, Homer might therefore seem to be guilty of an anachronism. However, in the sixth city of Troy, which may be that of the Homeric war and is contemporary with the Hittite Empire, there is abundant evidence of cremation, and it is possible that the Achaean heroes adopted the practice from the Trojans as a convenient method of disposing of their dead in a foreign land. Whether or not this is so, the fact of cremation in Troy VI shows from which direction this method of burial could have reached the Hittites and at the same time provides a foundation for the Homeric account of the ritual.

Note to second edition

P. 166. In 1952 Dr Bittel found that another of the outcrops of rock on the way to Yazilikaya had been used by the Hittites as a place of burial over a period of many centuries. It contained seventy-two burials, of which fifty were cremations, the ashes being deposited in pottery vessels of various shapes and sizes. Thus cremation is seen to have been practised by the Hittites from the earliest days of their history, and there is nothing to indicate that the persons cremated belonged to a socially superior class. It can no longer be said that the practice of cremation distinguishes the rulers from the ruled, and if there is any connexion between the Hittite ritual and that of the Homeric poems it must be due to a common tradition rather than to borrowing.

CHAPTER VIII

Literature

I. OFFICIAL LITERATURE

THE typical Hittite state document opens tersely with the formula: 'Thus speaks King NN, great king, king of Hatti, the hero, son of MM, great king, king of Hatti, the hero' (with variations in the titles, and sometimes omitting, sometimes expanding, the genealogy). What follows may be either a royal decree on a particular matter of moment, the annals of the king's military campaigns, or a 'treaty' containing the terms of the oath of fealty dictated to a vassal king. Formally, these are all branches of a single stem, the root of which may be traced back to the earliest times.

The earliest of the royal inscriptions is that of Anittas, the authenticity of which is discussed above (p. 20); but in form, as in so much else, this inscription is anomalous. The narrative which occupies most of the tablet purports to be copied from a stela set up in the gate of the king's city, and concludes with a curse upon any future prince or malefactor who might destroy or alter it. To this extent it belongs to a type of inscription common in Babylonia and Assyria, a fact which lends support to the view that the original text of the stela was in the Akkadian language. This type of inscription is unknown in Anatolia until after the downfall of the kingdom of Hattusas, and thus the document stands apart from the main Hittite tradition.

There are good reasons for supposing that Hittite cuneiform was introduced during the reign of Hattusilis I, for the main purpose of recording verbatim the pronouncements which the king delivered from time to time before his assembled noblemen. The so-called 'political testament' of Hattusilis is a remarkable example of this type of verbatim report. It is the record of an address delivered by the king on the occasion of the adoption of the boy Mursilis as heir to the throne (see above, pp. 24, 67). The king speaks freely and naturally to his people, without any conscious literary form. Some excerpts will illustrate the spontaneity and the vigorous style of this oration:

Great King Labarnas[1] spoke to the fighting men of the Assembly and the dignitaries (saying): Behold, I have fallen sick. The young Labarnas I had proclaimed to you (saying) 'He shall sit upon the throne'; I, the king, called him my son, embraced him, exalted him, and cared for him continually. But he showed himself a youth not fit to be seen: he shed no tears, he showed no pity, he was cold and heartless. I, the king, summoned him to my couch (and said): 'Well! No one will (in future) bring up the child of his sister as his foster-son! The word of the king he has not laid to heart, but the word of his mother, the serpent, he has laid to heart.' ... Enough! He is my son no more! Then his mother bellowed like an ox: 'They have torn asunder the womb in my living body! They have ruined him, and you will kill him!' But have I, the king, done him any evil? ... Behold, I have given my son Labarnas a house; I have given him [arable land] in plenty, [sheep in] plenty I have given him. Let him now eat and drink. [So long as he is good] he may come up to the city; but if he come forward(?) [as a trouble-maker], ... then he shall not come up, but shall remain [in his house].

Behold, Mursilis is now my son. ... In place of the lion the god will [set up another] lion. And in the hour when a call to arms goes forth ... you, my servants and leading citizens, must be [at hand to help my son]. When three years have elapsed he shall go on a campaign. ... If you take him [while still a child] with you on a campaign, bring [him] back [safely]. ...

Till now no one [of my family] has obeyed my will; [but

1. This was apparently the king's proper name; he adopted that of Hattusilis later in his reign. See above, p. 23.

thou, my son] Mursilis, thou must obey it. Keep [thy father's] word! If thou keepest thy father's word, thou wilt [eat bread] and drink water. When maturity [is within] thee, then eat two or three times a day and do thyself well! [And when] old age is within thee, then drink to satiety! And then thou mayest set aside thy father's word.

[Now] you (who are) my chief servants, you (too) must [keep] my, the king's, words. You shall (only) eat bread and drink water. [So] Hattusas will stand high and my land (will be) at peace. But if you do not keep the king's word ... you will not remain alive – you will perish.

My grandfather had proclaimed his son Labarnas (as heir to the throne) in Sanahuitta, [but afterwards] his servants and the leading citizens spurned(?) his words and set Papadilmah on the throne. Now how many years have elapsed and [how many of them] have escaped their fate? The houses of the leading citizens, where are they? Have they not perished? ...

And thou (Mursilis) shalt not delay nor relax. If thou delayest (it will mean) the same old mischief. ... What has been laid in thy heart, my son, act thereupon always! ...

In the opening words of this text we already have the forerunner of the introductory formula used in the later inscriptions. Attention may be drawn also to the historical example (the story of the conspiracy of Papadilmah) with which the warning against discord is here illustrated. Fragments of other contemporary texts show that this was a favourite rhetorical device of the period, and we possess a comparatively well-preserved document which consists entirely of such 'admonitory anecdotes', e.g.:

Zitis was a cup-bearer. The king's father ordered a *harhara*-vessel of wine for the Lady Hestaiara and for Marattis. He (i.e., Zitis) offered good wine to the king, but to them they gave other wine. The former (i.e. Marattis?) came and told the king: 'They have not given the same wine.' When the king saw it, he (i.e., Zitis?) came and said it was so. So they took him away and 'dealt with' him, and he died.

Santas, a man of Hurma, was a palace-servant in Hassuwa. He served the Hurrians and went to see his lord (i.e., the king of the Hurrians). The king heard of it and they mutilated him.

Was this peculiar document perhaps used as a reference book from which orators might select a story to suit their purpose? However this may be, the practice seems to show an attitude to history which became a marked feature of all the later royal decrees.

Between the reign of Mursilis I (the successor of Hattusilis) and that of Telipinus there is a gap in the series of inscriptions, and when we come to the great decree of Telipinus regulating the conduct of the royal family and enacting the law of succession, the later form is already almost fully developed. Like the speech of Hattusilis, this text was evidently read out before the assembled nobility, but unlike the earlier document its arrangement is orderly and must have necessitated careful preparation. The historical example has become a long preamble (the first few paragraphs of which are quoted above, p. 21), illustrating the disastrous results of discord in the body politic and so leading up to the main theme, which is introduced in the second half of the proclamation. This historical preamble became henceforward an indispensable part of all Hittite royal decrees, including the so-called treaties, in which it served to recall the past benefits conferred on the vassal and so to arouse his sense of duty and gratitude. Finally, under Mursilis II it divested itself of the decree altogether, and we find for the first time the history of the reign recorded *sui juris* in the form of Annals. But even here the narrative is not a mere chronicle of events; there is still a theme, generally a religious one, the whole record of the king's successes being piously laid before his patron-deity as a thank-offering. This may be illustrated by a paragraph from the introduction to the Annals of Mursilis:

When I, the Sun,[1] seated myself upon my father's throne, before I moved against any of the hostile countries which had declared war upon me, I attended to the recurrent festivals of the Sun-goddess of Arinna, my lady, and celebrated them, and to the Sun-goddess of Arinna, my lady, I raised my hand and spoke thus: 'Sun-goddess of Arinna, my lady, the surrounding hostile countries which called me a child and made light of me and were constantly trying to seize thy territories, O Sun-goddess of Arinna, my lady – come down, O Sun-goddess of Arinna, my lady, and smite these hostile countries for me.' And the Sun-goddess of Arinna heard my prayer and came to my aid, and in ten years from the time when I sat down on my father's throne I conquered those hostile countries and destroyed them.

The annals of these first ten years are inscribed on a single large and exceptionally well-preserved tablet (see Plate 25), at the end of which the king returns to his theme with the following words:

Now since I had seated myself on my father's throne, I had reigned for ten years. And these hostile countries I conquered in ten years with my own hand; the hostile countries which the princes and the lords conquered are not included. Whatsoever the Sun-goddess of Arinna, my lady, further vouchsafes to me, I will record it and lay it before her.

Accordingly, this document may be called the 'personal annals' of Mursilis II. A comprehensive edition of the annals of the whole reign, covering many tablets, also existed, but much of this is now missing. Several excerpts illustrating the style of the annals have been quoted above in the chapter on Warfare.

King Mursilis was the annalist *par excellence*. He recorded not only his own reign but also that of his father Suppiluliumas in annalistic form. No such record exists of his successor Muwatallis, and a small fragment is all that survives

1. Note the new title, replacing 'I, the king' of the old period. See above, p. 64.

to indicate that the example of Mursilis was followed by his second son Hattusilis III. The annals of Tudhaliyas IV are also badly mutilated.

From the reign of Hattusilis III, however, we possess a well-preserved text in which the traditional form is used to serve a special purpose. Hattusilis had driven his nephew Urhi-Teshub from the throne and so committed an offence against that old law of Telipinus which had stood the kingdom in such good stead. It was to justify himself for this high-handed action that he composed this elaborate document, which has been called his autobiography. It opens as follows:

Thus speaks *Tabarna* Hattusilis,[1] the great king, king of Hatti, son of Mursilis, the great king of Hatti, grandson of Suppiluliumas, the great king, king of Hatti, descendant of Hattusilis, king of Kussara.

I tell the divine power of Ishtar; let all men hear it, and in the future may the reverence of me, the Sun, of my son, of my son's son, and of my Majesty's seed be given to Ishtar among the gods.

This is the traditional theme. But the narrative is not concerned primarily with the military victories won in the god's name. The king tells of his childhood (in which he suffered from ill-health) and describes how he was dedicated to the goddess Ishtar, how he was surrounded by jealous enemies, and how Ishtar enabled him always to prevail against them. As governor of the northern provinces she continued to aid him, until Urhi-Teshub succeeded to the throne and out of jealousy for his successes joined the ranks of his adversaries.

But out of respect for my brother (writes the king), I loyally did not act selfishly, and for seven years I complied. But then that man sought to destroy me . . . and he took away from me Hakpissa and Nerikka, and then I complied no more but revolted from him.

1. On the title *Tabarna* see above, p. 64.

Yet though I revolted from him, I did not do it sinfully, by rising against him in the chariot or rising against him in the house, but I (openly) declared war on him (saying): 'Thou didst pick a quarrel with me – thou art the Great King, while as for me, of the one fortress thou hast left me, of just that one fortress I am king. Up now! Let Ishtar of Samuha and the Weather-god of Nerik pass judgement on us.' Now whereas I wrote thus to Urhi-Teshub, if some one says: 'Why did you previously raise him to the throne, yet now you are writing to him to make war on him?' Yet (I reply) if he had never quarrelled with me, would (the gods) have made him, a great king, lose to a petty king? But because now he has picked a quarrel with me, the gods by their verdict have made him lose to me. ... And because my lady Ishtar had previously promised me the throne, so now she visited my wife in a dream (saying): 'I am helping thy husband, and all Hattusas will turn to the side of thy husband.' ... Then I saw great favour from Ishtar. She deserted Urhi-Teshub, and in none other but (her own) city of Samuha she shut him up like a pig in a sty, ... and all Hattusas returned to me.

Hattusilis here tells how he disposed of Urhi-Teshub and his other enemies without vindictiveness by banishment, and recapitulates briefly his triumphant progress under Ishtar's guidance. There follow two paragraphs recording the dedication of certain buildings to Ishtar and of the prince Tudhaliyas as her priest, and in conclusion the text returns to the original theme with the words: 'Whoever in future, whether the son, the son's son, or the descendant of Hattusilis and Puduhepa may succeed, let him be a worshipper of Ishtar of Samuha among the gods.'

The kernel of this document is the passage about Urhi-Teshub. This is a piece of reasoned argument, amounting almost to legal pleading, of a type which occurs elsewhere in Hittite literature but has few parallels in that of the other peoples of pre-classical antiquity. If the reasoning appears transparently unsound, that is only because we have long since ceased to believe that war is an 'ordeal', in which the just cause must prevail; but, as we have already seen, this doctrine was axiomatic to the Hittites, and to them the reasoning of Hattusilis would have carried conviction. The evidence which the document provides of a highly developed political conscience has been noted (above, p. 37).

Space does not permit an extensive description of all the lesser types of state document comprised in the Hittite archive. We possess charters, or letters patent, in which certain individuals or institutions are declared free of tax and other imposts; deeds of gift, by which great estates are conveyed to new owners by royal decree; rescripts settling disputed frontiers or indicting rebellious vassals for treasonable conduct; minutes of courts of inquiry (cf. p. 94); and standing orders for various officials and dignitaries.

It will be seen from the above that for purposes of government and statecraft the Hittites created their own literary forms and style, which contrast strikingly with those of the other contemporary nations. The annalistic form, it is true, has long been familiar to orientalists from the records of the Assyrian kings; but these works belong to the centuries following the downfall of the Hittite Empire, and in this respect the Assyrians were the heirs of the Hittites.

2. MYTH, LEGEND, AND ROMANCE

The number of texts in these categories is not large, and formally they are of no great artistic merit. The narrative is couched in the simplest and baldest prose, and there is no attempt at verse or metre.[1] Yet there are frequent touches of vivid detail, and the stories themselves, though primitive, are of considerable interest. There are a few myths relating to Hittite deities; but the more elaborate compositions of

1. The Song of Ullikummi (p. 192) appears to be an exception, having a rudimentary rhythmic structure.

this kind belong strictly speaking not to Hittite but to Hurrian religion. There are legends based on the early history of the Hittite kingdom, and there are Hittite versions of Babylonian legends and epics. The various shorter tales seem again to be of Hurrian origin. The presence of these alien myths, legends, and tales in the Hittite archives is to be explained by the political and cultural dominance of the Hurrians during the period between the Old and New Kingdoms; even the Babylonian legends probably found their way into the archives by way of the Hurrians, who were steeped in Babylonian traditions.

A. Legend

Of the purely Hittite legends only one is tolerably well preserved: the tale of the Siege of Urshu. The text is in the Akkadian language, but is undoubtedly derived from Hittite tradition. The scene is laid outside the city of Urshu (somewhere in North Syria), which is besieged by a Hittite army, the operations being directed by the king from the town of Luhuzantiya. Urshu is in contact with, perhaps allied with, the Hurrian state, the city of Aleppo, and the city of Zaruar, perhaps also with the city of Carchemish, the forces of which are ensconced on a mountain overlooking the city and keeping watch. After some scarcely intelligible paragraphs we read:

They broke the battering-ram. The king waxed wroth and his face was grim: 'They constantly bring me evil tidings; may the Weather-god carry you away in a flood!' (The king continues:) Be not idle! Make a battering-ram in the Hurrian manner and let it be brought into place. Make a 'mountain' and let it (also) be set in its place. Hew a great battering-ram from the mountains of Hassu and let it be brought into place. Begin to heap up earth. When you have finished let every one take post. Only let the enemy give battle, then his plans will be confounded. (Later he speaks to his general Santas, perhaps the same ill-fated general whom we have already met as the subject of an 'admonitory anecdote'): Would anyone have thought that Iriyaya would have come and lied saying: 'We will bring a tower and a battering-ram' – but they bring neither a tower nor a battering-ram, but he brings them to another place. Seize him and say to him: 'You are deceiving us and so we deceive the king.'

What happened after this is lost in a lacuna. When Santas again reports to the king he finds him again in a rage at the perpetual delay.

'Why have you not given battle? You stand on chariots of water, you are almost turned into water yourself(?) ... You had only to kneel before him and you would have killed him or at least frightened him. But as it is you have behaved like a woman.' ... Thus they answered him: 'Eight times (i.e., on eight fronts?) we will give battle. We will confound their schemes and destroy the city.' The king answered, 'Good!'

But while they did nothing to the city, many of the king's servants were smitten so that many died. The king was angered and said: 'Watch the roads. Observe who enters the city and who leaves the city. No one is to go out from the city to the enemy.' ... They answered: 'We watch. Eighty chariots and eight armies surround the city. Let not the king's heart be troubled. I remain at my post.' But a fugitive came out of the city and reported: 'The subject of the king of Aleppo came in five times, the subject of Zuppa is dwelling in the city itself, the men of Zaruar go in and out, the subject of my lord the Son of Teshub goes to and fro.' ... The king waxed wroth. ...

The rest of the text is lost. It will be seen that the story consists of a series of incidents which provoked the wrath of the king at the incompetence of his officers; it seems therefore to have some affinity with the type of decree illustrated above, which consisted of admonitory anecdotes. A similar document is the badly broken text concerning the legendary history of the city of Zalpa and its relations with three generations of Hittite kings.

The legends which are of Babylonian origin are represented in the Hittite version only by fragments, and a full
account of their Babylonian originals would be out of place
here. There are many fragments of the Epic of Gilgamesh,
of which not only a Hittite but also a Hurrian version existed. The episode of Huwawa (Humbaba), the scene of
which is laid in Syria and the Lebanon, fills a large proportion of the text as preserved, and may well have been given
greater prominence than in the original Babylonian epic.
Similarly, the other Babylonian legends represented are
those concerned with Syria and Anatolia, namely the tales
of the expeditions of the ancient kings of Akkad to the
countries on their north-western borders. We have a fragment of a Hittite translation of the tale of Sargon entitled
'King of Battle' (the original Akkadian text of which was
found at Tell el Amarna), describing how that famous king
went to the assistance of the merchants settled at Burushkhatum (see above, p. 19), and free versions of the
legends of Naram-Sin, especially that of his war against a
coalition of seventeen kings. It is of some interest to note
that in the last-mentioned text the names of some of the
kings and their kingdoms are not the same as those in the
Babylonian original but have apparently been adapted to
suit the Hittite (or Hurrian) environment. 'Scientific'
works of Babylonian origin, such as handbooks on the
interpretation of omens of various kinds, horoscopes,
models of livers, and medical texts have also been found in
considerable numbers at Boghazköy.

B. Myth

The mythological texts relating to Hittite or Hattian
deities fall into two groups, which may be called the Myth
of the Slaying of the Dragon and the Myth of the Missing
God. Whether other myths about Hittite or Hattian gods
existed it is difficult to say, since the texts are smashed into

small fragments from which no connected narrative can be obtained. There are, however, several slightly different versions of these two myths.

The Slaying of the Dragon is a typical new-year myth of the kind represented by the Babylonian Epic of Creation, the English Mummers' Play, and similar stories and dramas in many parts of the world. Its essence is a ritual combat between a divine hero and an opponent who represents the forces of evil. There are two versions. Both begin baldly with the statement that at their first encounter the Weather-god (for he is the hero) was worsted by the dragon Illuyankas. So, according to the first version, the Weather-god appealed to all the gods, and the goddess Inaras planned a simple ruse. She prepared a great banquet with barrels of every kind of drink. Then she invited a man called Hupasiyas to assist her. Hupasiyas replied: 'If I may sleep with you, I will come and do what you wish.' So she slept with him. She now invited the Dragon to come up from his hole and partake of the food and drink.

So up came the Dragon Illuyankas with his children; they ate and drank and emptied every barrel and quenched their thirst. They could not go back into their hole. So Hupasiyas came up and bound the Dragon with a rope. Then the Weather-god came and slew the Dragon Illuyankas, and the gods were with him.

There follows a strange episode, the end of which is lost.

Inaras built a house on a rock in the district of Tarukka and gave the house to Hupasiyas to dwell in. And Inaras instructed him saying, 'Farewell! I am now going out. Do not look out of the window; for if you look out you will see your wife and children.' But when twenty days had passed, he pushed open the window and saw his wife and children. Now when Inaras returned from her journey, he began to moan, saying, 'Let me go home!'

At this point the tablet becomes fragmentary and

unintelligible, but we may be sure that Hupasiyas was destroyed as punishment for his disobedience.

According to the second version of the story, the Dragon not merely defeated the Weather-god but incapacitated him by getting possession of his heart and his eyes. In order to recover them the Weather-god himself devised a ruse. He begot a son by the daughter of a poor man. When this son was grown up, he took as his bride the daughter of the Dragon, and the Weather-god instructed him saying: 'When you enter the house of your bride, demand from them my heart and my eyes.' This he did, and the stolen organs were handed to him without demur.

Then he brought them to his father, the Weather-god, and restored his heart and his eyes to the Weather-god. When his body had thus been restored to its former state he went off to the sea to do battle, and when they came out to battle with him he succeeded in defeating the Dragon Illuyankas.

Here again there follows a curious episode. The son of the Weather-god happened to be in the Dragon's house at the time. So he cried to his father: 'Smite me too! Do not spare me!' Thereupon the Weather-god slew both the Dragon and his own son.

The primitive character of both these versions is obvious. The stories belong to folk-lore, and there has been no attempt to sublimate them in either a literary or religious sense. Typical of folk-lore, as Dr Theodor Gaster has pointed out, are the motifs of the stupidity and gluttony of the dragon, who is defeated by trickery, and of the human agent who performs the deed on behalf of the god. It was evidently thought necessary that the human agent should come to grief in the end, and the two versions conclude, as we have seen, with different accounts of how this was brought about. The first account, which had previously been mistranslated, is now clear: the incarceration of Hupasiyas on an inaccessible cliff and the prohibition against his seeing his wife and family are explained by the goddess's recognition that she would be powerless to hold her lover if he were allowed to see his family. In the second version Dr Gaster has suggested that the son's appeal to his father to 'smite him too' is to be explained by his belief that he had unwittingly betrayed the laws of hospitality, a deadly sin after which he could not bear to remain alive.

The text states explicitly that this myth was recited at the

Fig. 12 – Bas-relief from Malatya

purulli festival, which, as we have seen, was probably an annual spring festival. There is therefore every justification for comparing this myth with others of the same type which were likewise recited at seasonal festivals. For such comparisons the reader may refer to Dr Gaster's book *Thespis*.

The bas-relief from Malatya (fig. 12), illustrates either this myth or one of a similar kind; the god, followed by a smaller figure, advances against a coiling serpent with uplifted spear. Flames seem to issue from the serpent's body.

The Myth of the Missing God describes the paralysis of all life on earth caused by the disappearance of the god of fertility, the search for the god, and finally the re-invigoration of the earth when he is discovered and brought home. Within this general scheme there are several versions differing considerably from each other. There is a closely related group of texts in which the missing god is Telipinu, and for this reason the myth has been called the Myth of Telipinu. But since a version has now been found in which the object of the search is the Weather-god himself, and, moreover, the fragment known as the Yuzgat tablet contains a myth which conforms to the same general scheme but in which several deities, including the Sun-god, disappear, it seems preferable to adopt a more comprehensive title for the myth.

In the main version, which is concerned with Telipinu, the god of agriculture, the beginning of the story is lost, but seems to have described the normal state of life before the blight. Then, for some reason which is not stated, the god goes off in a temper 'putting his right boot on his left foot and his left boot on his right foot' (apparently a sign of haste). There follows the description of the ensuing blight, in which the precise meaning of some of the words is uncertain:

Dust(?)-clouds beset the window, smoke(?) besets the house, the embers on the hearth were choked(?), the gods stifled [in the temple], the sheep stifled in the fold, the oxen stifled in the stall, the ewe spurned her lamb, the cow spurned her calf. ... Barley and emmer wheat throve no more, oxen, sheep and humans ceased to conceive, and those who were pregnant could not bear.

Trees withered and the meadows and springs dried up. So there was a famine, and both gods and men began to starve.

The great Sun-god gave a feast and invited the thousand gods; they ate but they were not satisfied, they drank but they quenched not their thirst. Then the Weather-god remembered his son Telipinu (saying): 'Telipinu is not in the land; he was angry and has gone away and taken all good things with him.' The gods great and small set out to search for Telipinu. The Sun-god sent out the swift eagle, saying: 'Go, search the high mountains, search the hollow valleys, search the dark-blue waters.' The eagle went forth; but he found him not, and reported to the Sun-god, saying: 'I have not found him, Telipinu, the mighty god.'

The Weather-god myth, which is fragmentary, runs closely parallel throughout this passage, only the part of Telipinu is taken by the Weather-god and that of the Weather-god in the Telipinu myth by the 'Father of the Weather-god'. At this point, however, the versions begin to diverge. We follow the Telipinu myth, which is more complete:

Then the Weather-god spoke to the goddess Hannahannas: 'What shall we do? We shall die of starvation.'

The goddess in reply urged the Weather-god to go himself and look for Telipinu, and accordingly he set out.

He knocked at the gate in his town, but he could not get it opened and (merely) broke the shaft of his hammer. So the Weather-god ... gave up and sat down (to rest).

Hannahannas then proposed to send a bee to look for the missing god. The Weather-god protested:

The gods great and small have sought him but have not found him. Shall this bee now search and find him? His wings are small and he also is small.

But the goddess dismissed these objections and sent forth the bee, ordering it to sting Telipinu, when it found him, in his hands and feet and make him wake up, then to smear him with wax and bring him back home. The bee went forth, searched the mountains, the rivers, and the springs, and found Telipinu: according to one text he was discovered sleeping on a meadow near the town of Lihzina (a cult centre of the Weather-god). On being stung by the bee the god awoke, but broke out into a fresh storm of anger.

Then said Telipinu: 'I am furious! Why when I am sleeping and nursing a temper do you force me to make conversation?' [1]

So far from returning home with the bee, he proceeded to destroy mankind, oxen, and sheep. The text becomes very fragmentary at this point, but apparently the god was eventually brought home on the back of an eagle.

Then came Telipinu hastening. There was lightning and thunder. Below the dark earth was in turmoil. Kamrusepas saw him. The eagle's wing brought him from afar. She stilled his anger, she stilled his wrath, she stilled his rage, she stilled his fury.

These follow a series of magical spells performed by Kamrusepas to exorcise the wrath of Telipinu. Finally

Telipinu returned to his temple. He took thought for the land. He released the dust(?)-cloud from the window, he released the smoke from the house. The altars of the gods were made ready. He released the embers in the hearth, he released the sheep in the fold, he released the oxen in the stall. The mother attended to her child, the ewe attended to her lamb, the cow attended to her calf.

Telipinu (took thought for) the king and queen, he took thought for them to grant them life and vigour for the future. (Yea) Telipinu took thought for the king.

Then before Telipinu an evergreen was set up. On the evergreen the skin of a sheep was hung. In it was put mutton fat, in it were put corn, cattle(?) and wine(?), in it were put oxen and sheep, in it were put length of days and progeny, in it was put the soft bleating(?) of lambs, in it were put prosperity(?) and abundance(?), in it were put ...

Here the text breaks off.

In the Weather-god myth a passage of dialogue between the father of the Weather-god and his grandfather is preserved, in which the grandfather apparently accuses the father of having 'sinned' and threatens to kill him. The

1. Translation taken from Gaster, *op. cit.*

father of the Weather-god seeks the aid of the Gulses goddesses (Fates?) and Hannahannas. The rest of the story is lost; there is at least no trace of the episode of the bee, and it is not clear how the Weather-god is brought home. The final passage about the evergreen is preserved in a practically identical form.

The fragment known as the Yuzgat Tablet (because it was originally acquired by Sayce at Yuzgat, near Boghazköy, in 1905) ascribes the blight on earth to *hahhimas*, perhaps 'torpor', which is personified and plays an active part in the narrative. 'Hahhimas has paralysed the whole earth, he has dried up the waters, Hahhimas is mighty!' In these words at the beginning of the preserved portion of the text the Weather-god sums up the situation. He is apparently addressing his sister, who has appealed to him for help, but the dialogue is obscure. He then turns to 'his brother the wind' and says: '[Breathe on] the waters of the mountains, the gardens, and the meadows, let thy soothing breath go forth and let him cease to paralyse them.' But the wind seems to achieve nothing. He merely reports to the Weather-god: 'That Hahhimas is saying to his father and his mother: "Eat this, drink (this)! Care nothing for shepherd or oxherd!" And he has paralysed the whole earth.'

The narrative here becomes clearer.

The Weather-god sent for the Sun-god (saying): 'Go! Fetch ye the Sun-god!' They went to search for the Sun-god, but they found him not. Then said the Weather-god: 'Although you have not found him nearby(?), behold, my limbs are warm, (so) how can he have perished?' Then he sent out Wurunkatti (Zababa)[1] (saying): 'Go! Fetch the Sun-god!' But Hahhimas seized Wurunkatti. (Then said he): 'Summon "the Protective Genius".[2] He

1. See above, p. 136.
2. The name of this god is probably Tuwatas; 'Protective Genius' is an attempt to render the Sumerogram with which his name is written (see above, p. 137).

will revive him,[1] he is a child of the open country.' But him also
Hahhimas seized. (Then said he): 'Go! Summon Telipinu! That
son of mine is mighty; he harrows, ploughs, irrigates the field; and
makes the crops grow.' But him too Hahhimas seized.

(Then said he): 'Summon Gulses and Hannahannas.'

There follow some rather obscure lines which suggest
that the Weather-god fears that if these goddesses too are
seized, Hahhimas will end by demanding his own surrender; so he gives them as an escort the brothers of Hasam-
melis, a god who seems to have had the power of protecting
travellers, or even of rendering them invisible. He utters a
warning to Hahhimas; but here the text breaks off.

When it resumes again, we are at the very end of the re-
citation – the lacuna amounts to more than half the tablet.
There is a colophon, or title, which runs: '[Tablet] of the
invocation of the Sun-god and of Telipinu; finished.' However, the text continues with the description of a ritual, the
purpose of which is clearly to attract these two gods back
into the temple. Two tables are laid, one for the Sun-god
and one for Telipinu, and various foods and drinks are put
ready for them. The end is lost.

It must be admitted that as literature these stories are not
of a high order. The Yuzgat tablet is especially infantile. It is
their religious aspect that constitutes their main interest.
The descriptions of the disastrous effects of the absence of
the god, of the search for him over hill and dale, and of the
re-invigoration of the earth on his return have close parallels
in the mythological literature associated with Adonis, Attis,
Osiris, and Tammuz: they are just as typical elements of the
myths of the annual spring festivals as is the ritual combat,
illustrated by the myth of the Slaying of the Dragon. Yet
none of these texts is explicitly connected with a seasonal

1. As frequently in Hittite texts, it is not clear to whom the pronoun
refers, whether to Wurunkatti or to the Sun-god.

festival. They are 'invocations' (*mugawar* or *mugessar*) and belong as such to a type of religious performance of which there are numerous examples in the Hittite archives. The god is supposed to have removed himself to a distance and is persuaded to return home by a combination of prayer and ritual; the difference here lies solely in the inclusion of the myth describing the events in the divine world which it was desired to bring about. In the Telipinu myth even the ritual acts are included in the myth, the performer taking the part of the goddess Kamrusepas. The reference to the king and queen in the Telipinu myth might lead one to believe that the myth was recited at least on an occasion of national importance; but this is belied by the fact that one recension of the myth substitutes an individual named Pirwas, and it is apparently his house that is afflicted with blight and finally freed from the affliction. The evidence seems to show that, however these myths originated, they were used by the priests as occasion demanded, whenever any person wished to regain the divine favour. That they originated as the 'book of words' for a spring festival remains a possibility for which direct evidence is at present lacking.

The episode of the mission of the bee is of considerable interest. The ideas that honey is a purifying agent capable of expelling evil spirits and that the sting of a bee or an ant can cure paralysis of the limbs are widespread in folk-lore, and there is a remarkable parallel in the Finnish *Kalevala*, in which the hero Lemminkainen, who has been slain by his enemies, is eventually revived by magic honey brought by a bee, at the instance of the hero's mother, from the ninth heaven. In the Telipinu myth it is perhaps significant that the bee is dispatched by the goddess Hannahannas, whose name is a reduplicated form of the word meaning 'grandmother' and is generally replaced by an ideogram meaning 'great'; if the bee was specially sacred to this goddess, an echo of this belief may possibly be seen in the fact that, according to Lactantius, the priestesses of Cybele the 'Great Mother' were called *melissai*, 'bees'.

The most remarkable literary compositions are those of Hurrian origin, in particular the cycle of myths concerned with the god Kumarbi. This deity in Hurrian mythology was the father of the gods and is equated with the Sumero-Babylonian god Enlil. The main texts in which he plays a major role are two: a myth about the struggle for kingship among the gods; and a long epic in three tablets entitled 'The Song of Ullikummi'.

The myth of the divine kingship runs as follows. Once upon a time Alalu was king in heaven. Alalu sat upon the throne and 'the mighty Anu, the first among the gods, stood before him, bowed down at his feet and handed him the cup to drink'.

Alalu reigned in heaven for nine years. In the ninth year Anu made war on Alalu and conquered him, and Alalu fled before him to earth (i.e., the underworld?). Anu then sat on the throne, while 'the mighty Kumarbi' ministered to him and bowed down at his feet.

Anu too reigned for nine years, and in the ninth year Kumarbi made war on Anu. The latter abandoned the struggle and flew like a bird into the sky, but Kumarbi seized his feet and pulled him down. Kumarbi bit off Anu's member (called euphemistically his 'knee') and laughed for joy. But Anu turned to him and said: 'Do not rejoice over what thou hast swallowed! I have made thee pregnant with three mighty gods. First, I have made thee pregnant with the mighty Weather-god(?), secondly, I have made thee pregnant with the River Aranzakh (the Tigris), and thirdly I have made thee pregnant with the great god Tasmisu (a minion of the Weather-god). Three terrible gods I have planted within thee as fruit of my body.'

With these words Anu flew up to the sky and disappeared

from sight. But Kumarbi 'the wise king' spat out what was in his mouth, and in the sequel apparently the Earth, thus impregnated in her turn, gave birth to the three 'terrible gods'. Unfortunately the tablet is badly mutilated from this point onwards, and the rest of the text is largely unintelligible in consequence.

The editor of this text, Dr H. G. Güterbock, has already pointed out its striking resemblance to the 'Theogony' of the Greek poet Hesiod. There the Earth (Gaia) gives birth to Heaven (Uranos); then Uranos and Gaia together become the parents of Kronos and the Titans. Uranos hates his children and seeks to prevent their birth, but Kronos, incited by Gaia, emasculates his father with a sickle, and out of the blood which flows come forth the Erinyes (Furies), the Giants, and the Melian nymphs, while Aphrodite is born from the foam which arises when the severed member falls into the sea. Kronos and his wife Rhea then beget the Olympian gods, foremost among whom is Zeus. Kronos swallows all his children except Zeus, who is saved by the substitution of a stone which Kronos swallows instead of him. Zeus, on growing to manhood, forces Kronos to spit out the gods whom he has swallowed, and the stone, which comes out first, is set up as a cult-object at Pytho (Delphi). The poem ends with the battle of the gods and Titans, and the final victory of the Olympians.

Hesiod's sequence Uranos–Kronos–Zeus is matched in the Hittite version by the sequence: Anu (Sumerian *an* = heaven) – Kumarbi, father of the gods, – Weather-god, though Alalu in the Hittite version represents a still older generation unknown to Hesiod. The emasculation of the Sky-god occurs in both myths, though the motif of the swallowing and spitting out seems to have become attached to a different incident. In the broken part of the tablet there is some reference to Kumarbi eating and to a stone which may possibly correspond to the Pythian 'omphalos' of

Hesiod's version; and it is probable that the Hittite myth ends with the victory of the Weather-god. These points of resemblance are enough to establish a strong probability that both versions derive ultimately from the same Hurrian myth.

The 'Song of Ullikummi' is preserved only in the form of a number of fragments, none of which yields more than a short passage of consecutive narrative, and even the order of these is uncertain. It is the story of a conspiracy by Kumarbi against his son Teshub, who had displaced him as king of the gods. Kumarbi planned to create a mighty rebel who

Fig. 13 – Seal-impression, probably Mitannian

would defeat the Weather-god for him and destroy his city Kummiya. He enlisted the support of 'The Sea' in his plan, and according to one version of the myth (or possibly another myth) married the Sea's daughter; but the principal version names as his mate a 'great mountain peak'. In due course a son was born to him and was named Ullikummi, which may mean 'destroyer of Kummiya' or the like. The body of this child (evidently a true child of his mother) was made of diorite stone. Kumarbi summoned the Irshirra deities, and they carried the child down to earth and placed him on the shoulders of Upelluri (an Atlas figure) where he grew apace in the midst of the sea. When he had grown so big that the sea reached only to the middle of his body, the Sun-god espied him and was filled with anger and dismay.

He hastened to inform Teshub, and the latter with his sister Ishtar climbed to the top of Mount Hazzi (the Mons Casius near Antioch), whence they could see the monstrous Ullikummi rising out of the sea. Teshub wept bitterly, and Ishtar tried to comfort him. Thereupon Teshub apparently decided to give battle. He ordered his minister Tasmisu to fetch his bulls Serisu and Tella and adorn them, and to summon the thunder and rain. Battle was then joined; but the gods were powerless against Ullikummi, who reached the very gates of the Weather-god's city Kummiya and forced him to abdicate. His queen, Hebat, received the bad news while watching from a tower and nearly fell off the roof in horror. 'If she had made a single step she would have fallen from the roof, but her women held her and did not let her fall.' Teshub, following the advice of his minister Tasmisu, went and appealed for help to Ea the all-wise in his 'city' Abzuwa (a misunderstanding of the Sumerian *abzu* or Nether Sea, which was Ea's proper home). Ea summoned the gods to council and called Kumarbi to account, but the latter boastfully revealed his plot, and the council apparently broke up in dismay. Ea proceeded to Enlil to tell him what had happened, and then paid a visit to old Upelluri, on whose shoulder Ullikummi had grown up. But Upelluri had not even noticed, for he addressed Ea as follows:

'When heaven and earth were built upon me[1] I knew nothing of it, and when they came and cut heaven and earth asunder with a copper tool, that also I knew not. Now something is hurting my right shoulder, but I know not who that god is.' When Ea heard this, he turned Upelluri's right shoulder round and there stood the Diorite Stone on Upelluri's right shoulder like a post(?).

But Upelluri's words seem to have given Ea an idea. He ordered the ancient store-houses to be opened and the ancient saw with which heaven and earth were divided to be

1. Fig. 13 shows the Mitannian conception of an Atlas figure supporting a winged disc which represents the sky.

brought forth. With this potent tool he severed the Diorite Stone at its feet and so destroyed its power. He then announced his deed to the gods and urged them to renew the battle with the monster, which was now powerless against them. The end of the story is lost, but we may be sure it closed with the restoration of Teshub and the defeat of Kumarbi and his monstrous son.

This tale also has its parallel (though with considerable differences in detail) in Greek mythology, namely in the story of Typhon, a monster whose head reached to heaven and who made war on Zeus on behalf of his mother Gaia (Gê). This story is attached to the end of Hesiod's Theogony as a sequel to the War of the Gods and Titans, and is also found in Apollodorus and Nonnos. Such myths, however, were as alien to the Greeks as they were to the Hittites, and doubtless reached them directly from their oriental source by the sea-route, either from the North Syrian port of Poseideïon, through which, as we now know (as a result of Sir Leonard Woolley's excavations), a flourishing trade passed between Greece and the Asiatic hinterland for many centuries, or through the Phoenicians, who possessed similar myths.

These are only the best preserved of the texts of this class. Many other similar compositions are represented by small and scarcely intelligible fragments; such as the Myth of the serpent Hedammu, who loved the goddess Ishtar; the Epic of Gurparanzakhus, in which the River Aranzakh (the Tigris under its Hurrian name) plays a prominent part; the Epic of Kessis the hunter; and the Tale of Appus and his two sons named Good and Bad. All these stories show clear signs of their Hurrian origin, though ultimately it is possible that many motifs which appear in them go back to the mythology of the Sumerians. There are also a few fragments of Canaanite myths, such as that concerning the Goddess Ashertu and her husband El-kunirsa.

CHAPTER IX

Art

HITHERTO this book has been concerned mainly with the Hittite kingdom and empire of Hattusas. It has been possible to present a fairly complete picture of this kingdom and its civilization on the basis of the ample information gleaned from the clay tablets which formed its royal archives. When we turn to the works of art and the material products of Hittite civilization the political background becomes of less importance and the limits of time and space are changed. For the period of the Old Kingdom of Hattusas there is little to show but potters' vessels. Sculpture begins with the Empire, but does not end with its downfall. On the contrary, the successor-kingdoms are known to us above all by a profusion of rock-carvings, statues, and bas-reliefs which cannot be separated from the sculpture of the kingdom of Hattusas, even though, especially in the Syrian kingdoms, Mesopotamian characteristics become increasingly apparent.

Rather by way of contrast, this account must start with such evidence as exists for pre-Hittite art in central Anatolia. At Alaja Hüyük the Turkish excavators discovered a number of tombs dating from the third millennium and containing a remarkable collection of objects. They included figures of animals in silver and bronze, golden jugs and goblets, golden ornaments, and a series of 'standards' (their purpose is unknown) the form of which is thought to be derived from the sun-disc, and some of which contain small figures of stags. The stag, as we have seen, was the sacred animal of a god who was widely worshipped in Anatolia during Hittite times. But in general these finely wrought objects are quite unparalleled in later periods (though it is, of course, possible that this is due only to the chances of excavation).

Equally unique are the primitive stone idols from Kültepe, the body of which has the form of a disc covered with geometrical designs, and is surmounted by a head on a long neck (Plate 1*b*). In some instances there are two or even three heads, and in the more primitive examples the head is reduced to nothing more than a pair of eyes, which perhaps suggests a connexion with the 'eye-idols' found in large numbers by Professor Mallowan at Tell Brak in northern Mesopotamia. The type of face represented on the more elaborate specimens is quite unlike anything dating from the Hittite period.

The characteristic pottery of this early age is the fine hand-made polychrome ware formerly known as Cappadocian. The vessels are painted with geometric designs in black, red, and white paint; occasionally stylized representations of birds are introduced. The shapes are of great variety, with a fondness for a cut-away lip; rhytons in the form of animals, such as that illustrated on Plate 23*b*, and the model shoe, shown on Plate 24, are examples of special products of the potter's art. The geometrical designs link this type of pottery closely with the disc-idols described in the last paragraph.

Simultaneously with this type of pottery there was in use a wheel-made, burnished, generally red-slipped ware characterized by very graceful shapes and proportions and suggesting metallic prototypes (Plate 24), and this ware gradually became predominant as the painted ware went out of use. However, by the time of the Hittite Empire metal seems to have largely taken the place of pottery, and the only ware produced in this period was a plain, domestic type, of little artistic merit.

The most highly developed form of art in the early

second millennium in Anatolia is the glyptic represented by the impressions of cylinder-seals on the tablets of the Assyrian trading colonies. The cylinder-seal is a small stone cylinder perforated longitudinally for stringing, the design being engraved on the circumference and impressed by rolling. It was a Mesopotamian invention, and although these designs are provincial in style and contain several peculiarly Anatolian motifs, such as the worship of the sacred bull, they are essentially a foreign intrusion in Anatolia, and must be regarded as an offshoot of Babylonian art. After the disappearance of the Assyrian colonists such seals and their impressions are extremely rare. It is important to note, however, that stamp-seals and their impressions, closely resembling those of the later period (see below), are also occasionally found associated with the tablets of the Assyrian colonies, and thus have a very long history in Anatolia.

For the representation of the human form at this period we are dependent on a few sporadic finds which offer as yet insoluble problems. The bronze statuette shown in Plate 1a was found by local inhabitants at Boghazköy many years ago, and therefore cannot be accurately dated, though it is usually ascribed to about 2000 B.C. However, this bearded figure with the woollen mantle is strangely unlike the head of the disc-idol shown in Plate 1b. In fact, statuettes of this type have been found in Syria, and it may therefore be an import from that region.[1] The lead figurine from Kültepe (Plate 5c), showing a man with an apparently artificial beard dressed in a short fringed kilt with a belt, is probably later; it was found in a stratum which belongs to the Hittite Old Kingdom, and is perhaps the earliest representation of the human form that can be considered genuinely Hittite.

With the beginning of the New Kingdom all is changed. Monumental bas-reliefs in stone, often associated with the

1. See C. F. A. Schaeffer, *Ugaritica* I, pp. 136–7.

hieroglyphic script, appear suddenly, carved either on the massive blocks of stone which formed the lowest course of the wall-fronts of Hittite palaces and temples, or (characteristically) on isolated rock-faces at widely separated points of the country. All these are undoubtedly manifestations of the central Hittite power and were carved at the direct bidding of the king. Many of them represent the king himself, usually as a priest, in the act of worshipping his god (see Figs. 11, 17, and Plate 16). This figure of the king in his mantle and shawl (see above, p. 66) and carrying the 'lituus' becomes the hallmark of the sculpture of the Hittite imperial age; but within that period it has proved impossible for the most part to date the sculptures accurately. The most interesting of these representations of the king is in the small gallery at Yazilikaya (Plate 15), where he appears in the embrace of his god; this is also one of the finest and least weathered of the rock-carvings, and moreover, since the name of the king, Tudhaliyas, is given in hieroglyphic signs, it can be accurately dated to the later period of the Hittite Empire; for it is impossible to ascribe such highly developed sculpture to any of the earlier kings of that name.

In the scenes of worship the deity is sometimes represented as a life-size figure, either standing (Fig. 17), or seated, sometimes he or she is replaced by an animal (Fig. 11) or by a symbol (Plate 20a). The outstanding monument of Hittite religion is, of course, the great gallery of Yazilikaya, which has already been described. Here every deity of the official pantheon was depicted according to his type and is distinguishable by the weapon which he carries, the sign which is carved above his outstretched hand, and the animal on which he stands. The dress of the gods is the short belted tunic (sometimes also a cloak) with upturned shoes, or moccasins and fluted conical head-dress, while the goddesses wear a long pleated skirt, a loose upper garment draping the arm, similar upturned shoes, and a kind of 'mural crown'; there is no veil. Both sexes wear earrings and bracelets. This costume doubtless represents the most fashionable attire of the time, though the headdresses are of religious significance.

Many theories have been held about the meaning of the two converging processions at Yazilikaya. Texier, who was the first to report the existence of the sanctuary, interpreted the scene as the meeting of the Amazons and the Paphlagonians; Hamilton saw in the two parties Medes and Lydians, Kiepert Scythians and Cimmerians. The religious interpretation began to take shape with Ramsay, who thought of Baal and Astarte. The fullest discussion in English based on a knowledge of Hittite history is that of Garstang,[1] who suggests that the scene depicts a sacred marriage; either an annual ritual of the type familiar from other oriental religions, or an event unique in the divine world, namely the union of the Weather-god of Hatti with Hebat of Kizzuwatna (Kummanni), each with their retinue, on the occasion of the marriage of Hattusilis III to the priestess Puduhepa. The idea is very attractive; the difficulty is that there is no hint in the texts that such a ceremony was ever performed or even imagined by the Hittites. We are not in fact obliged to see in this sanctuary anything more than a holy place in which the 'thousand gods of Hatti' were thought to be present and were represented by the artist in a conveniently symmetrical arrangement by which the supreme divine family was brought together at the focal point on the innermost wall of the shrine. The appearance of two converging processions is probably an illusion created by the conventional attitude in which all the figures are shown, as if in the act of stepping forward; for this attitude is universal in Hittite bas-reliefs, and may be seen even where there can be no question of forward movement (e.g.,

1. *The Hittite Empire*, pp. 111 et seq.

Plates 4, 5a, 5b, 18, 28). The outstretched arms are also conventional, as may be seen from the fact that cult-statues are described in the texts as holding their symbols in their left hand, exactly as do the figures at Yazilikaya. The only figures which are certainly in motion are the twelve gods who bring up the rear of the male 'procession', and it may be argued that the fact that some of the figures are moving proves that the whole line is really a procession in motion. But we cannot yet identify these twelve gods, and there may be some special reason why they should be represented as if running. They appear also in the side gallery (Plate 14), where they certainly do not form part of a procession.[1]

As a further point of style it may be noted that whereas the gods at Yazilikaya and elsewhere are shown in the manner of Babylonian and Assyrian sculpture with the torso in full-face although the head and legs are in profile, the goddesses are shown (somewhat awkwardly) in true profile, as are the figures in the scene of worship at Alaja Hüyük. This seems to be an innovation in oriental art.

The great divine figure carved on the jamb of one of the gateways at Boghazköy has already been described (above, p. 107). This is in some ways the finest of all the Hittite bas-reliefs, even though here again we see the conventional twisting of the torso (see Plate 4). On account of the very full modelling of the breasts (which are covered with a design of little spirals) some have believed that this figure represents a female, an Amazon, clad in chain mail. But if we compare the bronze figurine which has been referred to above (p. 107) and the conventional representation of hair on animals such as the lion from Malatya (Plate 27) it seems more probable that the Guardian of the Gate is a male warrior stripped to the waist, for chest-hair was re-

---

1. The side gallery seems to have been a mortuary temple in honour of one of the kings named Tudhaliyas, whose statue once stood beside his 'monogram' at the end of the recess.

garded as a sign of strength. So high is the relief in which this figure is carved that the face is clearly seen in the side view (Plate 4b); a somewhat similar feature may be observed at Yazilikaya, where the central figures in the main gallery stand out in a remarkable way from the background and have the surface very carefully moulded.

One figure deserves special mention, namely the 'dirk-god' in the side-gallery at Yazilikaya (Fig. 14). This carving represents a sword of which the hilt is in the form of four crouching lions, two facing the point of the sword on opposite sides of the axis, two others facing outwards back-to-back (these are compressed, their hinder quarters being omitted). An iron axe with a similar hilt has been found at Ras Shamra in Syria, and it has been suggested that the sword depicted at Yazilikaya was a trophy of war captured from a Syrian or Mitannian enemy, since there is no evidence that the Hittites used such swords. But what of the human head which surmounts the whole design? This head wears the typical Hittite conical hat of the gods, and no such

Fig. 14 – The 'dirk-god', Yazilikaya

head is found on the axe from Ras Shamra. In view of the position of the figure in the rock-sanctuary it is clear that the figure represents a deity – more precisely, we may now add, an Underworld deity, for according to certain recently discovered texts a group of Underworld deities were represented in the form of swords.

The sculptured blocks of the palace(?) at Alaja Hüyük

show musicians playing the lute and bagpipes, jugglers, a shepherd leading his flock (probably part of the religious procession, the sheep being led to sacrifice), and scenes of hunting (Plate 17). All this is in a lighter vein than anything yet found elsewhere in the Hittite area. Mention must also be made of the double eagle carved on the side of one of the sphinxes at the same site. This heraldic creature (which has had such a distinguished history) may be seen beneath the feet of two goddesses at Yazilikaya (Fig. 8, p. 143), and was probably their sacred animal. The remains of a female figure may also be seen above the eagle at Alaja Hüyük.

The nearest approach to sculpture in the round from the central Hittite area may be seen in the sphinxes and lions from the gates at Boghazköy and Alaja Hüyük (Plates 8, 9, 10), in which at least the front parts of the animals emerge fully from the block. It cannot be said that these are altogether successful. None the less, the heads of these sphinxes are carefully executed, and may be thought to provide some evidence of the Hittite ideal of female beauty. A similar intermediate stage between bas-relief and sculpture in the round is represented by the colossal statue now lying on a hill-side near Fasillar, the only example of a Hittite cult-statue of the imperial age (if such it be).

The lack of monumental sculpture in the round is to some extent made good by a few exquisite miniature figures in metal. Plate 5a shows a young man wearing a short kilt clasped by a belt, and probably also boots, thus closely resembling on a smaller scale the great Guardian of the Gate (cf. pp. 107, 200). The head was undoubtedly surmounted by a helmet. The beautiful little figure shown in Plate 5b is a noteworthy example of the art of the goldsmith. This man wears a full tunic with short sleeves, covering the body down to the knees.

Hittite glyptic has little connexion with the art of the

Mesopotamian cylinder-seals. True Hittite cylinder-seals are quite exceptional, and the designs on them are not derived from the Babylonian repertoire. The typical Hittite seal is a conical stamp surmounted by a ring or perforated boss for attachment to the wearer's person; but many other shapes are known. The body of the seal may be expanded into the form of a drum or cylinder, and a further design may then be engraved on the circumference in addition to that on the end; or it may take the form of a cube, in which case the four side-surfaces may be engraved (Plate 21, top). The handle in such instances is a separate attachment, sometimes in the form of a tripod with perforated hammer-shaped head. The main engraved surface was usually flat, but was in some instances sharply convex; button- or lens-shaped seals having two convex surfaces have also been found (Plate 21*b*). A rarer type of seal was the signet ring.

The designs of the comparatively few actual seals that are extant can be amply supplemented by the large number of impressions found on lumps of clay used for sealings (so-called *bullae*). In general, there is a central field which may (if the field is large enough) be surrounded by one, two, or three bands of ornament or writing. This surrounding band of ornament may be in the form of running spirals, guilloches, or plaited strands; in the royal seals only does cuneiform writing, giving the name of the king and sometimes other details, take their place. The central field contains in most cases a group of hieroglyphic signs or symbols, the significance of which is uncertain. In the more distinguished pieces there is a figure of a god, or of an animal which is the god's symbol; some examples are given in Fig. 15, from which it will be seen that the repertoire is largely identical with that of the rock-sculptures and other reliefs. The royal seals show for the most part the 'monogram' of the king under the winged sun-disc (Fig. 16). Only very rarely do such royal seals show figures or scenes which are not symbolic;

Fig. 15 – Impressions of Hittite seals

Fig. 16 – Impressions of royal seals: (1 and 2) Muwatallis, (3) Suppiluliumas, (4) Urhi-Teshub, (5) Tudhaliyas, (6) Hattusilis

one instance would seem to be the embracing scene, familiar from Yazilikaya, which appears on three seals of Muwatallis (note that the god is here the bearded Weather-god, not the youthful deity who protects King Tudhaliyas at Yazilikaya). The seal-impression on the silver tablet of the treaty with Egypt was evidently that of a similar seal used by King Hattusilis, for it is described in the Egyptian text as showing 'a figure with a likeness of Setekh (the Egyptian Storm-god), embracing a likeness of the Great King of Hatti'. The silver seal of 'Tarkondemos' shows the king himself in his priestly robes (Plate 20*b*); it is still one of the most perfect and typical examples of Hittite glyptic (see introduction, p. 8).

Three exceptional seals are illustrated in Plates 21 and 22. The gold signet-ring is a beautiful example of Hittite workmanship, and shows a winged deity standing on his sacred animal. The cylindrical and cuboid seals are quite outside the ordinary repertoire, and are alike in depicting on their cylindrical or lateral surfaces ritual scenes which in spite of much speculation still defy interpretation. The designs on the ends of these pieces seem to link them with the Hittite artistic tradition, but since all were purchased from dealers, their provenance is uncertain. The only other known cylinder of this type was bought at Aydin in western Anatolia, where other influences would be at work.

Hittite glyptic did not survive the downfall of Hattusas. The glyptic art of the Syrian successor-kingdoms is that of the cylinder-seal, and is thoroughly Mesopotamian in outlook.

When Hattusas fell, it was in the kingdom of Milid (Malatya) that Hittite artistic tradition was most faithfully preserved. On a whole series of bas-reliefs from that site we see scenes of libation before deities who can easily be identified with their counterparts at Yazilikaya. An outstanding example is Fig. 17, which shows the king with his lituus (but

Fig. 17 – Libation scene, from Malatya

Fig. 18 – Stag-hunt, from Malatya

without his shawl) pouring a libation before the Weather-god, who appears in two forms, first borne in his archaic chariot with solid wheels and drawn by his two bulls, then standing alone and brandishing a thunderbolt. The artist of Malatya has united in this scene the Anatolian and the Syrian conceptions of the Weather-god. The scene of the slaying of the serpent is new but illustrates a Hittite myth (see above, p. 183). The Syrian influence is particularly apparent here in a number of scenes of hunting by chariot (Fig. 18); for the archer of Alaja Hüyük (Plate 17) is on foot. This scene of hunting by chariot, which first appears in Syrian art, was to become one of the most favourite motifs of the sculpture of the Assyrian palaces.

In the foot-hills of Taurus the little state of Sam'al (now Zinjirli) likewise maintained the Hittite artistic tradition for a time with some success. From Zinjirli we have some pon-derous stone lions, very much in the style of those from the gate of Boghazköy, a cult-statue (which may be compared with that from Fasillar, though the curious running atti-tude of the little figure between the lions is typically Syrian), a lion-headed genius such as may be seen guard-ing the entrance to the side-gallery at Yazilikaya, and a figure of the Elder Weather-god (Plate 28) which in dress at least (short tunic, belt and sword, upturned shoes) re-sembles the art of Hattusas, though the attitude is that of the Syrian Baal. This kingdom fell very early to an Aramean dynasty, but the Arameans were a nomadic people without an artistic tradition of their own, and it is not therefore sur-prising that the Hittite style lasted there for so long.

In the kingdoms of northern Syria the Hittite tradition had to compete with a developed indigenous culture based on Mesopotamian origins, and we find there a mixture of styles. Most fully known is the art of Carchemish, which has twice been excavated by expeditions from the British Museum (see pp. 5, 8). An awe-inspiring statue of the

Weather-god in his lion-drawn chariot is a development of several Hittite motifs. The human head with the conical hat added incongruously to the shoulders of the winged lion (Fig. 19), presumably to indicate divinity, is to be seen already on the gold ring from Konya (Plate 22) and may be compared with the similar head on the 'dirk-god' of Yazilikaya (Fig. 14). Many figures on the earlier

Fig. 19 – Fabulous monster, from Carchemish

reliefs from this site still wear the short tunic, belt, and up-turned shoes. But on the later tableaux, in spite of the presence of Hittite hieroglyphic inscriptions, the dress is the long Assyrian fringed cloak with the Assyrian head-dress and straight shoes, while great attention is paid to the hair and beard, also in the Assyrian manner. The scene of hunt-ing by chariot is well represented, and there are other scenes which are new to Hittite art. At Sakje-gözü near Marash, though the sculptures are late and largely in the Assyrian style, there is a survival of the curious fashion of carving a figure in such high relief that the face can be seen in the side view.

Even across the Euphrates at Guzana (now Tell Halaf) a feeble current of Hittite tradition can be traced. Here the emphasis is on winged monsters and genii, the prototypes of some of which can often be found in Hittite art of the imperial age, especially on seals. But for the most part the repertoire of this outlying principality is derived from Sumerian or Syrian originals.

In general, the use of bas-reliefs (orthostats) in the manner of a dado to adorn the lower part of a wall-face is an architectural feature which unites the art of all these successor-states with that of imperial Hatti (as represented at Alaja) with the proviso that, whereas in buildings of the second millennium, both at Carchemish and Alaja, the reliefs are carved on large blocks which are actually part of the structure of the wall, in the Neo-Hittite period the slabs are superimposed on the wall and are purely ornamental. The general plan of Hittite temples as described above (p. 145) was not passed on to the Syrian principalities. The view that the characteristic Syrian *bît hilani* (a two-storied gate-house with pillars, approached by a flight of steps and leading into a wide but shallow hall) was derived from a feature of the earlier Hittite temple has become much less plausible since the interpretation of the remains of the Hittite temples in question has been shown to be rather fanciful. Moreover, the term *bît hilani* has now been read on a tablet from Mari dating from the eighteenth century B.C.,[1] when Hittite Asia Minor had not yet begun to exert any appreciable influence on the civilization of the Syrian plains. It seems then that this type of building and its name are both of Syrian origin.

1. G. Dossin, *Archives Royales de Mari*, I, 3 rev. 10.

SOME PROBLEMS

The sudden appearance of stone sculpture at the beginning of the Hittite New Kingdom has inevitably raised the question of the origin of its inspiration. It has even been asserted that Hittite art as a whole is not Hittite but Hurrian, on the ground that many characteristic features of it are more commonly represented in Syria and particularly at Tell Halaf than on the plateau. On this theory the Hittites would have borrowed the main motifs of Hurrian art during the fifteenth century, when the Hurrians were exercising such a profound influence on their religion and literature, and the Hittites themselves could only be credited with developing certain artistic characteristics and motifs within the framework of a style which was fundamentally foreign to them. The weakness of this theory lies in the fact that the plastic art of the Mitannian and Hurrian kingdoms has never been discovered and is entirely hypothetical; all we have is a certain number of cylinder seals which form a provincial branch of Mesopotamian glyptic, going back directly to Sumerian prototypes.

That the Hittites borrowed many subjects from Syria and so indirectly from the Mesopotamian repertoire cannot be denied. Foremost among them is the figure of the god standing on his animal, a type which has a long history reaching back to Sumerian times. The double eagle, the fabulous monsters, and some of the tableaux of profane activities from Alaja Hüyük are likewise of oriental origin. Egyptian influence may be seen in the human-headed sphinxes of Alaja and Boghazköy, but especially in the winged sun-disc which hovers over the head of every Hittite king and forms part of his 'monogram'. This was the Egyptian symbol of royalty, and to the Syrian and Anatolian kingdoms the prestige of the Egyptian Empire of the

Eighteenth Dynasty was immense. The symbol seems first to have been adopted by the kings of Mitanni and to have been assimilated to a concept of a sky symbol supported on a pillar, such as is mentioned in the Rigveda. The Hittites then adopted the symbol again from Syria, where it had become confused with the Babylonian sun-symbol, and that is why the Hittite symbol contains a radiant star-like sun instead of the Egyptian disc. Its use marked Hatti as one of the Great Powers of the time.

But the cult-scenes, and above all the figure of the king in the embrace of his tutelary god, are unquestionably Hittite innovations. None the less, the use of these motifs for bas-reliefs may well be secondary, for they are found also on seals, and it may be that the original inspiration of these ideas should be credited to the Hittite seal-cutters, whose work, as we have seen, is attested from very early times.

Another problem which may be dealt with here is that of the human types represented on these monuments. What did the Hittites look like? There seems to be a sharp distinction between the 'Armenoid' type, with large hooked nose and receding forehead, represented by the running figures at Yazilikaya, by the Guardian of the Gate at Boghazköy, or by the golden figurine in the British Museum (Plate 5b) and the flatter, more upright physiognomy to be seen in the heads of the sphinxes at Boghazköy and in the figurines from that site (Plates 5a and 10). That there were in fact at least two types of Hittites is apparently confirmed by the Egyptian monuments, which are very carefully executed. Plates 2a and 3 show the 'Armenoid' type in a pronounced form, whereas the two central figures in Plate 2b have a totally different type of face (those behind may not be Hittites). We might well suppose that the 'Armenoid' type represents the mass of the Hittite (perhaps rather Hattian) population, while the upright type of face belongs to the Indo-European ruling class, though the proud bearing of the 'Armenoid' charioteer in Plate 3 would show that in any case the types had become considerably intermingled.

However, these hypotheses seem to be belied by the evidence of excavation. Examination of the skulls which have been found on several sites in Anatolia shows that in the third millennium the population was preponderantly long-headed or dolichocephalic, with only a small admixture of brachycephalic types. In the second millennium the proportion of brachycephalic skulls increases to about 50 per cent. But in neither millennium is this brachycephalic element of the 'Armenoid' type, which is hyper-brachycephalic with flattened occiput, but is classified rather as 'Alpine'. It is not till the first millennium that the 'Armenoid' type appears.

It seems impossible to reconcile these facts with the monuments. If the contradiction were confined to Anatolia it might be evaded by supposing that the comparatively few skulls that have been excavated there are not truly representative, but the same contradiction has been observed in Persia and Iraq, where the craniological material is much more plentiful. The problem thus raised has so far proved insoluble.

The Egyptian portraits (Plates 2, 3) show a variety of hair-fashions. In general, the hair seems to have been left to fall uncut in a mass behind the neck, with or without a head-band; sometimes the forehead is shaved. One figure appears to have the whole head shaved except for a short pigtail at the back. The long appendage behind the helmet of the gate-figure at Boghazköy is not a pigtail but is attached to the helmet; the hair, however, can also be seen coming from under the helmet and flowing down over the shoulders. In the later figure from Zinjirli there is clearly a pigtail or mass of hair (Plate 28). All Hittites on the Egyptian monuments are clean-shaven except those who are in reality Syrian allies. Their own monuments of the imperial age in general confirm this, though it is noteworthy that the elder Weather-god is represented as a bearded figure (Plate 28 and Fig. 17), and the later monuments show that the fashion of wearing a beard spread from Syria to the whole of Hittite Anatolia.

Conclusion

THE civilization of the Hittites was most advanced in those aspects which can be referred to the ruling caste, namely in military genius, political organization, legislation, and the administration of justice. Literature and religion, though exhibiting many interesting features, remained primitive and are derived from the Hattian and Hurrian elements of the population. In the Old Kingdom the king was primarily the military leader of the nation, and it was only later that his religious functions became prominent. In art we may say that the Hittite people revealed a certain genius, but even here the powerful rupestrian art of the later Empire was probably stimulated by the rulers.

Many intriguing problems still await solution, such as the date and the route of the earliest penetration of the Indo-Europeans into Asia Minor, the origin of the Hittite cuneiform and hieroglyphic scripts and the full decipherment of the latter, the historical relation of the Hittite Law Code to the codes of Mesopotamia, above all the construction of a definitive map of Hittite Asia Minor which will render intelligible the very full accounts of the campaigns of the Hittite kings. It may be hoped that in the excavations at Boghazköy, and perhaps elsewhere, will be discovered many more cuneiform tablets, which may help to explain these major problems and the other innumerable details about which we still have too little information.

Table of Hittite Kings

Name	Dates (B.C.)	Relationship to Last King
Pitkhanas (of Kussara)		
Anittas (of Kussara)		Son

OLD KINGDOM

Name	Dates (B.C.)	Relationship to Last King
Tudhaliyas I (?)	1740–1710	?
Pu-sarrumas(?)	1710–1680	Son
Labarnas I	1680–1650	Son
Labarnas II=Hattusilis I	1650–1620	Son
Mursilis I	1620–1590	Adopted son
Hantilis I	1590–1560	Brother-in-law
Zidantas I	1560–1550	Son-in-law(?)
Ammunas	1550–1530	Son
Huzziyas I	1530–1525	Son(?)
Telipinus	1525–1500	Brother-in-law
Alluwamnas	1500–1490	Son-in-law
Hantilis II (?)	1490–1480	?
Zidantas II (?)	1480–1470	?
Huzziyas II (?)	1470–1460	?

EMPIRE

Name	Dates (B.C.)	Relationship to Last King
Tudhaliyas II	1460–1440	?
Arnuwandas I	1440–1420	Son
Hattusilis II	1420–1400	Brother
Tudhaliyas III	1400–1380	Son
Suppiluliumas	1380–1340	Son
Arnuwandas II	1340–1339	Son
Mursilis II	1339–1306	Brother
Muwatallis	1306–1282	Son
Urhi-Teshub (=Mursilis III)	1282–1275	Son
Hattusilis III	1275–1250	Uncle
Tudhaliyas IV	1250–1220	Son
Arnuwandas III	1220–1190	Son
Suppiluliumas II	1190–?	Brother

NOTE ON THE KING-LIST AND CHRONOLOGY

THE relation of Pitkhanas and Anittas to the kings of the Old Kingdom of Hattusas is obscure (see above, p. 21).

The order of the kings of the Old Kingdom as far as Alluwamnas is assured, though there is some doubt whether Tudhaliyas I, the grandfather of Labarnas, was a king of Hatti. The existence of the last three kings of the Old Kingdom is less certain, but has become more probable in view of the latest evidence.

A text published by Dr Kemal Balkan in 1948 established the existence of Suppiluliumas II at the end of the Empire, but it was only in 1953 that E. Laroche demonstrated in *Revue d'Assyriologie*, XLVII, 70–8, that a number of other texts previously ascribed to Suppiluliumas I belong in reality to the later king of that name. It follows, as shown by Laroche, that the insertion of a king Arnuwandas II between Tudhaliyas III and Suppiluliumas I was an error and that Suppiluliumas I succeeded his father directly. This Arnuwandas has accordingly been deleted from the list. The existence of Arnuwandas I is also somewhat uncertain.

All dates are approximate, but two of them are directly linked with events in Babylonia and Egypt respectively. The death of Mursilis I occurred shortly after his attack on Babylon which caused the downfall of the First Babylonian Dynasty; the death of Suppiluliumas occurred four years after that of Tutankhamun. The dates for the Old Kingdom have to be entirely reconstructed, in accordance with the average length for a generation, from that of the death of Mursilis I. Those of the Empire are to some extent controlled by a network of synchronisms, which cannot be explained here.

The absolute chronology adopted in this book is that of Dr Sidney Smith, as proposed in his *Alalakh and Chronology* (1940), combined with the new low dates for Egyptian kings worked out by M. B. Rowton in *Iraq*, vol. VIII (1946), pp. 94–110, and *Journal of Egyptian Archaeology*, vol. XXXIV (1948), pp. 47–74. Mr Rowton's chronology differs by about ten years from that most generally accepted. It will be observed that even with this scheme it is scarcely possible to accommodate the three kings at the end of the Old Kingdom. To lower the Babylonian dates by sixty years, as proposed by Professor Albright and others, would create serious difficulties in Hittite chronology.

NOTE TO REVISED EDITION, 1962

MR ROWTON has now abandoned the low dates for the Egyptian kings of the Eighteenth and Nineteenth Dynasties. The latest chronology would raise all the dates in this book after *c.* 1500 B.C. by 14 years. See 'Chronology', by W. C. Hayes, M. B. Rowton, and Frank H. Stubbings, in *Cambridge Ancient History*, rev. ed., Vol. I, Chap. VI (1962).

Select Bibliography

SYNOPSIS OF SECTIONS

I. GENERAL

BITTEL, K. *Die Ruinen von Boğazköy.* Berlin and Leipzig, 1937.

— 'Hethiter und Protohattier'. *Historia*, I, 267–86. 1950

— and NAUMANN, R. *Boğazköy-Hattuša.* (Deutsche Orientgesellschaft, Wissenschaftliche Veröffentlichung no. 63) Stuttgart, 1952.

CAVAIGNAC, E. *Les Hittites.* (L'Orient ancien illustré.) Paris (Maisonneuve), 1950.

— *Le problème hittite.* Paris (Leroux), 1936.

CERAM, C. W. *Narrow Pass, Black Mountain.* London, 1956.

CONTENAU, G. *La civilisation des hittites et des hurrites du Mitanni.* Paris (Payot), 2nd ed., 1948.

DELAPORTE, L. *Les Hittites.* Paris (L'Évolution de l'humanité), 1936.

DROWER, M. S. 'Hittites'. Article in *Chambers Encyclopaedia*, 1950.

DUSSAUD, R. *Prélydiens, Hittites et Achéens.* Paris (Geuthner), 1953.

FORRER, E. O. 'Stratification des langues et des peuples dans le proche-orient préhistorique'. *Journal Asiatique*, 1930, 227–62.

GARSTANG, J. *The Land of the Hittites.* London (Constable), 1910.

— *The Hittite Empire.* London (Constable), 1929.

GOETZE, A. *Das Hethiter Reich.* (Der alte Orient, Band 27.) Leipzig, 1928.

— *Hethiter, Churriter und Assyrer.* Oslo, 1936.

— 'Hittite Dress'. *Corolla Linguistica.* Wiesbaden, 1955.

— 'Kleinasien'. (Müller, *Handbuch der Altertumswissenschaft*, III, 1, iii.) 2nd ed. München, 1957.

— 'The Cultures of Early Anatolia'. *Proc. of American Phil. Soc.*, 97, no. 2. 1953.

GÜTERBOCK, H. G. 'Boghazköy, the Capital of the Hittites'. *Archaeology*, VI, 1953.

— 'The Hurrian Element in the Hittite Empire'. *Cahiers d'Histoire Mondiale*, II, 1954.

HROZNÝ, B. 'Hittites'. Article in *Encylopaedia Britannica*, 14th ed., 1929.

LAROCHE, E. 'La Bibliothèque de Hattusa'. *Archiv. Orientalni*, XVII, 7–23. 1949.

— *Recueil d'onomastique hittite.* Paris, 1952. Additions in *Revue Hittite*, XIII/57, 1955.

MERCER, S. A. B. *The Tell El-Amarna Tablets.* Toronto, 1939. (Reviewed by C. J. Gadd in *Palestine Exploration Quarterly*, 1950, 116–23.)

O'CALLAGHAN, R. 'Aram Naharaim. A contribution to the history of Upper Mesopotamia in the Second Millennium B.C.' *Analecta Orientalia*, 26. Rome, 1948. (Reviewed by A. Goetze in *Journal of Cuneiform Studies*, II, 309–14.)

RIEMSCHNEIDER, M. *Die Welt der Hethiter*. Sutttgart, 1954. (Reviewed by Güterbock in *Orientalistische Literaturzeitung*. 1956.)

SAYCE, A. H. *The Hittites. The Story of a Forgotten Empire*. 5th ed., London, 1910.

SOMMER, F. *Hethiter und Hethitisch*. Stuttgart, 1947.

WRIGHT, W. *The Empire of the Hittites*, with decipherment of the Hittite inscriptions by Prof. A. H. Sayce. London, 1884.

2. HISTORICAL AND CHRONOLOGICAL PROBLEMS

BALKAN, K. *Observations on the Chronological Problems of the Kārum Kanis*. Ankara, 1955.

CAVAIGNAC, E. 'L'Affaire de Iaruvatta'. *Revue Hittite et Asianique*, I, 189–200. 1932.

— 'Le premier royaume d'Arménie'. *Ibid.*, III, 9–14.

— 'La Date et l'ordre des campagnes de Mursil'. *Ibid.*, II, 193–8. 1934.

— 'L'Égypte, le Mitanni et les Hittites de 1478 à 1350'. *Ibid.*, I, 61–71. 1931.

— 'L'Égypte et le Hatti vers 1302'. *Mélanges Maspero*, I (= *Mémoires de l'institut français d'archéologie orientale*, LXVI), 357–60. Cairo, 1935–6.

— 'L'Histoire politique de l'orient de 1340 à 1230; succession des événements'. *Revue Hittite et Asianique*, III, 117–26. 1935.

— 'La lettre de Ramsés II au roi de Mira'. *Ibid.*, III, 25–9. 1935.

— 'La Maison de Subbiluliuma'. *Ibid.*, III, 237–9. 1936.

— *Subbiluliuma et son temps*. Paris, 1932.

— 'Synchronismes assyriens, égyptiens et hittites (XIVe–XIIIe siècles)'. *Revue Hittite et Asianique*, II, 180–9. 1933.

CORNELIUS, F. 'Chronology, eine Erwiderung'. *Journal of Cuneiform Studies*, XII. 1958.

DUSSAUD, R. 'Un Point de chronologie hittite et assyrienne'. *Syria*, XVI, 323. 1935.

EDEL, E. 'Ni-ip-hu-ru-ri-ia-aš'. *Journal of Near Eastern Studies*, VII, 14–15. 1948.

GOETZE, A. 'On the Chronology of the Second Millennium B.C.'. *Journal of Cuneiform Studies*, XI. 1957.

GÜTERBOCK, H. G. 'The Deeds of Suppiluliuma as Told by his Son Mursili II'. *Journal of Cuneiform Studies*, X. 1956.

— 'Kaneš and Neša, Two Forms of one Anatolian Name'. *Eretz-Israel*, V. 1958.

GURNEY, O. R. 'Anatolia *c.* 1750–1600 B.C.' *Cambridge Ancient History*, rev. ed., Vol. II, chap. VI. Cambridge, 1962.

HARDY, R. S. 'The Old Hittite Kingdom'. *American Journal of Semitic Languages*, LVIII, 177–216. 1941.

LAROCHE, E. 'Chronologie hittite, état des questions'. *Anadolu* II. Paris, 1955.

— 'Un point d'histoire: Ulmi–Teššub'. *Revue Hittite et Asianique*, VIII, 40–8. 1947–8.

Laroche, E. 'Šuppiluliuma II'. *Revue d'Assyriologie*, 47, 70–8. 1953.

Mellaart, J. 'Anatolian Chronology in the Early and Middle Bronze Age'. *Anatolian Studies*, VII. 1957.

Nougayrol, J. *Le palais royal d'Ugarit*, IV. Paris, 1956. (Reviewed by E. Cavaignac in *Revue Hittite*, XV/61, 1957.)

Otten, H. 'Die hethitischen "Königslisten" und die altorientalische Chronologie'. *Mitteilungen der deutschen Orientgesellschaft*, 83, 47–71. 1951.

— 'Zu den Anfängen der hethitischen Geschichte'. *Ibid.*, 33–45.

— 'Ein althethitischer Vertrag aus Kizzuwatna'. *Journal of Cuneiform Studies*, V, 129–32. 1951.

— 'Aitiologische Erzählung von der Überquerung des Taurus'. *Zeitschrift für Assyriologie*, LV (1963), 156–68.

— 'Neue Quellen zum Ausklang des Hethitischen Reiches'. *Mitteilungen der deutschen Orientgesellschaft*, 94 (1963), 1–23.

Özgüç, T. 'The Dagger of Anitta'. Türk Tarih Kurumu, *Belleten*, XX. 1956.

Rowton, M. B. 'The Date of the Hittite Capture of Babylon'. *Bulletin of the American Schools of Oriental Research*, 126, 20–4. 1952.

3. BATTLE OF KADESH

Alt, A. 'Zur Topographie der Schlacht bei Kades'. *Zeitschrift des deutschen Palästina-Vereins*, LV, 1–25. 1932.

Breasted, J. H. *The Battle of Kadesh*. Chicago, 1903.

Burne, A. H. 'Some Notes on the battle of Kadesh'. *Journal of Egyptian Archaeology*, VII, 191–5. 1920.

Gardiner, Sir A. *The Kadesh Inscriptions of Ramesses II*. Oxford, 1960.

Goetze, A. 'Zur Schlacht bei Qadeš'. *Orientalistische Literaturzeitung*, XXXII, col. 832–8. 1929.

Kuentz, C. 'La Bataille de Qadech'. *Mémoires de l'Institut français d'Archéologie Orientale*, LV, 81–398. 1934.

Sturm, J. 'Der Hettiterkrieg Ramses II'. *Wiener Zeitschrift für die Kunde des Morgenlandes*, Beiheft IV. 1939.

Yeivin, S. 'Canaanite and Hittite Strategy in the Second Half of the Second Millennium B.C.' *Journal of Near Eastern Studies*, IX, 101–7. Chicago, 1950.

4. NEO-HITTITE KINGDOMS

Bossert, H. T. 'Zur Geschichte von Kargamiš'. *Studi Classici e Orientali*, I. Pisa, 1951.

Cavaignac, E. *Le Problème hittite*. Paris (Leroux), 1936.

Hogarth, D. G. 'The Hittites of Syria'. *Cambridge Ancient History*, III, vi. Cambridge, 1929.

— *Kings of the Hittites*. (Schweich Lectures.) London, 1926.

Landsberger, B. *Sam'al. Studien zur Entdeckung der Ruinenstätte Karatepe*. Turkish Historical Society, 1948.

Laroche, E. 'Chronologie hittite, état des questions'. *Anadolu* II, Paris, 1955.

NASTER, P. *L'Asie Mineure et l'Assyrie*. Louvain, 1938.
SMITH, S. 'The Greek Trade at Al Mina'. *Antiquaries' Journal*, XXII, 87–112. 1942.
TAYLOR, J. Du PLAT, and others. *Iraq*, XII, 64–73. 1950.

4A. KARATEPE

ALKIM, B. 'Les Résultats archéologiques des fouilles de Karatepe'. *Revue Hittite et Asianique*, IX (50), 1948–9. (With full bibliography.)
BOSSERT, H. T. 'Found at last: a bi-lingual key to the previously unde-cipherable Hittite Hieroglyphic inscriptions'. *Illustrated London News*, 14 May 1949, 664–8.
— 'Sur quelques problèmes historiques des inscriptions de Karatepe'. *Revue Hittite et Asianique*, IX (49), 1–9.
DUPONT-SOMMER, A. 'Azitawadda, roi des Danouniens'. *Revue d'Assyriologie*, XLII, 161–88, 1948.
GORDON, C. H. 'Azitawadda's Phoenician Inscription'. *Journal of Near Eastern Studies*, VIII, 116–20. 1949.
HONEYMAN, A. M. 'Epigraphic Discoveries at Karatepe'. *Palestine Exploration Quarterly*, 21–39. 1949.
LAROCHE, E. 'Adana et les danouniens'. *Syria*, XXXV, 263 ff. 1958.
LÉVY, I. 'Les Inscriptions de Karatepe'. *La Nouvelle Clio*, II. 1950.
MARCUS, R., and GELB, I. J. 'The Phoenician Stele Inscription from Cilicia'. *Journal of Near Eastern Studies*, VIII, 116–20. 1949.
OBERMANN, J. *New Discoveries at Karatepe. A complete text of the Phoenician royal inscription from Cilicia*. New Haven, 1949.
O'CALLAGHAN, R. 'The Great Phoenician Portal Inscription from Karatepe'. *Orientalia*, XVIII, 173–205. Rome, 1949.
— 'An approach to some religious problems of Karatepe'. *Archiv Orientalni*, XVIII, 354–65. 1950.
See also Section 15 *s.v.* Bossert.

5. RELIGION

ALBRIGHT, W. F. 'The Anatolian Goddess Kubaba'. *Archiv für Orientforschung*, V, 229–31. Berlin, 1929.
BOISSIER, A. *Mantique babylonienne et mantique hittite*. Paris, 1935.
BRANDENSTEIN, C. G. 'Hethitische Götter nach Bildbeschreibungen in Keilschrifttexten'. *Mitteilungen der Vorderasiatisch-ägyptischen Gesellschaft*, XLVI (2), 1943. (Reviewed by Güterbock in *Orientalia*, XV, 1946, 482–96.)
DUSSAUD, R. (Chapters in:) *La religion de Babylonie et d'Assyrie; la religion des Hittites et des Hurrites, des Phéniciens et des Syriens*. (Mana, no. 1.) Paris (Presses Universitaires de France), 1945.
FRANZ, L. 'Die Muttergöttin im Vorderen Orient und in Europa'. (*Der Alte Orient*, XXXV, 3.) Leipzig, 1937.
FURLANI, G. *La Religione degli Hittiti*. Bologna, 1936.
— 'The Basic Aspect of Hittite Religion'. *Harvard Theological Review*, XXXI, 231–62. 1938.

GASTER, T. *Thespis*. New York (Schuman), 1950.

GOETZE, A. *The Hittite Ritual of Tunnawi*. (American Oriental Series, vol. 14.) New Haven, 1938. (Reviewed by Gurney in *Journal of the Royal Asiatic Society*, 1941, 56–61.)

GÜTERBOCK, H. G. 'Hethitische Götterdarstellungen und Götternamen'. *Belleten*, Turkish Historical Society, Ankara, 1943.

— 'Hittite Religion'. In V. Ferm, *Forgotten Religions*. New York, 1949.

GURNEY, O. R. 'Hittite Prayers of Mursili II'. *Annals of Archaeology and Anthropology*, XXVII. Liverpool, 1940.

— 'Hittite Kingship' in *Myth, Ritual and Kingship* (ed. S. H. Hooke). Oxford, 1958.

KAN, A. H. *Juppiter Dolichenus*. Leiden (Brill), 1943. (See also Bossert in *Jahrbuch für kleinasiatische Forschung*, II, 206–8, 1952.)

KRAUSE, K. 'Boğazköy Tempel V'. *Istanbuler Forschungen*, XI, 1940.

LAROCHE, E. 'Divinités lunaires d'Anatolie'. *Revue de l'Histoire des Religions*, 148. 1955.

— 'Le panthéon de Yazilikaya'. *Journal of Cuneiform Studies*, VI, 115–23. 1952.

— *Recherches sur les noms des dieux hittites*. Paris, 1947. (Also in *Revue Hittite et Asianique*, VII.)

— 'Teššub, Hebat et leur cour'. *Journal of Cuneiform Studies*, II, 113–36. 1948.

LESKY, A. 'Ein ritueller Scheinkampf bei den Hethitern'. *Archiv für Religionswissenschaft*, XXIV, 73–82, 1927.

MASSON, O. 'À propos d'un rituel hittite pour la lustration d'une armée'. *Revue de l'Histoire des Religions*, 137, 5–25, 1950.

MERLAT, P. *Juppiter Dolichenus*. Paris, 1960.

OTTEN, H. 'Die Gottheit Lelvani der Boğazköy-Texte'. *Journal of Cuneiform Studies*, IV, 119–36. 1950.

— 'Ein Bestattungsritual hethitischer Könige'. *Zeitschrift für Assyriologie*, XLVI, 206–24. 1942.

PETTAZZONI, R. 'Confession of Sins in the Hittite Religion'. *Occident and Orient ... Studies in honour of Dr M. Gaster's 80th birthday*. London, 1936.

RANSOME, H. M. *The Sacred Bee in Ancient Times and Folklore*. London (Allen and Unwin), 1937.

WOHLER, L. 'Die altrömische und die hethitische evocatio'. *Archiv für Religionswissenschaft*, XXV, 206–9. 1928.

6. LAW

A. TRANSLATIONS OF THE CODE

FRIEDRICH, J. *Die Hethitischen Gesetze*. Leiden, 1959.

GOETZE, A. In Pritchard, *Ancient Near Eastern Texts relating to the Old Testament*, 188–96. Princeton, 1950.

STURTEVANT, E. H. 'Selections from the Code'. In Sturtevant and Bechtel, *A Hittite Chrestomathy*. Philadelphia, 1935.

SELECT BIBLIOGRAPHY

WALTHER, A. In J. M. P. Smith, *The Origin and History of Hebrew Law.* Chicago, 1931.

B. DISCUSSIONS

COLLINET, P. 'Droit babylonien, droit assyrien, droit hittite'. *Journal des Savants*, 68–81, 122–8. 1932.

CUQ, E. *Études sur le droit babylonien, les lois assyriennes et les lois hittites.* Paris, 1929.

GUTERBOCK, H. G. 'Authority and Law in the Hittite Kingdom'. *Journal of the American Oriental Society*, Supp. 17. 1954.

HOLT, J. 'Quelques interprétations du Code Hittite'. *Archiv Orientalni*, XVII, 315–19. 1950.

KOROŠEC, V. 'Beiträge zum hethitischen Privatrecht'. *Zeitschrift der Savigny-Stiftung*, LII, 156–69. 1932.

— 'Die Kollektivhaftung im hethitischen Recht'. *Archiv Orientalni*, XVIII$_3$, 187–289. 1950.

— 'Ehe in Hatti'. *Reallexikon der Assyriologie*, II, 293–6.

— 'Einige Beiträge zum hethitischen Sklavenrecht'. *Festschrift P. Koschaker*, III, 127.

— *Hethitische Staatsverträge.* Leipzig, 1931.

— 'Le problème de la codification dans le domaine du droit hittite'. *Revue Internationale des Droits de l'Antiquité*, Sér. 3, Tome IV, 93–105. 1957.

KOSCHAKER, P. 'Fratriarchat, Hausgemeinschaft und Mutterrecht in Keilschriftrechten'. *Zeitschrift für Assyriologie*, XII, 1–89. 1933.

— 'Zum Levirat nach hethitischem Recht'. *Revue Hittite et Asianique*, II, 77–89. 1933.

NEUFELD, E. 'Notes on Hittite Laws'. *Archiv Orientalni*, XVIII$_4$, 116–30. 1951.

PRICE, J. 'The so-called Levirate-Marriage in Hittite and Assyrian Laws'. *Oriental Studies (Paul Haupt Anniversary Volume)*. Baltimore, 1926.

PUUKKO, A. F. 'Die altassyrischen und hethitischen Gesetze und das alte Testament'. *Studia Orientalia*, I, 125–66. 1925.

— 'Die Leviratsehe in den altorientalischen Gesetzen'. *Archiv Orientalni*, XVII, 296–9. 1949.

ROSENKRANZ, B. 'Zur Chronologie der hethitischen Gesetze'. *Zeitschrift für Assyriologie*, XLIV, 210–14. 1938.

SAN NICOLÒ, M. 'Zur Frage der Schriftlichkeit des Abschlusses von Rechtsgeschäften bei den Hethitern'. *Zeitschrift der Savigny-Stiftung*, LVI, 236–8. 1936.

SOMMER, F., and FALKENSTEIN, A. 'Die hethitisch-akkadische Bilingue des Hattušili I (Labarna II)'. (*Abhandlungen der Bayrischen Akademie der Wissenschaften*, phil.-hist., Abt., Neue Folge, XVI.) München, 1938.

SMITH, J. M. P. *The Origin and History of Hebrew Law.* Chicago, 1931.

7. LITERATURE

BARNETT, R. D. 'The Epic of Kumarbi and the Theogony of Hesiod'. *Journal of Hellenic Studies*, XLV, 100–1. 1945.

GÜTERBOCK, H. G. 'The Hittite version of the Hurrian Kumarbi Myths; Oriental Forerunners of Hesiod'. *American Journal of Archaeology*, LII, 123–34. 1948.

— 'Die historische Tradition und ihre literarische Gestaltung bei Babyloniern und Hethitern bis 1200'. *Zeitschrift für Assyriologie*, XLII (1933) and XLIII (1934).

— 'Hittite Mythology'. In *Mythologies of the Ancient World*, ed. S. N. Kramer. New York, 1961.

8. TRANSLATION OF TEXTS

For individual texts translated up to 1957, see Laroche, 'Catalogue des textes hittites', in *Revue Hittite et Asianique*, XIV/58–XVI/62 (summary by categories, XVI/62 p. 62).

FRIEDRICH, J. 'Aus dem hethitischen Schrifttum'. *Der Alte Orient*, XXIV (3) and XXV (2). 1925.

— 'Churritische Märchen und Sagen in hethitischer Sprache'. *Zeitschrift für Assyriologie*, XLIX, 213–55. 1950.

— 'Der churritische Mythus vom Schlangendämon Hedammu in hethitischer Sprache'. *Archiv Orientalni*, XVII, 230–54. 1949.

— 'Die hethitischen Bruchstücke des Gilgameš-Epos'. *Zeitschrift für Assyriologie*, XXXIX, 1–82. 1930.

— 'Ein hethitisches Gebet an die Sonnengöttin der Erde'. *Rivisia degli Studi Orientali*, XXXII. 1957.

— 'Staatsverträge des Hatti-Reiches in hethitischer Sprache'. *Mitteilungen der Vorderasiatisch-Aegyptischen Gesellschaft*, XXXI (1926) and XXXIV (1930).

GOETZE, A. 'Die Annalen des Mursilis'. *Mitteilungen der Vorderasiatisch-Aegyptischen Gesellschaft*, XXXVIII, 1933.

— Madduwattas. *Ibid.*, XXXII, 1928.

— 'Die Pestgebete des Mursilis'. *Kleinasiatische Forschungen*, I, 161–251. 1929.

— and PEDERSEN, H. *Mursilis Sprachlähmung*. Copenhagen, 1934.

GÜTERBOCK, H. G. 'The Deeds of Suppiluliuma as Told by his Son Mursili II'. *Journal of Cuneiform Studies*, X, 1956.

— 'The composition of Hittite prayers to the Sun'. *Journal of the American Oriental Society*, LXXVIII, 1958.

— *The Song of Ullikummi*. New Haven (American Schools of Oriental Research), 1952.

GURNEY, O. R. 'Mita of Pahhuwa'. *Annals of Archaeology and Anthropology*, XXVIII, 32–44, 1948.

LUCKENBILL, D. D. 'Hittite Treaties and Letters'. *American Journal of Semitic Languages*, XXXVII, 161–211, 1921.

OTTEN, H. 'Die erste Tafel des hethitischen Gilgamesch-Epos'. *Istanbuler Mitteilungen* 8. 1958.

— *Hethitische Totenrituale*. Berlin, 1958.

— 'Neue Fragmente zu den Annalen des Mursili'. *Mitteilungen des Instituts für Orientforschung*, III. 1955.

— 'Ritual bei Erneuerung von Kultsymbolen hethitischer Schutzgottheiten'. *Festschrift Johannes Friedrich*. Heidelberg, 1959.

SELECT BIBLIOGRAPHY

PRITCHARD, J. B. *Ancient Near Eastern Texts relating to the Old Testament.* Princeton University Press, 1950. (Translations of Hittite texts by A. Goetze.)

SCHULER, E. VON. *Hethitische Dienstanweisungen für höhere Hof- und Staatsbeamte.* (*Archiv für Orientforschung,* Beiheft 10.) 1957.

STURTEVANT, E. H., and BECHTEL, G. *A Hittite Chrestomathy.* Philadelphia, 1935.

WEIDNER, E. F. *Politische Dokumente aus Kleinasien.* Boghazköi-Studien, Hefte 8–9. 1923.

See also Section 5 *s.v.* Boissier, Brandenstein, Goetze, Gurney, Otten; Section 6 *s.v.* Walther, Sommer-Falkenstein; Section 7 *s.v.* Güterbock; Section 10 *s.v.* Sommer (1932); Section 12 *s.v.* Garstang and Gurney; and Section 2 *s.v.* Otten.

9. ART

AKURGAL EKREM. *Remarques stylistiques sur les reliefs de Malatya.* Ankara, 1946. (Reviewed by J. Garstang in *Annals of Arch. and Anthr.,* XXVIII 105–7.)
— *Späthethitische Bildkunst.* Ankara, 1949.

BARNETT, R. D. 'The Phrygian rock façades and the Hittite monuments'. *Bibliotheca Orientalis,* X, 77–82. 1952.

BITTEL, K. *Boğazköy. Die Kleinfunde der Grabungen 1906–12.* (Deutsche Orientgesellschaft, Wissenschaftliche Veröffentlichung Nr. 60.) Leipzig, 1937.
— *Die Felsbilder von Yazilikaya.* Istanbul, 1934.
— 'Nur hethitische oder auch hurritische Kunst?' *Zeitschrift für Assyriologie,* 49, 256–90. 1950.
— and others. *Yazilikaya.* (Deutsche Orientgesellschaft, Wissenschaftliche Veröffentlichung Nr. 61.) 1941.

BOSSERT, H. T. *Altanatolien.* Berlin, 1942.
— 'Zur Chronologie der Skulpturen von Malatya'. *Felsefe Archivi,* Istanbul, 1947, 85–101.

COUISSIN, P. 'Le dieu-épée de Iasili-kaia et le culte de l'épée dans l'antiquité'. *Revue Archéologique,* XXVI, Paris, 1928.

DELAPORTE, L. *Malatya. La porte des lions.* Paris (Boccard), 1940.

DUSSAUD, R. 'Datation des reliefs de Malatya'. *Comptes rendus de l'Académie des Inscriptions et des Belles Lettres,* 432–42, 1945.

FRANKFORT, H. 'The Origin of the Bît Hilani'. *Iraq,* XIV, 120–31. 1952.

GARSTANG, J. 'The First Imperial Hittite Sculpture found South of the Taurus Range'. *Illustrated London News,* 210–11. 1937.
— *The Hittite Empire,* London (Constable), 1929.

GELB, I. J. *Hittite Hieroglyphic Monuments.* Univ. of Chicago, Or. Inst. Publ., vol. 45. 1939. (Contains full bibliography of monuments known up to that date.)

DE GENOUILLAC, H. *Céramique cappadocienne.* Paris, 1926.

GÜTERBOCK, H. G. 'Siegel aus Boğazköy, I and II'. *Archiv für Orientforschung,* Beihefte 5 and 7, 1940 and 1944.

HOGARTH, D. G. *Hittite Seals with particular reference to the Ashmolean Collection, Oxford.* Oxford, 1920.

KRAUSE, K. *Boğazköy Tempel V. Ein Beitrag zum Problem der hethitischen Baukunst.* Istanbuler Forschungen II, 1940.

MOORTGAT, A. *Die bildende Kunst des alten Orients und die Bergvölker.* Berlin, 1933.

— 'Nur hethitische oder auch churrische Kunst?' *Zeitschrift für Assyriologie,* 48, 152–60. 1944.

OPPENHEIM, M., BARON VON. *Tell Halaf. A new culture in oldest Mesopotamia.* London, 1933.

OSTEN, H. H. VON DER. *Four Hittite Rhytons.* Parnassus, New York, 1932.

PUCHSTEIN, O. *Boghazköi, die Bauwerke.* Deutsche Orientgesellschaft, Wissenschaftliche Veröffentlichung Nr. 19. Leipzig, 1912.

VIEYRA, M. *Hittite Art.* London (Tiranti), 1953.

See also Section 13 *s.v.* Özgüç, Osten, Woolley, Thureau-Dangin.

10. AHHIYAWA AND GREEK LEGENDS

ALBRIGHT, W. F. 'Some Oriental Glosses on the Homeric Problem'. *American Journal of Archaeology,* LIV, 162–76. 1950.

ANDREWS, P. B. S. 'The Mycenaean Name of the Land of the Achaians'. *Revue Hittite et Asianique,* 1954.

BARNETT, R. D. 'Mopsos'. *Journal of Hellenic Studies,* 73, 140–3. 1953.

CAVAIGNAC, E. 'Hépat et les Amazones'. *Ibid.,* I, 48–55. 1950.

— 'Hittites et Achéens'. *Revue Hittite et Asianique,* III, 149–52. 1935.

— 'La question hittito-achéenne après les dernières publications'. *Bulletin de Correspondence Hellénique,* LXX, 58–66. 1946.

FORRER, E. O. 'Vorhomerische Griechen in den Keilschrifttexten von Boghaz-köi'. *Mitteilungen der Deutschen Orientgesellschaft,* LXIII, 1924.

— 'Die Griechen in den Boghaz-köi Texten'. *Orientalistische Literaturzeitung,* 1924, col. 113–18.

— 'Ahhijawā'. *Reallexikon der Assyriologie,* I, 1932.

FRIEDRICH, J. 'Werden in den hethitischen Keilschrifttexten die Griechen erwähnt?' *Kleinasiatische Forschungen,* I, 87–107; also in: *Zeitschrift der Deutschen Morgenländischen Gesellschaft,* LXXXI, I, 1929.

GÜTERBOCK, H. G. 'Neue Ahhijawā-Texte'. *Zeitschrift für Assyriologie,* XLIII, 321–7. 1934.

HALL, H. R. 'Mursil and Myrtilos'. *Journal of Hellenic Studies,* XXIX, 19–22. 1909.

HUXLEY, G. L. *Achaeans and Hittites.* Oxford, 1960.

KRETSCHMER, P. Articles in *Glotta,* XIII, XV (168), XVIII, XXI, and XXIV (1924–35).

PAGE, D. L. *History and the Homeric Iliad.* Berkeley and Los Angeles, 1959.

POISSON, G. 'Tantale, roi des hittites'. *Revue Archéologique,* Sér. 5, XXII, 75–94, 1925.

PUGLIESE CARRATELLI, G. 'Ahhijawa, Lazpa et leurs divinités dans KUB. V, 6'. *Jahrbuch für kleinasiatische Forschung,* I, 156–63. 1950.

SAYCE, A. H. 'Perseus and the Achaeans in the Hittite tablets'. *Journal of Hellenic Studies,* XLV, 161–3. 1925.

SCHACHERMEYR, F. *Hethiter und Achäer*. Mitteilungen der Altorientalischen Gesellschaft, IX, 1/2. 1935.
SHEWAN, A. 'Hittite Names'. *Classical Review*, XLV, 2–4. London, 1931.
SOMMER, F. *Die Ahhijavā-Urkunden*. Abhandlungen der *Bayrischen Akademie der Wissenschaften*, Phil.-hist. Abt., Neue Folge 6. 1932.
— *Ahhijavā-Frage und Sprachwissenschaft*. *Ibid.*, Neue Folge 9. 1934.
— 'Ahhijavā und kein Ende?' *Indogermanische Forschungen*, LV, 169–297. 1937.
VÖLKL, K. 'Achchijawa'. *La Nouvelle Clio*, IV. 1952.

II. HITTITES IN PALESTINE

DELAPORTE, L. 'Les Hittites sont-ils nommés dans la Bible?' *Revue Hittite et Asianique*, IV, 289–96. 1938.
FORRER, E. O. 'The Hittites in Palestine'. *Palestine Exploration Quarterly*, LXVIII, 190–209, and LXIX, 100–15. 1936–7.
JIRKU, A. 'Eine hethitische Ansiedlung in Jerusalem zur Zeit von El-Amarna'. *Zeitschrift des deutschen Palästina-Vereins*, XLIII, 58–61. 1920.
SAYCE, A. H. 'The Hittite name Araunah'. *Journal of Theological Studies*, XXII, 267, 1921.
SCHROEDER, O. 'Uria der Hettiter'. *Zeitschrift für Alttestamentliche Wissenschaft*, XXXV, 247–8. 1915.
VIEYRA, M. 'Parallèle hurrite au nom d'Urie "le hittite" '. *Revue Hittite et Asianique*, V, 113–16.
VINCENT, H. 'La sépulture des patriarches'. *Revue Biblique*, 1920, 515–17.

12. HITTITE POLITICAL GEOGRAPHY. MAPS OF HITTITE ASIA MINOR

CAVAIGNAC, E. *Les Hittites* (Paris, 1950), 8–9.
— *Revue Hittite et Asianique*, III, opp. p. 24.
CORNELIUS, F. 'Hethitische Reisewege'. *Revue Hittite*, XIII/57. 1955.
— 'Zur hethitischen Geographie'. *Ibid.* XVI/62. 1958.
— 'Geographie des Hethiterreiches'. *Orientalia* 27. 1958.
DELAPORTE, L. *Atlas historique. I. L'antiquité*. Presses Universitaires de France, 1948. Map IV.
FORRER, E. O. *Forschungen* I, 1 (Berlin, 1926), at end.
— 'Kilikien zur Zeit des Hatti-Reiches'. *Klio*, XXX, 135–86 and 267–9. 1937.
GARSTANG, J., and GURNEY, O. R. *The Geography of the Hittite Empire*. British Institute of Archaeology at Ankara, Occasional Publications, No. 5. London, 1959.
GOETZE, A. *Kuzzuwatna and the Problem of Hittite Geography*. New Haven, 1940. (Reviewed by S. Smith in *Journal of the Royal Asiatic Society*, 1942, 61–6, and by W. F. Albright in *American Journal of Archaeology*, XLIV, 444–6.)

GOETZE, 'The Roads of Northern Cappadocia in Hittite Times'. *Revue Hittite*, XV/61. 1957.

TOYNBEE, A. *A Study of History*, Vol. XI. 1959.

13. EXPLORATION AND EXCAVATION

For bibliography up to 1955 see Seton Lloyd, *Early Anatolia* (1956), pp. 213–19 See also the annual 'Summary of Archaeological Research in Turkey', in *Anatolian Studies* (*Journal of the British Institute of Archaeology at Ankara*), for recent work.

ALKIM, U. B. 'Excavations at Domuztepe'. *Türk Tarih Kurumu, Belleten*, XVI, 238–50, 1952.

ANDERSON, J. G. 'Exploration in Asia Minor during 1898'. *Ann. of Brit. Sch. at Athens*, IV, 48–78. 1899.

BITTEL, K. Reports of excavations at Bogazköy, in *Mitteilungen der Deutschen Orientgesellschaft*, LXX–LXXVIII, 1932–9 and LXXXVI (1953) ff.

— and others. *Yazilikaya*. Deutsche Orientgesellschaft, Wissenschaftliche Veröffentlichung, Nr. 61. 1941.

BURCKHARDT, J. L. *Travels in Syria and the Holy Land*. London, 1821.

CHARLES, B. B., OLMSTEAD, A. T., and WRENCH, J. E. *Travels and Studies in the Near East* (*Cornell Expedition*), I, II, Ithaca, 1911.

DAVIS, E. J. 'On a new Hamathite inscription at Ibreez'. *Transactions of Society for Biblical Archaeology*, IV, 336–46. 1876.

GARSTANG, J 'Notes on a Journey through Asia Minor'. *Annals of Archaeology and Anthropology*, I, 1–12. Liverpool, 1908.

GOLDMAN, H *Excavations at Gözlü Kule, Tarsus*, II. Princeton, 1956.

HAMILTON, W. T. *Researches in Asia Minor, Pontus and Armenia*. London, 1842.

HUMANN, K., and PUCHSTEIN, O. *Reise in Kleinasien und Nord-Syrien*. Berlin, 1890.

KOŞAY, HAMIT ZUBEYR. 'A Great Discovery'. (Excavations at Alaja Hüyük.) *Illustrated London News*, 21 July 1945, 78–81.

LLOYD, SETON. *Early Anatolia*. Pelican Books, 1956.

MACRIDY BEY. 'La porte des sphinx à Euyuk. Fouilles du Musée Impérial Ottoman'. *Mitteilungen der Vorderasiatisch-Aegyptischen Gesellschaft*, XIII, 177–205. 1908.

OSTEN, H. H. VON DER. *The Alishar Hüyük. Seasons of 1930–32*. Univ. of Chicago Or. Inst. Publ. XXVIII, XXIX, XXX. 1937.

— *Explorations in Central Anatolia. Season of 1926*. Univ. of Chicago, Or. Inst. Publ. V, 1929.

— *Explorations in Hittite Asia Minor*, 1927–9. Univ. of Chicago, Or. Inst. Comm., 6 and 8. 1929–30.

— *Discoveries in Anatolia, 1930–31. Ibid.*, 14, 1933.

OZGÜÇ, T. 'Excavations at Kültepe, Level II Finds'. *Belleten*, XIX. 1955.

— *Karahüyük Kazisi Raporu*. Ankara, 1949.

— *Kültepe Kazisi Raporu*. Ankara, 1950.

— 'Where the Assyrians built a commercial empire in second-millennium Anatolia: excavating the "karum" of Kanes'. *Illustrated London News*, 14 January 1950, 68–71.

SELECT BIBLIOGRAPHY

RAMSAY, W. M., and HOGARTH, D. G. 'Pre-Hellenic Monuments of Cappadocia'. *Recueil de Travaux*, XIV, 1893, 74–94; XV, 1893, 89–97.
TEXIER, C. *Description de l'Asie Mineure*. Paris, 1839–48.
THUREAU-DANGIN, F., and others. *Til-Barsib*. Paris, 1936.
WOOLLEY, C. L. *A Forgotten Kingdom*. Penguin Books, 1953.
— *Alalakh, an account of the Excavations at Tell Atchana, 1937–1949*. Oxford, 1955.

14. HITTITE LANGUAGE

A. GRAMMARS

FRIEDRICH, J. *Hethitisches Elementarbuch*. Heidelberg, 1940.
STURTEVANT, E. H *A Comparative Grammar of the Hittite Language*. Philadelphia, 1933. 2nd edit., 1951.

B. GLOSSARY

FRIEDRICH, J. *Hethitisches Wörterbuch*. Heidelberg, 1952.
STURTEVANT, E. H. *A Hittite Glossary*. 2nd ed., Philadelphia, 1936; with Supplement, 1939.

C. DECIPHERMENT

HROZNÝ, B. 'Die Lösung des hethitischen Problems'. *Mitteilungen der Deutschen Orientgesellschaft*, LVI, 17–50. 1915.
— 'Hittites'. Article in *Encyclopaedia Britannica*, 14th ed., 1929.

D. COMPARATIVE STUDIES

BONFANTE, G. 'Indo-Hittite and Areal Linguistics'. *American Journal of Philology*, LXVII, 289–310. 1946.
BONFANTE, G. 'La Position du hittite parmi les langues indo-européennes'. *Revue Belge de Philologie et d'histoire*, 1939, 381–92.
COUVREUR, W. 'Le Hittite et la doctrine de Ferdinand de Saussure'. *Revue Hittite et Asianique*, V, 132–41. 1939.
CROSSLAND, R. A. 'A reconsideration of the Hittite evidence for the existence of laryngeals in primitive Indo-European'. *Transactions of Philological Society*, 1951, 88–130.
CUNY, A. 'Le Phonème ḫ du hittite résulte de la fusion de plusieurs phonèmes nostratiques'. *Ibid.*, VI (43), 66–99, 1942.
DEVOTO, G. 'Nota sulla formazione della lingua ittita'. *Archiv Orientalni*, XVIII₃, 55–64.
JURET, A. *Vocabulaire étymologique de la langue hittite*. Limoges, 1942.

229

KEITH, A. B. 'The Relation of Hittite, Tocharian and Indo-European'. *Indian Historical Quarterly*, XIV, 201–23. 1938.

MEILLET, A. 'La Chronologie des langues indo-européennes et le développement du gendre féminin'. *Comptes Rendus de l'Académie des Inscriptions et des Belles Lettres*, 1930. 149–54.

— 'Essai de chronologie des langues indo-européennes'. *Bulletin de la Société Linguistique de Paris*, XXXII, 1–28. 1931.

OTTEN, H. 'Hethitisch und Indogermanisch'. *Wissenschaftliche Annalen*, II₅, 322–330. 1952.

PEDERSEN, H. *Hittitisch und die anderen indo-europäischen Sprachen*. Copenhagen, 1938.

PETERSEN, W. 'Hittite and Tocharian'. *Language*, IX, 12–34. 1933.

PISANI, V. 'La Question de l'indo-hittite et le concepte de parenté linguistique . *Archiv Orientalni*, XVII, 251–64. 1949.

SOMMER, F. *Hethiter und Hethitisch*. Stuttgart, 1947.

STURTEVANT, E. H. *The Indo-Hittite Laryngeals*. Philadelphia, 1942. (Reviewed by Goetze in *Language*, XIX, 165 ff.)

— 'Hittite and Areal Linguistics'. *Language*, XXIII, 376–82. 1947. (Reply to Bonfante, 1946.)

— 'The Relationship of Hittite to Indo-European'. *Transactions of American Philological Association*, LX, 25–37. 1929.

— (See also above, Sub-section A.)

15. HITTITE HIEROGLYPHIC LANGUAGE AND LUWIAN

For earlier bibliography, see Goetze, *Kleinasien* (above, section 1), pp. 48–9 and 51–3.

ALBRIGHT, W. F. 'Hittite Scripts'. *Antiquity*, VIII, 453–5. 1934.

ALP, S. *Zur Lesung von manchen Personennamen auf den hieroglyphen-hethitischen Siegeln und Inschriften*. Ankara, 1950.

BARNETT, R. D. 'Karatepe, the Key to Hittite Hieroglyphs'. *Anatolian Studies*, III, 53–95. 1953

BOSSERT, H. T. Articles in *Mitteilungen des Instituts für Orientforschung*, II, III (1954–5), *Rivista degli Studi Orientali*, XXXII (1957), and *Oriens Extremus*, I (1959).

— *Ein hethitisches Königssiegel*. Berlin, 1944.

— 'Das hieroglyphenhethitische Zahlwort "Fünf"'. *Archiv Orientalni*, XVIII, 123–5. 1950.

— 'Die Phoenizisch-hethitischen Bilinguen vom Karatepe'. *Oriens*, I, 163–92, 1948, and II, 72–120. 1949. *Archiv Orientalni*, XVIII₃, 1–38, 1950. *Jahrbuch für kleinasiatische Forschung* I, 264–95; II, 167–89 and 293–339. 1951–2. *Gedenkschrift Paul Kretschmer* (Wien, 1956), 40 ff.

— 'Zu drei hieroglyphen-hethitischen Inschriften'. *Jahrbuch für Kleinasiatische Forschung*, I (2), 218–24. 1950.

— 'Zur Geschichte von Kargamis'. *Studi Classici e Orientali* (Pisa), 1951.

— 'Das H–H Wort für Malstein'. *Türk Tarih Kurumu, Belleten*, XVI, 495–544. 1952.

BOSSERT, H. T. 'Wie lange wurden hethitische Hieroglyphen geschrieben?' *Welt des Orients*, 1952, 480–4.

FRIEDRICH, J. 'Zur Lesung der hethitischen Bilderschrift'. *Archiv Orientální*, XXI. 1953.

— 'Luwische Kleinigkeiten'. *Corolla Linguistica*. Wiesbaden, 1955.

GÜTERBOCK, H. G. 'Die Elemente *MUWA* und *ZITI* in den hethitischen Hieroglyphen'. *Archiv Orientální*, XVIII/1–2. 1950.

— 'Notes on Luwian Studies'. *Orientalia*, XXV. 1956.

KAMMENHUBER, A. 'Beobachtungen zur hethitisch-luwischen Sprachgruppe'. *Revue Hittite*, XIV/58. 1956.

LAROCHE, E. Articles in *Revue Hittite*, XIII/57 (1955), XIV/59 (1956), XVI/63 (1958); in *Syria*, XXXI (1954), XXXIII (1956), XXXV (1958); and in Schaeffer, *Ugaritica III* (Paris, 1956).

— *Dictionnaire de la langue louvite*. Paris, 1959.

— 'Comparaison du louvite et du lycien'. *Bulletin de la Société de Linguistique de Paris*, LIII, 1957–8.

— *Les Hiéroglyphes Hittites*, I. Paris, 1960.

MERIGGI, P. 'Die längsten Bauinschriften in "hethitischen" Hieroglyphen'. *Mitteilungen der Vorderasiatisch-Aegyptischen Gesellschaft*, XXIX, no. 1. 1934.

— 'Le iscrizione in eteo geroglifico del Tabal'. *Rivista degli Studi Orientali*, XXXII, 1957.

— 'Listes des hiéroglyphes hittites'. *Revue Hittite et Asianique*, IV (27), 69–114. 1937.

— 'Schizzo della declinazione nominale dell'eteo geroglifico'. *Archivio Glottologico Italiano*, XXXVII, 1953.

PALMER, L. R. 'Problems of Hieroglyphic Hittite'. *Transactions of the Philological Society*. 1958.

TRITSCH, F. J. 'Lycian, Luwian and Hittite'. *Archiv Orientální*, XVIII/1–2. 1950.

16. OTHER ASIANIC LANGUAGES AND PEOPLES

CARRUBA, O. 'Lydisch und Lyder'. *Mitteilungen des Instituts für Orientforschung*, VIII (1963), 383–408.

FORRER, E. O. 'Die acht Sprachen der Boghazköi-Inschriften'. *Sitzungsberichte der Preuss. Akad. d. Wiss.*, 1919.

— 'Die Inschriften und Sprachen des Hatti-Reiches'. *Zeitschrift der Deutschen Morgenländischen Gesellschaft*, LXXVI, 174–296. 1922.

FRIEDRICH, J. *Kleinasiatische Sprachdenkmäler*. Berlin, 1932.

— 'Arier'. *Reallexikon der Assyriologie*, I, 1932.

GELB, I. J. *Hurrians and Subarians*. Chicago, 1944. (Reviewed by S. Smith in *Pal. Expl. Quart.*, 1949, 117–26, and E. A. Speiser: see below.)

—, PURVES, P. M., and MACRAE, A. A. *Nuzi Personal Names*. Chicago, Or. Inst. Publ. no. 57. 1943.

HAAS, O. 'Zur Deutung der phrygischen Inschriften'. *Revue Hittite et Asianique*, XI (53), 1–30. 1951.

JONKEES, J. H. 'Zur Transcription des Lydischen'. *Mnemosyne*, VII, 157–60. 1939.

KAHLE, P., and SOMMER, F. 'Die lydisch-aramäische Bilingue'. *Kleinasiatische Forschungen*, I, 1–86. 1927.

KAMMENHUBER, A. 'Das Palaische: Texte und Wortschatz'. *Revue Hittite*, XVII/64. 1959.

KRETSCHMER, P. 'Die Leleger und die ostmediterrane Urbevölkerung'. *Glotta*, XXXII, 161–204. 1953.

LAROCHE, E. 'Une conjuration bilingue Hatti-Hittite'. *Jahrbuch für Klein-asiatische Forschung*, I (2), 174–81. 1950.

— 'Études "proto-hittites"'. *Revue d'Assyriologie*, XLI, 67–98. 1948.

— 'Hattic Deities and their Epithets'. *Journal of Cuneiform Studies*, I, 187–216. 1947.

— 'Problèmes de la linguistique Asianique', *Conférences de l'Institut de Linguistique de l'Université de Paris*, IX, 1949. Paris, 1950.

LESNÝ, V. 'The language of the Mitanni chieftains; a third branch of the Aryan group'. *Archiv Orientalni*, IV, 257–60. 1932.

MENTZ, A. 'Zu den lydischen Inschriften'. *Glotta*, XXIX, 148–55. 1942.

OTTEN, H. 'Zum Paläischen'. *Zeitschrift für Assyriologie*, XLVIII, 119–45. 1944.

PARROT, A., and NOUGAYROL, J. 'Un Document de fondation hurrite'. *Revue d'Assyriologie*, XLII, 1–20. 1948.

PEDERSEN, H. *Lykisch und Hittitisch*. Copenhagen, 1945.

SAYCE, A. H. 'Indians in Western Asia in the fifteenth century B.C.' *Oriental Studies in Honour of Cursetji Erachji Pavry*. London, 1933.

SCHAFER, R. 'Pisidian'. *American Journal of Philology*, 71, 239–70. 1950.

SPEISER, E. A. 'Introduction to Hurrian'. *Annual of American Schools of Oriental Research*, XX, 1941. (Reviewed by Goetze in *Language*, XIX, 1943, 170–6.)

— Review of Gelb, *Hurrians and Subarians*, in *Journal of American Oriental Society*, LXVIII, 1–13. 1948.

STEINHERR, F. 'Zu den neuen karischen Inschriften'. *Jahrbuch für klein-asiatische Forschung*, I, 328–36. 1951.

STOLTENBERG, H. L. 'Neue Lesung der karischen Schrift'. *Die Sprache*, IV. 1958.

17. CRANIOLOGY

ŞENYÜREK, M. Appendix I, in Seton Lloyd, *Early Anatolia* (above, section 13). 1956.

18. CLIMATE

DE PLANHOL, M. X. 'Limites antique et actuelle des cultures arbustives méditerranéennes en Asie Mineure'. *Bulletin de l'Association de Géographes français*, No. 239–240. 1954.

Index

233